IN THE STEPS OF THE ROMANOVS:

Last Two Years of the Last Russian Imperial Family (1916-1918)

HELEN AZAR

ISBN: 1986893278
ISBN-13: 978-1986893275

ACKNOWLEDGMENTS

Many thanks to George Hawkins; Ferrah Arslan; Fathers at Mesa Potamos Monastery in Cyprus; Staff at State Archives of Russian Federation (GARF), Beinecke Library at Yale University and G.E.T. Educational Tours; Eva & Dan McDonald, Deborah Brown, Laura Mabee and Russian imperial history enthusiasts.

Emperor Nicholas II Alexandrovich Tsar of Russia (1868-1918)

Empress Alexandra Feodorovna, nee Princess Alix of Hesse (1872-1918)

Grand Duchess Olga Nikolaevna eldest daughter of Nicholas and Alexandra (1895-1918)

Grand Duchess Tatiana Nikolaevna second daughter of Nicholas and Alexandra (1897-1918)

Grand Duchess Maria Nikolaevna third daughter of Nicholas and Alexandra (1899-1918)

Grand Duchess Anastasia Nikolaevna fourth daughter of Nicholas and Alexandra (1901-1918)

Tsesarevich Alexei Nikolaevich youngest child and only son of Nicholas and Alexandra (1904-1918)

In the Steps of the Romanovs

Introduction by George Hawkins

July 17, 2018 is the hundredth anniversary of the murder of the last Russian Tsar Nicholas II, his wife Alexandra Feodorovna, their only son, the Heir-Tsesarevich Alexei Nikolaevich, daughters – the Grand Duchesses Olga, Tatiana, Maria and Anastasia Nikolaevna and their remaining servants: Dr Eugene Sergeyevich Botkin, chambermaid Anna Stepanovna Demidova, footman Alexei Yegorovich Trupp and cook Ivan Mikhailovich Kharitonov in Yekaterinburg.

The story of the Russian Revolution and the exile and execution of the Romanovs has been the subject of many books but here for the first time, author/translator Helen Azar has compiled the writings of the Imperial Family themselves, presenting in their own words the momentous events they lived through in the last two years of their lives.

Importantly this book is presented without subjective commentary from the author – leaving it to the reader to form their own impressions of the Imperial Family, their personalities and lives. For many years, the children – in particular the Tsar's daughters – have been presented as somewhat sheltered, naïve and childish side-notes of history. This book shows this to be far from the reality. The diaries of the Grand Duchesses show that they led busy socially active lives, interacting with a wide range of people.

While the Grand Duchesses have left no extant diaries from after the revolution, their letters to their friends are full of fascinating detail about their every-day lives and the circumstances they found themselves in. Their younger brother Alexei likewise has in his letters provided a wealth of information about the last few months of this devoted family.

In translating the personal writings of the Imperial Family, author Helen Azar has preserved the particular idiosyncrasies and writing style of them. While at times this may make for some unusual turns of expression or use of language, it actually gives the reader a feeling for the true 'voices' of the Imperial Family and how they thought.

The book opens in 1916 where we see how the Imperial Family were dedicated to the war effort. The Tsar's daughters were devoted to their patients at the hospitals and their diaries and letters are full of their interactions with them. While Grand Duchesses Maria and Anastasia were not nurses like their older sisters, they too spent much time visiting the wounded. All four wrote detailed letters to their father and brother when they were away at General Headquarters. Included in this section are large amounts of 12-year-old Tsesarevich Alexei's diaries.

Of particular interest is the large amount of material, newly translated into English, from Nicholas II's 1917 diary, detailing the Romanov's day-to-day lives in a time of tumultuous change. Initially, in the first two months of 1917, everything is as usual. Then comes the abdication and the adjustment to a new way of life as prisoners in the Alexander Palace at Tsarskoe Selo. The ex-Emperor writes in detail about how he and the family pass their days.

In August the family is transferred by train and steamer to the provincial town of Tobolsk in Siberia. The Tsar's diary outlines the events of this journey and how they spent their time on the river steamer after it was found that the Governor's House in Tobolsk was not yet ready for them. At the Governor's House, the family had to adjust to living in much more confined circumstances than before, while still having some freedoms. Diary entries and letters detail their daily lives in Tobolsk. During this time, despite all correspondence being checked, the Imperial Family wrote long, detailed and informative letters about how they passed their days. Occasionally signs of frustration show through but in general the family remained cheerful and optimistic.

In April 1918, Nicholas, Alexandra and Maria are transferred to Ekaterinburg while the three other Grand Duchesses and Alexei remain in Tobolsk as the Tsesarevich convalesces from a bout of haemophilia. There is a flurry of letters between the parties, coded instructions and details of the journey to Ekaterinburg and how both sides were coping with separation from each other. The huge worry the Grand

Duchesses have for their parents and sister is evident in their letters.

Following the transfer of Olga, Tatiana, Anastasia and Alexei to Ekaterinburg the Tsar and Tsaritsa's diaries provide the reader with a glimpse into life at the 'House of Special Purpose', interspersed with their guards' observations and impressions of the Imperial Family. The book concludes with a translation of a letter Dr Botkin was writing on 16 July 1918 and the recollections of the night of 16-17 July 1918 by the Romanov's chief executioner, Yakov Yurovsky.

This book should be seen as a valuable and important resource for historians of the Russian Revolution, as well for anyone interested in this fascinating period of history and the Romanov family, providing many diary entries, letters and recollections for the first time in English. After one hundred years the Imperial Family are now able to tell the story of their last years in their own words. Follow them, in their steps, from Tsarskoe Selo to Tobolsk and on to Ekaterinburg...

* * *

Note from the author/translator

The story of the downfall of the last ruling Romanov family is fairly well-known: following the Russian revolution, members of the family were arrested, imprisoned and ultimately executed without a trial. For many years, mystery surrounded the details around their murders, but after the fall of the Soviet Union, archives were gradually opened and investigations began. Around that time, the remains of the last Tsar and his family were found, and later, thorough scientific testing confirmed that the bodies of the entire family were accounted for (although the Russian Orthodox Church has not accepted them as authentic at the time of this writing).

The discovery of imperial remains led to a revival of interest in the family, as many of their personal documents—all carefully preserved—came to light. Today, after more than a quarter of a century, it seemed unlikely that anything new could be said about the last months and days of the Romanovs. But as it turned out - even to my own surprise - there was.

I started working on this manuscript with the intention of creating a simple, relatively short companion book for the 2018 centennial tour to Russia, called "In the Steps of the Romanovs", organized by myself and managed by GET Educational Tours. I decided to strictly use primary documents and photographs to recount the final two years of Russia's last imperial family in the places the tour would be covering.

However, as I did my research and translations, the manuscript seemed to take on a mind of its own, and kept growing. I was discovering more and more primary documents that I did not even realise existed, which I felt had to be included in this book.

So, before you is an almost 700 page volume, which of course is no longer a mere tour companion but a fully fledged book, which not only tells the familiar story in a unique way, but also provides a significant amount of new details.

I feel that this final result is one of the most accurate accounts of the last months of the Romanov imperial family, since it consists strictly of first hand accounts, with very minimal subjective commentary from the author. I hope you feel the same way and enjoy reading it as much as I enjoyed creating it.

Helen Azar

April 2018

YEAR 1916: Last full year of reign

From the 1916 diary of Alexei Romanov

January 1. Got up late today. Had tea at 10 o'clock, then went to [see] Mama. Mama is not feeling well, so she was lying down all day. Sat at home, because I have a cold. Had breakfast[1] with Olga, Tatiana, Maria and Anastasia. In the afternoon went to Kolya's[2] and

---

[1] What the family referred to as "*zavtrak*" ("breakfast") was a midday meal eaten at around noon or 1pm, so it actually corresponded to lunch. The morning meal was at around 8 - 9am and usually consisted of a small portion of bread with butter and tea.

[2] Alexei's playmate Nikolai Vladimirovich Derevenko, son of imperial physician Dr. Vladimir Nikolaevich Derevenko

played there. It was really fun. Had dinner at 6 o'clock, then played. At 8 o'cl. was at Mama's during their dinner. At 10 o'cl. was in bed.

Tatiana to Nicholas Alexandrovich

Tsarskoe Selo. **1 January**. Papa darling! So lonesome without You today. We went to *Obednya*[3] alone, before that [were] at our infirmary for a bit. Mama is in bed, so we 5 had breakfast alone in Mama's. Terribly cold today. - In the morning it was 20 [degrees], now a little less [cold] because the sun is shining. Yesterday evening we had a *moleben*[4] at 10.30 and then went to bed. Alexei received a touching telegram from all his foreign Stavka[5] friends. He was very pleased. How are you in Mogilev, is it cold there, a lot of snow or not? Anya[6] recently invited us five: Irina Tolstaya, Rita Khitrovo[7] and her little sister Lyuba. [We] played different games and hide and go seek with them. Although not very much, but we put out the lamps, it was better that way. [Your] very loving *Voznesenetz*[8].

---

[3] Divine liturgy

[4] Prayer service

[5] General military headquarters in Mogilev

[6] Anna Alexandrovna Vyrubova, close friend of the imperial family

[7] Countess Margarita Khitrovo, lady in waiting and friend of the family

[8] Tatiana was honourary commander-in-chief of Voznesensky regiment

From the 1916 diary of Alexei Romanov

2 January. Got up late. Did not take a walk. Read in English. Had breakfast with O., T., M., A.[9] Mama stayed in bed. Did not walk during the day. Played with Alexei[10] and Sergei. Had dinner at 6 o'clock. At 8 o'cl. was at dinner at Mama's. Went to bed late.

From the 1916 diary of Maria Romanov

5 January. In the morning went to church with O[lga], T[atiana] and Al[exei]. Mama is in bed. In the afternoon walked around town with T. and Isa.[11] Had tea with O., T. and Anya near Mama. Went to *vsenoshnaya*[12] with O., T. and Alexei. Had dinner 3 and Mama [was] on the sofa. Anastasia was in bed as she has a cold, she has high fever. Got a letter from darling Papa.

---

[9] Olga. Tatiana, Maria and Anastasia, aka "OTMA", as they often referred to themselves

[10] Another boy named Alexei, one of Tsesarevich's playmates

[11] Baroness Sophia Karlovna von Buxhoeveden, lady-in-waiting to the Empress

[12] Evening prayer services, the all-night vigil

Maria in the Empress's Mauve sitting room at Alexander Palace

From the 1916 diary of Alexei Romanov

6 January. Got up late. At 11 o'clock in the morning went to the Palace infirmary. Had breakfast with O., T., M. Mama and Anastasia stayed in bed all day. Anastasia has bronchitis. During the day took a walk outside then went to Kolya's. Had dinner at 6 o'cl. Sat at Mama's after their dinner. To bed at half [past] 10 o'cl.

Alexei in front of Circular Hall of the Alexander Palace

Tatiana to Nicholas Alexandrovich

10 January. My dear Papa darling! I am writing to you now before *Obednya*. It is snowing mixed with rain because it is one degree of warmth[13], we have had this weather for three days already. We saw Nik.[olai] Pav.[lovich][14], he alone came over two or three times, and yesterday he left for Helsingfors. One of these days

[13] "Of warmth" refers to above zero Celsius, "of frost" below zero

[14] Nikolai Pavlovich Sablin – aide-de-camp to the tsar

N.N. Rodionov[15] is supposed to arrive, and I am very happy. We have not seen him for almost a year. Alexei and Anastasia are both moving their beds into the playroom, where they lie next to each other all day. During the day we all have tea up there. The [Christmas] tree still stands, so cozy. It will be sad to take it down, but for now it is not dropping its needles, so it is fine. So tiresome that Mama still does not feel well, but she still gets up during the day and lies on the sofa a little there. We take turns going to Anya's so that she doesn't get too bored lying in bed. The other day Emelyanov had surgery, remember him? He was at the Christmas party at the Arena. They removed a bullet fragment from his bone. Now he is in a lot of pain, but the rest are fine. Well, goodbye. Papa my darling dear. We have to go to church. May God bless you, I kiss You very very hard as I love you. Your faithful *Voznesenetz.*

Anastasia to Nicholas Alexandrovich

11 January, 1916. Tsarskoe Selo. My dear Papa Darling! I am still in bed, but I think tomorrow I will get up for the first time. My bronchitis is gone now.

---

[15] Nikolai Nikolaevich Rodionov, lieutenant from the imperial yacht The Standart

In the morning before breakfast I stay in bed in my room and write or Shura[16] reads to me, and I go to the playroom for breakfast, and there get into bed. Mama comes for tea and sits until 6 o'cl. Yesterday Alexei was in a very military mood, what did he not do, he was so terribly funny. Now we have nice weather, the sun comes out and not much melting, so that it is rather warm and nice. Tomorrow is a month since the 1st Hundred left Mogilev. Yesterday we all wrote to Aunt Olga,[17] as some man was going there. It's such a shame that they took your little shovel, but hope that they gave you a new one, or the same one! Mordvinov[18] is probably charming, yes? We will soon have breakfast with Alexei, but he will not finish very fast, while I am done in 10 min. or faster. Mama will now sit on the balcony with Maria. "Ortipo"[19] and "Joy"[20] asked to send [you] big regards and to tell you that they miss you. I am so bored sitting in bed and being unable to go to our infirmary—this is desperately

---

[16] Alexandra Alexandrovna Tegleva, nurse to the imperial children and eventual wife of Pierre Gilliard

[17] Grand Duchess Olga Alexandrovna, younger sister of the tsar

[18] Colonel Anatoly Alexandrovich Mordvinov, of His Majesty's Own Life-Guards Cuirassiers Regiment

[19] Tatiana's pet French bulldog

[20] Alexei's pet spaniel

boring. I send you awfully big 1000 kisses. May God keep you. Your loving loyal and faithful *Kaspiyitz.*[21]

Maria's and Anastasia's infirmary

From the 1916 diary of Alexei Romanov

15 January. Got up at ½ [of] 9. In the morning studied French and God's Law. Did not take a walk. Had breakfast with O., T., M. and A. Mama was lying down all day. During the day [I] played with [toy] soldiers. Had tea at Mama's. Had dinner at 6 o'cl. Dinner was at Mama's. Went to bed early.

[21] Anastasia was commander-in-chief of Kaspiysky regiment

From the 1916 diary of Tatiana Romanov

Saturday, **16 January**. German lesson in the morning. At 10 o'clock [I] went to the infirmary. Dressings <....> At 12 o'clock went with Valentina Ivanovna back to the soldiers' ward for Popov's dressings. Under anesthesia. Kidney was removed. Then returned and went to [see] Tuznikov. Breakfast and tea with Mama. Had a history lesson. 4 with Isa rode in a *troika*[22]. Went to the Grand Palace[23] for a concert. Went to *Vsenoshnaya*. Had dinner with Mama and Anya. Later Nikolai Pavlovich came over. Said good-bye to him as he goes to the front with his battalion tomorrow.

From the 1916 diary of Alexei Romanov

17 January. Got up early. Went to *obednya*. Then [we] rode to the train station at 12 o'cl. to meet Papa. Had breakfast with Papa, Mama, O., T., M., A. Then rested and took a walk. Then had tea. Had dinner at 6 o'cl. Was at dinner at Papa's. Later [I] played. Went to bed early.

18 January. Got up early. Studied and took a walk. Had breakfast 5[24], Papa and Mama. Took a walk

---

[22] Carriage or sleigh drawn by three horses

[23] Aka Catherine Palace

[24] Meaning all five siblings

during the day by the W[hite] Tower. Then studied and did homework. Went to tea at Mama's. Had dinner at 6 o'cl. At 8 o'cl. went to *obednya.* Went to bed late.

OTMA in Alexander Park near the White Tower

From the 1916 diary of Tatiana Romanov

Tuesday, **19 January**. Had a lesson in the morning. Went to "*Znamenie*",[25] from there to the infirmary. Dressings <...> Went to [see] the others. 5 [had] breakfast with Papa, Uncle Sergei (Mikhailovich) and Gavriil. Mama in the other room on the sofa. At 2.15 we two with Isa went to Petrograd to the Anichkov.

---

[25] Church of Our Lady of *Znamenie* (The Sign), located near the palace

Went to Grandmama's[26], to Aunt Ella's[27] house for the infirmary consecration. Had *moleben.* Walked around all the wards, and then took photographs. Had tea. All the staff is English, came from England especially for this[28]. Wonderful infirmary. From 5 to 6 o'clock were at Tatiana's.[29] Had tea, then sat in her office and played with the children. Returned with Papa at 7.15. Had dinner with Papa, Mama and Gavriil. At 9.20 Anya came over with Nikolai Nikolaevich. Sat cozily until 11 o'clock. Was very pleased. Rita gave me an injection[30] in the morning.

Znamenie church

---

[26] Dowager Empress Maria Feodorovna

[27] Grand Duchess Elizaveta Feodorovna, sister of the Empress

[28] She refers to the British infirmary which opened in St Petersburg

[29] Tatiana Konstantinovna, daughter of Grand Duke Konstantin Konstantinovich

[30] Possibly arsenic, which at the time was used to treat various illnesses

From the 1916 diary of Alexei Romanov

24 January. Got up early. Took a walk. Had breakfast with Mama. Took a walk in the afternoon. At 5 o'cl. went to tea at Mama's, where Rodionov was [too]. At 6 o'cl. ate dinner. At 8 o'cl. was at dinner at Mama's. Went to bed late.

26 January. Got up early. In the morning studied, then took a walk. Had breakfast with Papa, Mama and we 5. Three days ago, a rabid dog bit Joy and Brom in Bablovsk. Took a walk during the day. At 5 o'cl. was at tea at Mama's. Had dinner at 6 o'cl. with V. Nikolaevich [Derevenko].[31] At 8 o'cl. was at Mama's for dinner. Went to bed late. In the evening Grigori[32] was here.

29 January. Got up early. Studied and took a walk. Had breakfast with Mama we 5. Walked during the day and sledded. Papa sent a telegraph. [He] saw lots of troops. At 5 o'cl. was at Mama's for tea. Had dinner at 6 o'cl. Prepared homework. At 8 o'cl. was at

---

[31] Dr. Vladimir Nikolaevich Derevenko, imperial physician
[32] Grigory Yefimovich Rasputin

Mama's for dinner. Went to bed late. Nagorny's[33] wallet was stolen with 90 rubles.

Alexei in Alexander Park

Tatiana to Nicholas Alexandrovich

1 February. My dear darling Papa. My *Voznesentzy* telegraphed that they saw You. I am terribly pleased for them and regret that I was not there too. Yesterday afternoon, they had a small concert at Anya's infirmary, we five went to see it. We and the soldiers liked it tremendously. De Lazari was there and told us a lot of funny things. Later they played the guitar and sang. Very nice. Nikolai Nikolaevich Rodionov was also there. He leaves today. How is Kedrov? Did you

[33] Klementy Gregorievich Nagorny, Alexei's sailor "uncle"/caretaker

get used to him and he to you? And what is Mordvinov doing? These days it is cold, five or more degrees of frost. Yesterday we received the [new] cadets entering our regiments from the Nikolaevsky Cavalry School. I had two: Viranovsky and Budim-Levkovich. I do not know if the former is a relative of our Crimean, but he said that his father was in the 8th corps, where is he do you know? Everything is the same, nothing new. [It is] lonesome without you. The only thing Maria does is talk. During breakfast, after, during rides. In short, whenever we are [with her], and there is no way to stop her. I am sitting in the classroom now before the lesson. Sitting across from me is P.V.P.[34] and daydreaming. At times, [he] says something, but I don't even hear him and don't respond, as I am writing. Well, goodbye. May God bless You. I embrace you firmly and gently. Your *Voznesenetz.*

From the 1916 diary of Maria Romanov

3 February. Had lessons in the morning. Breakfast 5 and Mama on the sofa. Went to our infirmary[35] with Anya. Rode around with A. and Shura. Had tea with

---

[34] Pyotr Vladimirovich Petrov, their tutor of Russian

[35] Maria and Anastasia were patrons of an infirmary located in Feodorovsky Gorodok (Village) in Tsarskoe Selo

Mama and A. and Anya. Did homework. Had French reading [lesson]. Had dinner 4 with Mama on the sofa. Anya was here. Our [army] took [the town of] Yerzerum.

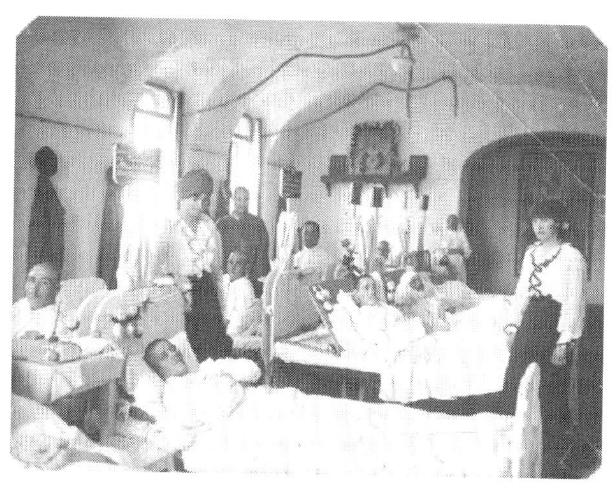

Maria and Anastasia with the wounded inside their infirmary

5 February. Had lessons. Rode around with Shura. Breakfast 4 and Mama on the sofa. Al.[exei] was in bed all day. Went to a concert at our infirmary with A.[nastasia]. Morfesi was there and also Sasha Makarov and De Lazari played the guitar. One of them played the accordion. In the afternoon had tea 4 with Mama and Anya. Rode around with O., T. and Shura. Had a music [lesson]. Had dinner 4 with Mama in the playroom. Anya was here.

Maria and Anastasia with officers in front of their infirmary

Tatiana to Nicholas Alexandrovich

5 February. My dear darling Papa. Today the poor Scout of the 10th Battalion is having surgery. He has a very badly shattered leg, and they fear that he may have tetanus because his friend, with whom he was [sharing a room] had serious tetanus, and they think that he has already died. I hope very much that he will have nothing. Later today I will have a meeting in town.[36] So horribly boring to go there. We very much

[36] Both eldest Grand Duchesses served on committees to benefit families of those fighting in the war

rejoiced that Yerzurum was taken, the wounded were all very happy about it. Do You walk a lot? And where - in the country or around somewhere? Mama's cheek is better, thank God, and the swelling is almost completely gone. I often recall the evenings when we sat with Mama, about "Olive, etc." Such a pity that it's all over. I wish it would continue. Are you reading something now? Well, good-bye, Papa darling. May God bless You. I embrace you firmly and kiss you, as [strongly as I] love [you]. Your *Voznesenetz*

From the 1916 diary of Maria Romanov

9 February. Had lessons in the morning. Breakfast 4 with Papa, and Mama on the sofa. Had a lesson in the afternoon. Went 4 to the Grand Palace. Rode in a *troika* 4 with Isa. Had tea 4 with Mama and Anya. Had a music [lesson]. Went to Zhilik's[37] concert at the gymnasium. Had dinner 4 with Papa, and Mama on the sofa. Anya was here. Pasted in the [photo] album with Papa.

---

[37] Nickname of the imperial children's French tutor, Pierre Gilliard

Alexandra's sofa in her Mauve boudoir

From the memoirs of Anna Vyrubova

For the benefit of those who imagine that the work of a royal nurse more or less has nature of play, I will describe the average routine of one of those mornings in which I was privileged to assist the Empress Alexandra Feodorovna and the Grand Duchesses Olga and Tatiana, the latter two were girls of nineteen and seventeen. Please remember that we were then only nurses in training. Arriving at the hospital shortly after nine in the morning we went directly to the receiving wards where the men were brought in after having first-aid treatment in the trenches and field hospitals. They had traveled far and were usually disgustingly dirty as well as bloodstained and suffering.

Infirmary on Gospitalnaya Street in Tsarskoe Selo, where Alexandra, Olga, Tatiana and Anna Vyrubova worked as nurses

Our hands scrubbed in antiseptic solutions we began the work of washing, cleaning, and bandaging maimed bodies, mangled faces, blinded eyes, all the indescribable mutilations of what is called civilized warfare. This we did under supervision and direction of trained nurses who had the skill to do the things our lack of experience prevented us from doing.

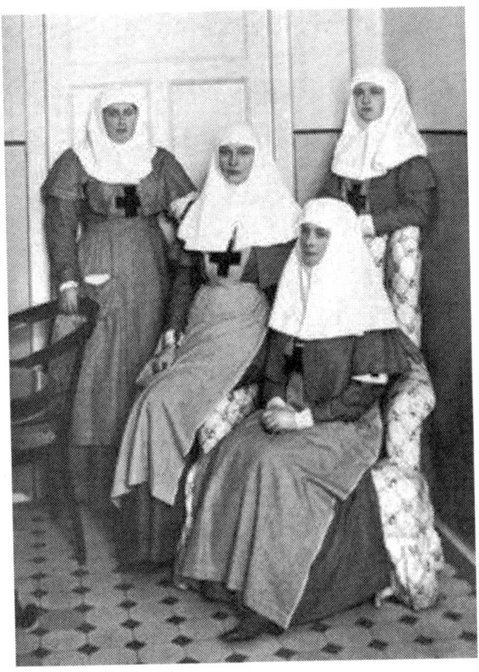

Olga, Tatiana, Alexandra and Anna Vyrubova in nurse uniforms

As we became accustomed to the work, both the Empress and Tatiana had extraordinary ability as nurses, and we were given more important work. I speak of the Empress and Tatiana especially because Olga within two months was almost too exhausted and too unnerved to continue, and my abilities proved to be more in executive and organizing than in the nursing end of hospital work. I have seen the Empress of Russia in the operating room of a hospital holding ether cones, handling sterilized instruments, assisting in the most difficult operations, taking from the hands of busy surgeons amputated legs and arms, removing bloody and even vermin-infected dressings, enduring all the sights and smells and agonies of that most dreadful of all places, a military hospital in the midst of war. She did her work with the humility and the gentle tirelessness of one dedicated by God to a life of ministration. Tatiana was almost as skillful and quite as devoted as her mother, and complained only that on account of her youth she was spared some of the more trying cases. The Empress was spared nothing, nor did she wish to be. I think I never saw her happier than on the day, at the end of our two months' intensive training, that she marched at the head of the procession of nurses to receive the red cross and the diploma of a certificated war nurse.

Anastasia to Nicholas Alexandrovich

15 February, 1916. Tsarskoe Selo. My Precious Papa Darling. It is so pleasant that the sun came out today, it has not been out for a long time. Yesterday we three little ones, so to speak, went to Anya's infirmary where they had a concert. It was really nice. One little 10-year-old girl danced a Russian [dance] with an accordion, it was so sweet, and I felt sorry for her. Delaware and Yu. Morfesi, Sasha Makarov and your friend Larsky were there as usual. He talked about an art lesson, it was so incredibly funny that the soldiers were crying from laughter. Then he talked about how you can hear the piano being played on three floors, also rather funny, and finally about the zoo, how they explain all the animals, etc. Nikolai Dmitrievich[38] was also there, and Irina Tolstaya.

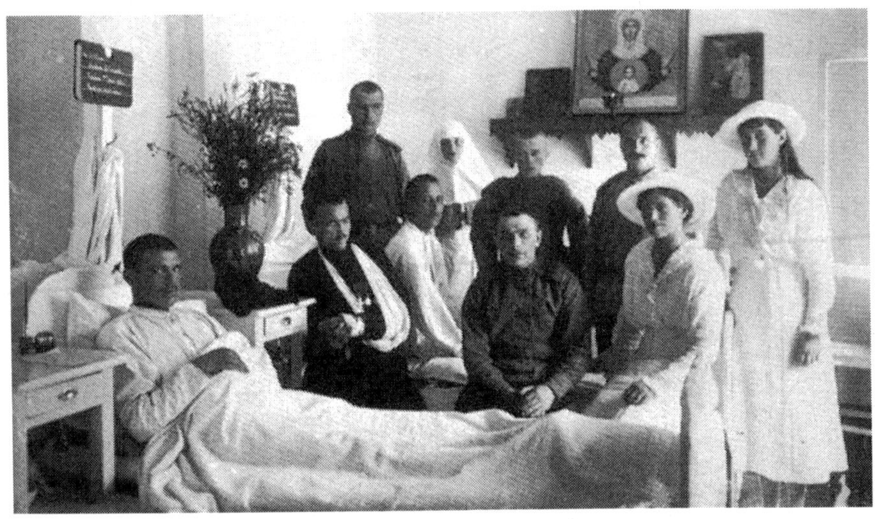

Maria and Anastasia with patients at their infirmary

While Olga and Tatiana were at their infirmary at this time, and they also had a concert. Fersen Bezobrazov and various young ladies played the *balalaikas* there, and many others. So, you think we are not going to [another] concert, right? You are mistaken, we are

[38] Nikolai Dmitrievich Demenkov, Grand Duchess Maria's romantic interest

going to the Grand Palace, where they will have something like a comedy of the crooked mirror, so we are going there because they begged us desperately. “Sleep the achievement of pride, everyone sleep.” Now I will have an arithmetic lesson. Maria and Alexei have colds and they don’t go out except to the infirmaries. Well, I will end. I send you an awfully big kiss. Regards to yours. Your loving loyal and faithful *Kaspiyitz.*

Grand Duchesses Olga and Tatiana greeting officers in front of Feodorovsky Cathedral. N. Demenkov is on the left

From the 1916 diary of Maria Romanov

20 February. Rode around with A. and Shura. Skip-walked with A. Breakfast 5 with Papa and Mama and

2 Englishmen. In the afternoon built the fortress[39] 4 with Papa and the sailors. Went to our infirmary with A. Sat with Sh.[akh]-N.[azarov]. Had tea with Papa, Mama and Uncle Pavel.[40] Went to *Vsenoshnaya* 4 with Papa. Had dinner with same with Mama on the sofa. Papa read, Anya was here.

Maria's and Anastasia's room in Alexander Palace

22 February. Had lessons. Then went to church 5 with Papa. Breakfast with same, with Vikitsky and Mama on the sofa. In the afternoon went to our infirmary with A. Sat with Sh.N. Walked 5 with Papa, built and jumped off the fortress. Had tea in the playroom. Had an English lesson. Went to church 5

[39] Snow fort they built every winter

[40] Grand Duke Pavel Alexandrovich, Nicholas's uncle

with Papa and Mama. Had dinner with same except Al. Papa read, Anya was here.

Playing at the snow fort

23 February. Had lessons. Went to church 5 with Papa. Breakfast with same, with Count Sheremetiev[41] and Mama on the sofa. Built the fortress, and jumped from it. Had tea in the playroom. Had music. Went to church 5 with Papa and Mama. Had dinner 4 with Papa, Count Sheremetiev and Mama on the sofa. Papa read, Anya was here.

[41] Count Alexander Sheremetiev

Alexandra's sofa in her boudoir

25 February. Lessons as usual. Went to church 5 with Papa. Breakfast with same and Mama on the sofa. Built the fortress. Went to our infirmary with A., sat with Sh.N. Had tea with Papa, Mama and O. and A. Went to church 5 with Papa and Mama. Had dinner with same except Al. Papa read. Anya was here.

Tatiana to Alexandra Feodorovna[42]

28 February, 1916 Tsarskoe Selo. Mama darling. Don't you want to put this bit of wadding on the little cut on your cheek. Olga Vl. gave it me [sic] long ago when I had such headaches – it lay on the grave of Simeon Verkhotur. Try it it'll help you if not then give it me back [sic] to-morrow. I hope God will help you + that you'll sleep well. God bless you. 1000 kisses fr yr own child Tatiana

[42] Originally written in English

From the 1916 diary of Maria Romanov

29 February. Had lessons. Breakfast 5 with Papa, Uncle Georgiy[43] and Ioann.[44] In the afternoon went to our infirmary with A. Sat with M.Z. Baron, Ton, and A.V. Walked and built the fortress. Had tea with A. and T. in the playroom. Had English and music lessons. Did homework. Dinner 3 with Papa, Ioann and Dmitri.[45] Papa read, Anya was here. Mama has neuralgia, and she stayed in bed almost the entire day.

Maria and Anastasia at their infirmary

[43] Grand Duke Georgiy Mikhailovich

[44] Prince Ioann Konstantinovich, son of Grand Duke Konstantin Konstantinovich

[45] Grand Duke Dmitri Pavlovich, first cousin of the tsar

Maria to Nicholas Alexandrovich

3 March. My sweet and dear Papa! Yesterday after we saw you off, Tatiana, Anastasia and I went to the cemetery[46] in a motor. We drove there for an unusually long time because the roads are so bad. We arrived there and went to the officers' graves, there was nothing there yet, and too much snow, then I wanted to visit the graves of our patients from the lower ranks. There was a big pile of snow on the side of the road, so I was able to climb up with great difficulty on my knees and jump down from it.

[46] Brethren military cemetery at Tsarskoe Selo

Down there the snow turned out to be above the knees, and although I was wearing long boots I was already wet, so I decided to continue ahead. Nearby I found one grave with the surname Mishenko, this was the name of our patient; I laid down some flowers there and walked ahead, and suddenly I saw the same surname again, I looked up at the board, [to see] which regiment he was from, and it turned out that he was one of our patients [too], but not the same one. So I laid down the flowers for him and was just starting to walk away when I fell on my back, and was lying there for almost a minute not knowing how to get up, there was so much snow that I could not reach the ground with my hand for leverage. I finally got up and walked ahead.

Contemporary photo of the Brethren cemetery

Earlier Tatiana and Anastasia said that they were going to go to another cemetery, to Sonia Orbeliani's[47] [grave] and that they will return for me. But instead they sent the man in charge of the graveyard to help me. He crawled over to me with great difficulty and we went to look for another grave together. We searched and searched and could not understand at all what happened to it. It turned out that it was closer to the fence and that we should have climbed over a ditch. He stood in the ditch and said to me "I will carry you over", I said "no", he said "let's try." Of course, he put me down not on the other side but right in the middle of the ditch. And so, we are both standing in the ditch, up to our bellies in snow, and dying from laughter. It was hard for him to climb out, as the ditch was deep, and for me too. So, he climbed out somehow and stretched his arms out to me. Of course, I slid back down into the ditch on my stomach about three times, but finally climbed out. And we performed all this with flowers in our hands. Then we couldn't fit between the crosses for a while, as we were both wearing our coats.

---

[47] Sonia Orbeliani was a Georgian princess and friend of the imperial family

Rare contemporary photo of the graves at Brethren cemetery

But in the end, I did find the grave. Finally, we were able to leave the cemetery. Tatiana and Anastasia were already waiting for me on the road. I felt half-dead from heat and dampness. We climbed into the motors and drove away. I took off one boot to shake out the snow. At this same time, we ran into a wagon. We were driving rather fast. We just swerved to the side a little, when Lapin's steering wheel spun [out of control] and our front tires slid into a snow bank, and frighteningly [we] turned on our side, I jumped out wearing one boot and put the other one back on out on the road. What could we do, no one was there any longer and it was already 1 o'clock 10 minutes. Then we 3 decided to walk home on foot, but luckily at this moment some squadron was walking back from shooting practice and they dug out the motor, while we walked almost all the way to the shooting gallery. The motor caught up to us and we got home safely. But the road was so bad the entire time that we were certain that the motor would break. Across from the Cuirassier Cathedral. And we were tossed up so high that Tatiana almost hit her head on the roof. In the afternoon during our *troika* ride we almost ran over another sleigh.

So, after all this, we went to our infirmary, and we were certain that we will fall into a ditch or something else will happen to us again. [We] went to the fortress yesterday. The sailors were all very sweet and worked hard. You were very much missed there. [...] In the evening Anya finished reading "Our People Abroad" to us. Olga went to bed early of course. And you are probably enjoying the English book. Grandmama sent the book "Olive," and Mama sent her another one. Well, farewell my darling. May Christ be with you. + Your *Kazanetz*[48]. I kiss you affectionately and squeeze you a lot and for a long time. Titanis, titanis. Dukchik Dukchik.

From 1916 diary of Alexei Romanov

5 March. Got up early. Studied and took a walk. Had breakfast we 5 with Mama. In the afternoon took a walk with Kolya. Had tea and dinner at Mama's. Had dinner at 6 o'cl. Went to bed early.

6 March. Got up early. Took a walk. Had breakfast with Mama, O., T., M. and A. Took a walk in the afternoon. Went to *obednya.* Had dinner at Mama's. Went to Anya's infirmary, a magician was there. Had dinner at 6 o'cl. Went to bed early.

---

[48] Refers to the 5th Kazansky Dragoons regiment, of which Maria was honourary captain

From the 1916 diary of Maria Romanov

7 March. Had lessons. Rode around with Shura, breakfast 5 with Mama on the sofa. Went to our infirmary with A. Ivan bid farewell to us as he is leaving from the Svodny regiment and returning to the Black Sea. Went to Vitebsk community infirmary with Isa, in the barracks of the 3rd St. Regiment. Had tea 4 with Mama and Anya. Had English and music lessons. Rode in a *troika* with O., A. and Shura. Had dinner 4 and Mama on the sofa. Lili Dehn[49] with [her] husband, Anya and Baron Taube were here. Sat and looked at a [photo] album, then went to tea. It was very cozy.

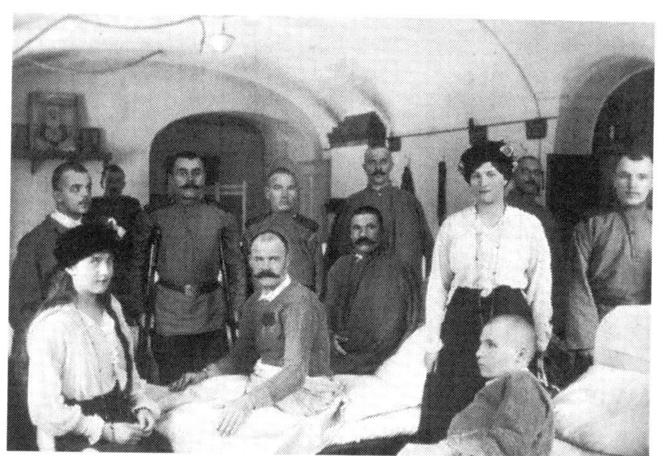

[49] Lili Dehn - born Yulia Alexandrovna Smolskaia, wife of a Russian naval officer on the imperial yacht The Standart, and friend of Empress Alexandra

Maria to Nicholas Alexandrovich

9 March. My dear darling Papa! Today is Spring already, but it's 7 [degrees] of frost here and snowing with wind. Completely unacceptable. [I] just finished breakfast. Olga and Tatiana are going to Petrograd for charities and committee, and will have tea at Grandmama's, and will also stop by Aunt Ksenia's[50] who feels terrible and does not leave the house. I will now go to our infirmary with A. Nikolai Dmitrievich[51] bade farewell to Mama. Before that, the regiment had a goodbye party for him in the evening at 7 o'clock, which only ended at 5 in the morning, so Resin looked rather sad, and when he was leaving the room [he] almost knocked over a vase with flowers, and his voice was not very nice either. But N.D. himself was very charming. I have not seen him since then, and don't even expect to anymore.

---

[50] Grand Duchess Ksenia Alexandrovna, Nicholas's sister

[51] Demenkov

Right now, Anastasia is sitting here and playing the *balalaika*. Well so long, my dear. I kiss you affectionately and apologize for a boring letter. Your *Kazanetz*. May Christ be with you. +

Maria and Anastasia in Feodorovsky Gorodok[52], near their infirmary

From 1916 diary of Alexei Romanov

10 March. Got up at 8 ½, studied and took a walk. Had breakfast with Mama and the sisters. In the afternoon took a walk and worked. Did homework. Had dinner at 6 o'cl. Went to Mama's for dinner. Went to bed as usual.

[52] Little village the Tsar built near the palace, in the old Russian style

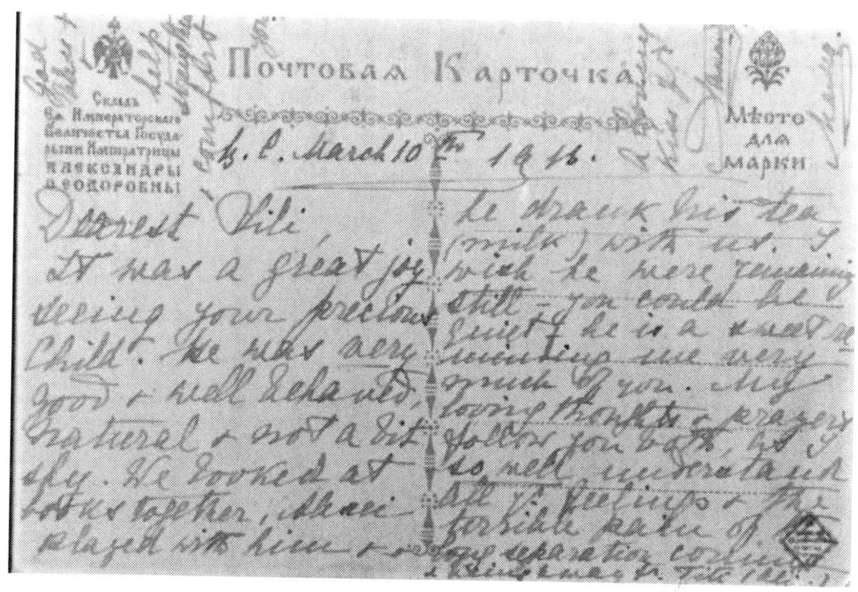

Почтовая Карточка

Мѣсто для марки

Ц. С. March 10th 1916.

Dearest Lili

It was a great joy seeing your precious Child. He was very good & well behaved, natural & not a bit shy. We looked at books together, Alexei played with him & he drank his tea (milk) with us. I wish he were remaining still – you could be quiet, he is a sweet reminding me very much of you. My loving thoughts & prayers follow you both, as I so well understand all yr feelings & the terrible pain of long separation.

Postcard from Alexandra to Lili Dehn dated **10 March**, 1916

From 1916 diary of Alexei Romanov

12 March. Got up early. Studied and took a walk. Had breakfast with Mama, O., T., M. and A. Took a walk in the afternoon. Titi[53] was here. Went to tea at Mama's and dinner. Had dinner at 6 o'cl. Went to bed early. ~~Yesterday it was~~ It was raining.

[53] Lili Dehn's son.

Tatiana to Nicholas Alexandrovich

12 March. Papa darling. Our fortress is growing frighteningly [fast]. Do you remember the spot where Mordvinov built the ladder? Well, we have leveled the entire top and will build another level. Yesterday 11 sailors worked [there], the weather was fine and wonderfully clear, sunny, but in the shade it was 12 of frost. But it was nice for working. Anastasia took a lot of photographs, so when they are ready, will send them to You. It's appalling to think that there are people who are enjoying Livadia [now], right? E.S.

Botkin[54] writes the longest letters to Mama about all the resorts and infirmaries. Do You play dominoes a lot? Do You take long walks or are You too busy nowadays? It will feel empty tonight [in church] again standing alone by our column. I will think about how You stand alone at your Stavka. Well, goodbye. Papa darling dear. May God bless You and help You at this difficult time. Firm firm hugs and kisses, as [strong as] I love [you]. Your *Voznesenetz.*

From the 1916 diary of Alexei Romanov

17 March. Got up early. Studied and took a walk. Had breakfast with Mama, O., T., M. and A. Took a walk in the afternoon. Went to Mama's for tea and dinner. Had dinner at 6 o'cl. Anya was at dinner.

From the 1916 diary of Maria Romanov

20 March. Went to church with Papa and Mama. Had breakfast 5, Papa and Mama on the sofa. 4 went to the Gr.[and] Pal.[ace]. Walked with Papa and Mama [rode] in a carriage. Broke ice 4 with Papa. Had tea in the playroom. 5 went to Anya's concert at the infirmary, "Ivanov Pavel" and the magicians. Went to

[54] Evgeny Sergeyevich Botkin, imperial physician

our infirmaries with A., 17 soldiers arrived from the train. Rode around with A. and Shura. Had dinner 5 with Papa, Mama, Silaev and Anya. Papa read.

Maria breaking ice with her father

From 1916 diary of Alexei Romanov

25 March. Got up early. Took a walk. Went to *obednya.* Had breakfast with Papa, Mama, O., T., M. and A. Took a walk in the afternoon. Dmitri had breakfast. Papa and Mama went to the city. Saw Papa off. Had dinner at 6 o'cl. Went to bed early. Was at Mama's for dinner.

From the 1916 diary of Maria Romanov

26 March. Walked with Trina[55], had lessons, rode around with Shura. Had breakfast 5 with Papa and Mama, Count Fredericks, and Count Kutaisov. Broke ice with Papa and the sailors. Mama was there. Papa departed, [we] saw him and Dmitri off. Had tea 4 and Mama. Went to *vsenoshnaya* 5 with Mama. Had dinner 4 and Mama on the sofa. Anya was here.

Maria at the Alexander Palace, circa 1916

27 March. Sunday. Went to Church 5 with Mama, breakfast with same and Isa. Went to our infirmary with A. Rode 4 with Mama and Anya. Went to a concert at Anya's infirmary 5 with Mama. Rode 2 with

[55] Catherine Schneider, one of imperial tutors

Shura. Had dinner 4 and Mama on the sofa. Anya was here.

Tatiana to Nicholas Alexandrovich

28 March. Papa, my darling dear. Today we worked on the ice, it was very nice. Mama sat in her chair beside us for a little while. Saw and heard as the Hundred Convoy passed by us. They sang very well. They, of course, stopped singing as soon as they noticed us, but I ordered them to continue, and pretended to be You, charming isn't it?! Mama was with us today at the infirmary, and bandaged three officers who just arrived from Proskurov. There was one colonel with an amputated left arm. I wanted to write to You more and say where he had served, but Mama tells me that she had already written to you all about him. Well, it is now very lonesome and empty standing in church alone in our spot. Ortipo is now lying on the floor and chewing on her football.

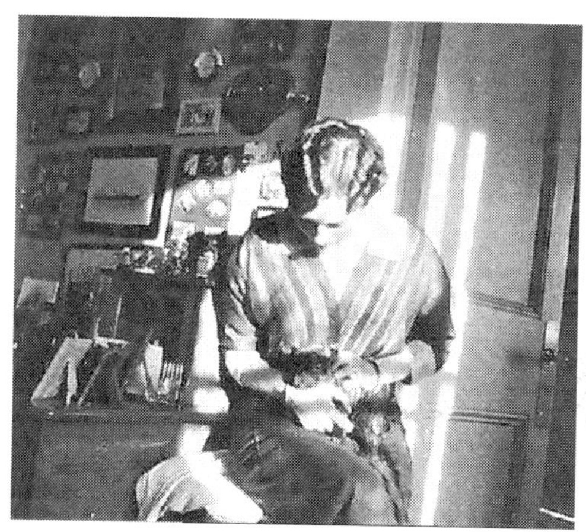

Tatiana with Ortipo

[We] just finished dinner. Mama is reading to herself, and Olga and Marie are composing mean verses about the sisters [nurses] of the Grand Palace. Of course there is no rhyme, since it will have to be sung, not read. Did you finish the book and was it interesting later on? Is Dimitri reading his book? If you see our Hundred and the Crimeans, send them our regards <...>. Goodbye, Papa darling. May God bless you. I kiss You very very affectionately. Dmitri also. Your very loving *Voznesenetz.*

Olga, Maria, Tatiana and Alexei with his sailor Derevenko in Alexander Park

Anastasia to Nicholas Alexandrovich

31 March, 1916. T.S. My precious Papa Darling. I am hurrying to write to you as we must go to the infirmary. Maria and I and Alexei had breakfast upstairs as Mama and the sisters are in Petrograd. We go outside and break ice. Yesterday Fedotov was not there. Krylov is terribly weak and showed up. Maria and I are now playing, she on the piano, and I on the balalaika, and it's turning out rather well, but it's even better with Olga.

The Grand Duchesses' rooms "upstairs" at the Alexander Palace

I am imagining how the 1st Hundred was happy to see you there in particular and I was a little envious of you. We will go break ice again today, and to two infirmaries, to ours and to the Grand Palace. I give you a terribly big kiss and squeeze you. Your loving loyal and faithful *Kaspiyitz.* +

Tatiana to Nicholas Alexandrovich

5 April. Today the weather is not very nice again, cold and no sun. Went to church twice today, very lonesome without you. I can't even imagine Easter and *Zautrenya*[56] without you. Saw my three Voznesentzy today, who came to the infirmary to visit their chief, which in my opinion was very charming. One of them, whom I know best, told me that all the officers and even the soldiers do not seem to like their regimental commander. Many left the regiment because of him and became pilots. <…> He used to command the 14th Yamburg Regiment. Something happened there, for which he left the regiment and was appointed to the reserves. From there, he got into my regiment. They all say to me, "can he be promoted faster to <…> his team, and give us someone better from the Guards or a Gen[eral]." Today Petya had breakfast with us. Imagine this, he got fatter. Oddly he is going to Crimea to Ai-Todor. Ksenia with Nikita[57] will go there too after Easter. They are really hoping that in the meantime Grandmama will go to Kiev to a.[unt] Olga's. It would be so nice for her. On 3 April we had tea with Dmitri, as always he talked a lot of nonsense, told us how you

[56] Matins of Easter

[57] Ksenia's son, Tatiana's cousin

rode and how he liked the book "Through the Postern Gate". Isn't it nice that the Cossacks, the soldiers and apparently Batushka's entire wonderful family will partake with us. Well, Papa darling, although the letter will not arrive in time I ask Your forgiveness before confession. You will be very missed during prayers before confession, near our icons when the Batushka reads "Lord have mercy" 12 times. Forgive the blots in the letter, but I have perfumed it and Mama said that it wouldn't smear, but that has turned out to the contrary. Well, goodbye. May God bless You. I am going to church and will pray for You. Big big kiss to you, as big as my love of you. Your very lonesome without You, Voznesenetz.

Nicholas Alexandrovich to Tatiana

Christ Has Risen! Thank you, dear Tatiana, for your letter and photos, whi[ich] I often look at. I am very sad to be alone these days. Constantly thinking about you, and regret that we cannot ride here together along the Dnieper. It is quite warm but no greenery yet. I wish you a pleasant holiday. I embrace you. Your Papa. 1916.

Tatiana to Nicholas Alexandrovich

9 April. Christ Has Risen! I thank you so much, Papa darling, for Your wonderful egg and postcard. We are also very, very lonesome without You. Today it is warm here, so that tonight it will probably be nice to walk around the church.[58] Yesterday it rained a little and was muddy. And by You? Did You also walk around the church? And where will You break the fast? I am glad for Silaev that he is getting into a regiment, but you will be one adjutant short. Again will have to choose. And when does he go to the regiment? Alexei already rode today, so we hope that he will go to *zautrenya.* Well, good-bye, Papa darling. I must finish, otherwise the man[59] will leave and the letter will be late. May God bless You. I kiss You very, very affectionately three times. It will be very lonesome and empty without Your very loving Voznesenetz.

10 April. My dear darling Papa. We just finished breakfast. Before that we had the Easter greetings. A lot of people, but finished fast, it lasted from 11 to 12 o'clock. In the afternoon we will drive to our infirmary,

[58] Procession of the Cross

[59] Messenger

Mama will be giving out [Easter] eggs[60] there. Yesterday [the weather] was wonderful during *zautrenya*. It was completely still during the procession of the cross. Even the candles did not have to be covered by hand. There were masses of people, needless public, of course. [There is] a new Scout in the Consolidated Regiment. His vision is very bad, poor thing, from contusions or injuries, I do not know which. Yesterday Rodionov had tea with us, he only came for a few days and is leaving today. The weather today is average, not hot and not cold and no sun, which is tiresome. Tomorrow we will do Easter greetings at the Grand Palace. Terribly strange to be at such things without you, Papa darling. Thanks again for a wonderfully attractive egg that I like very much, and a sweet card. Well, good-bye, Papa darling. Regards to Silayev, Mordvinov and Count Nikitin. May God bless you. I kiss You very very affectionately, [as much as I] love [you]. Your Voznesenetz.

From 1916 diary of Tatiana Romanov

Sunday, Paskha [Easter]. **10 April**. Returned from *zautrenya* at 1.50. Broke the fast 4 with Mama and

---

[60] Souvenirs for Easter

Anya. Very lonesome without Papa. For the first time without him. In the morning at 11 o'clock, greetings. Mama gave out eggs until 12 o'clock. All of us were there. Breakfast at 12.30 with Mama, had dinner and tea with her. Skated with Olga and Trina. At 3 o'clock we 4 went with Mama to our infirmary. Distributed eggs to ours in the sitting room. Later – to all the bedridden. Sat with Sedov, Iedigarov was also there. Very nice. Had tea at home. At 7 o'clock went to church until 7.40. Read after dinner.

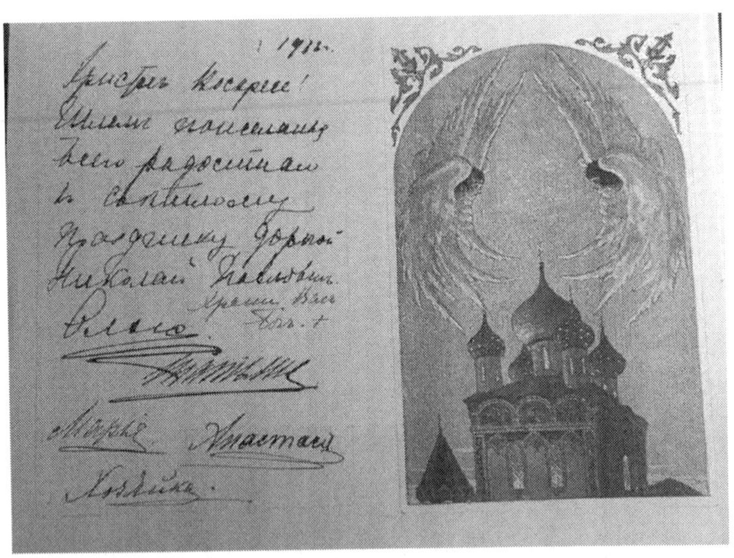

Easter postcard to N.P. Sablin[61] from the Romanov women. "*1916. Christ has risen! We are sending wishes of all happiness for the holy day, dear Nikolai Pavlovich. May God keep you + Olga Tatiana Maria Anastasia The Mistress*[62]"

[61] Nikolai Pavlovich Sablin, the tsar's aide-de-camp

[62] Empress Alexandra Feodorovna

From 1916 diary of Alexei Romanov

10 April. Got up at ½ 11. Exchanged Easter greetings with everyone. Mama was giving out eggs to everyone. Had breakfast with O., T., M. and A. In the evening rode around and visited Kolya. Went to bed early.

14 April. Got up early. Studied and took a walk. Had breakfast with Papa, Mama, O., T., M., A., Aunt Ksenia and Sandro. In the afternoon took a walk and misbehaved. Had dinner at 6 o'cl. Was at Mama's in the evening. Went to bed early.

Palisander room at the Alexander Place

15 April. Got up early. Studied and took a walk. Had breakfast with Papa, Mama, O., T., M., A., and Vilkitsky. In the afternoon took a walk and a ride. Papa, Mama and the sisters were at Aunt Mavra's.[63] Took a ride. Was at Mama's for dinner. Went to bed early.

16 April. Studied and took a walk. Had breakfast with Papa, Mama, O., T., M., A., Uncle Georgiy, Count Fredericks and Dmitri Sheremetiev. In the afternoon took a walk and a ride in boats. Had dinner at 6 o'cl. Was at Mama's for dinner. Went to bed early.

Boating in Alexander Park

[63] Grand Duchess Elizaveta Mavrikievna, wife of Grand Duke Konstantin Konstantinovich

From the 1916 diary of Tatiana Romanov

Tuesday, **3 May.** Did not do much of anything in the morning. Went to “Znamenie”. Drove to the infirmary. Dressings <...> Then sat with Sedov, and the others. Was with Bibi. Breakfast 5 with Mama, Mme. Zizi[64], and Trina. At 1.45 we two went with Isa to Petrograd to the Registration Bureau for refugees, where they are searching for them, then to the Winter Palace for the committee meeting. Then sat at Alya’s. Returned with Nastenka. There was [some] music. Had dinner with Mama. At 8:30 all went to the infirmary. Sat with Sedov, then fed Pavlov, then again with Sedov until 11 o’clock. Returned [and went] to bed.

The Grand Duchesses walking to Znamenie church

Wednesday, **4 May**. Packed in the morning. At 10.40 we two with Mama and Alexei went to "Znamenie." Met Bibi there. Took her on the motor and brought to the

[64] Elizaveta Naryshkina, former lady-in-waiting

infirmary. Walked around in full swing [to see] everyone, said goodbye to all and left. It was such a pity really. Picked up the sisters and drove to the train. At 11 o'clock departed. Breakfast, lunch and tea all together. In the afternoon sat at Mama's, and finished reading an English book. Then worked, read, wrote. After lunch, Olga played the piano, Nastasya[65] the balalaika, and we sang. Went to bed at 10 o'clock. At the stations went out, walked, Ortipo was with me.

From 1916 diary of Alexei Romanov

10 May. At 10 o'cl. ¼ went to the review. We saw the Russian soldiers and 3 regiments of the Serbian ones. When we returned from the parade, Papa and I saw the small museum. Had breakfast with Mama. 2 o'cl. 45 m. went to see the iodine producing factory. Then went to see the clinic for healing mud baths, in two places on the shore of the Black Sea. Had dinner with Mama on the train.

[65] One of Anastasia's nicknames

Photo from 10 May, 1916 in Odessa

Tatiana to Nicholas Alexandrovich

20 May 1916. Today it is 20 [degrees] in the sun, but cold in the shade. We will go to the infirmary, [our] lessons start. All our rooms were cleaned, they seem so big after the cozy train. Iedigarov told us many interesting things about how they are fighting over there, about the regiment and a lot of things in general. Well, good-bye, Papa darling. May God bless You. I kiss you both firmly and gently, my dears. Your Voznesenetz.

Tatiana coming out of an infirmary

From the 1916 diary of Tatiana Romanov

Monday, **23 May.** In the morning, went for a walk with Anastasia and Trina, from 9 to 10 o'clock. Then to *Znamenie* and to the infirmary. Olga rides with me, Mama too, a little. Surgery on a soldier, excised the leg bone. Handed the instruments. Bandaged Natarov. Sat on the balcony with Pavlov, Mitya and Borya[66] came [over]. Stayed with them. Breakfast 4 with Mama on the balcony. Had tea and dinner there. Had a lesson. Then rode "Kopriko." It was wonderful.

[66] Possibly Boris Ravtopulo

Around Pavlovsk. After tea [had a] lesson. Then rode around with Nastenka and the sisters. After dinner we all went to the infirmary. Picked up Bibi on the way. There we cleaned instruments and sewed compresses until 11:45. Borya and Mitya were there, too.

Tatiana and Alexandra

From the 1916 diary of Maria Romanov

25 May. Went to *obednya* with Mama. Had breakfast with same on the balcony.

Breakfast on the balcony

Went to our infirmary with A. Rode 4 with Nastenka. Had tea 4 on the balcony with Mama, Aunt Olga, Aunt Mavra, and Aunt Miechen.[67] Drove 4 with Mama to Anya's house, [where] we saw Grigori[68] and Munika[69]. Had dinner 4 with Mama. Went to the sisters' infirmary, put together a puzzle with Grekova, the Countess, Natarovich, Nikiforov, Karankozov and the Doctor.

[67] Grand Duchess Maria Pavlovna "the Elder," wife of Grand Duke Vladimir Alexandrovich.

[68] Rasputin

[69] Maria "Munya" Golovina

Anya Vyrubova's house (contemporary photo)

Anastasia to Nicholas Alexandrovich

27 May, 1916. T.S. My dear Papa Darling! I will soon send you the pictures that I took in Mogilev and Sevastopol, if you want them! Yesterday when I was riding around, a long distance passenger train passed by and suddenly I saw through the window a protective red beshmet and papakha,[70] and further in the window a grey cherkeska[71] and I thought I recognized Count Grabbe and his Cossack, and then during the day we ran into Voiekov, he was riding in a motor.

[70] Quilted half-caftan and cape, of Tatar origin

[71] A long caftan, tightened at the waist, without a collar and with a wedge-shaped neckline on the chest

The Grand Duchesses, Alexei and Nicholas with General Voiekov

Tell Alexei that I plan to write to him, but never have time. We now pick flowers; the lilac is here already but not that much of it. The weather is not great, it rains daily nevertheless we still have breakfast and tea on the balcony.

Alexander Palace balcony in the left wing

Right now, I don't have a lesson and therefore I can write. Have you heard anything about the 1st Hundred! They probably have enough to do now and are rather happy. Sometimes a Hundred comes by here for practice and returns with *zurna*[72], so of course we eye [them] and yesterday they passed and I watched. It's a shame there are too many bushes so they can't see us well, but the important thing, of course, is that we can see them. We will now accompany the sisters to their infirmary and ride back for our lessons. Everyone gives you a big kiss and Alexei too. Your loving loyal and faithful little *Kaspiyitz.* May God keep you!

[72] A type of musical instrument

Anastasia on the balcony

Nicholas Alexandrovich to Tatiana

Stavka **28 May, 1916**. Dearest Tatiana. Congratulations on your birthday and I wish you good health and all the best. I regret that I cannot spend time with you on this day! Thank you very much for writing the letters, which give me great pleasure. Alexei and I often remember our trip and especially Sevastopol! It was so nice to be there among the sailors! Alexei named this one place here with soft sand on the banks of the Dnieper— "Evpatoria", and [he] loves it. Every other day we ride on the river in motor boats and row boats. Tell Olga that I chose four photographs and [am] returning the rest and [I] thank her. How did you like Zhilik's letter; he was afraid to send it, but I insisted you get it. These days it is hot and the weather is wonderful and it is during this time that different ministers are pestering me! Thank God that things are going well for us in the south-west, now the total number of prisoners has reached 77,000 men. Grandmama will probably see a lot, because they all gather in Kiev first. I'm glad that you go horseback riding, but why not with the sisters? Today the miraculous icon of Our Lady of Vladimir arrived from Moscow and at 5 o'cl. they will solemnly take [it] to our church. Well, I've got to finish now. I embrace you and the sisters. May Christ be with you. + Your Papa.

Maria to Nicholas Alexandrovich

29 May. [At] the Feodorovsky Cathedral Imperial infirmary for the wounded. My dear Papa! I don't think I ever wrote to you on this paper before. Today it was hot here, but now [it is] not that [hot], as it rained a little. In the morning we went to *obednya* and had breakfast on the balcony, also had tea with Zizi.[73] She is leaving to her village tomorrow. I am all bitten up by some nasty beast, and therefore my entire body

[73] Elizaveta Naryshkina, mistress of the robes.

itches. It is extremely unpleasant, especially in public, when one has to scratch.

Grand Duchesses at Feodorovsky Cathedral entrance

These days we go to the sisters' infirmary almost every evening. They clean the instruments and prepare materials for the next day. Anastasia plays table croquet with the wounded, while I play bloshki or put together a puzzle. This afternoon we rode around, and then went to our infirmary. Almost all the wounded are lying in the tent, only the heavily [wounded] ones are not allowed.

Those who are able, walk to Catherine Park and sail around the lake in row boats. They really enjoy this and always ask the nurses to go with them. We go to our infirmary every day too, this is much better than the Grand Palace with Nurse Lyubushina. She of course noted that we got tan and all the nurses too.

The other day we went to Children's Island[74] with Poupse's[75] sister, and she weeded with us. There is so much decayed grass among the lilies of the valley that they are not growing well. We cleaned half, and will finish the other half in one of the next couple of days. I kiss you and Alexei very affectionately. May God keep you. + Your *Kazanetz.*

---

[74] Small island in Alexander Park, where a playhouse had been built in 1830 for the children of Tsar Nicholas I

[75] Presumably a nickname for one of the members of th suite or officers, literally means "baby doll"

Children's Island and house in Alexander Park

Tatiana to Nicholas Alexandrovich

29 May[76], 1916. My dear Papa! I thank You immensely for the dear letter and the congratulations, which made me terribly happy. Thank you very much also for the wonderful gifts. We all laughed terribly at Zhilik's letter. What rubbish – to write such letters. When I see him he will pay, the old smart alec. This morning it was 30 [degrees], now 25 in the shade. Very nice, just a little stuffy. I received a touching telegram from Nik. Dm. Demenkov. Made me very happy. The Yerivantzy also wrote. Yesterday Nikolai Pavlovich had tea with us. [He is] very tan and looks good. Congratulations to Alexei on the Lance, so charming! Well, goodbye Papa

[76] Tatiana's birthday

darling. May God bless You. I kiss both of you darlings firmly, my dears. Your *Voznesenetz.*

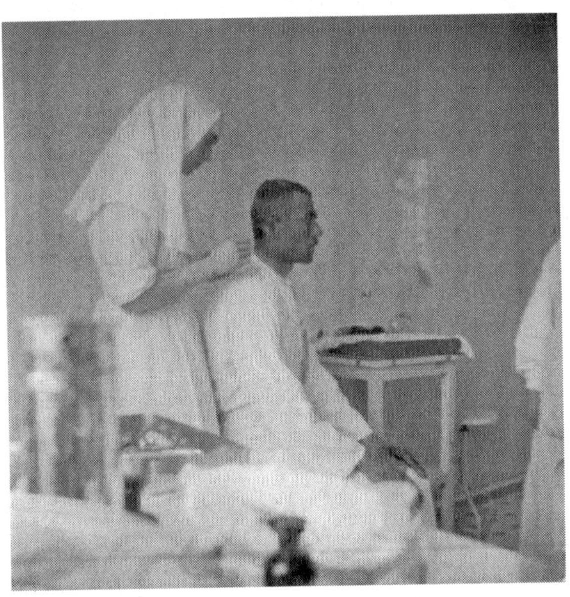

Anastasia to Nicholas Alexandrovich

31 May 1916. Tsarskoe Selo. We are having lessons now, but as of tomorrow we will still have lessons but not during the day anymore, and this will be very pleasant. These days Maria and I swing on giant steps[77] a lot. We are almost never nauseous (although we fell a bunch of times already, but so far have not hurt ourselves). We were riding around now as there is no lesson and now we are waiting for Mama and the sisters [to return] from the infirmary. We go there in

[77] A swing-like game

evenings and I play croquet which is sitting on a table. It is very small, but it is really fun to play. I play with 3 officers the entire evening until they send me to bed, although most of the time I go without an invitation.

Anastasia in Alexander Palace, circa 1916

Now I must finish writing as it is time for *frishtyk*[78] on the balcony. Today it is windy but sunny and warm. I listen to your and Alexei's letters with great gusto during *zakuski*[79] or breakfast. I apologize that I am

---

[78] Type of appetisers (German)
[79] Appetisers (Russian)

using different ink, but I am writing in Mama's room. Well now! I give awfully big kisses to your sweet little cheeks and hands, and Alexei. May God keep you. Your loving loyal and faithful 14-year-old Kaspiyitz.

From the 1916 diary of Olga Romanov

Saturday, **4th June.** Viktor Erastovich[80] was wounded. Skvortsov too, but lightly, and 7 Cossacks. 1 was killed. Shurik is ill with typhus. To *Znamenie* and to the infirmary with Mama. Mitya and Borya came before 1 o'clock. Did everything as usual. Raining and cold. Anya and Emma Fredericks with her father had breakfast again. During the day rode with Mama in 2 carriages. [We] were cold and wet. Saw Mitya from the Silayevs' window.

[80] Viktor Erastovich Zborovsky (aka "Vik.Erast."), one of imperial officers close to the family

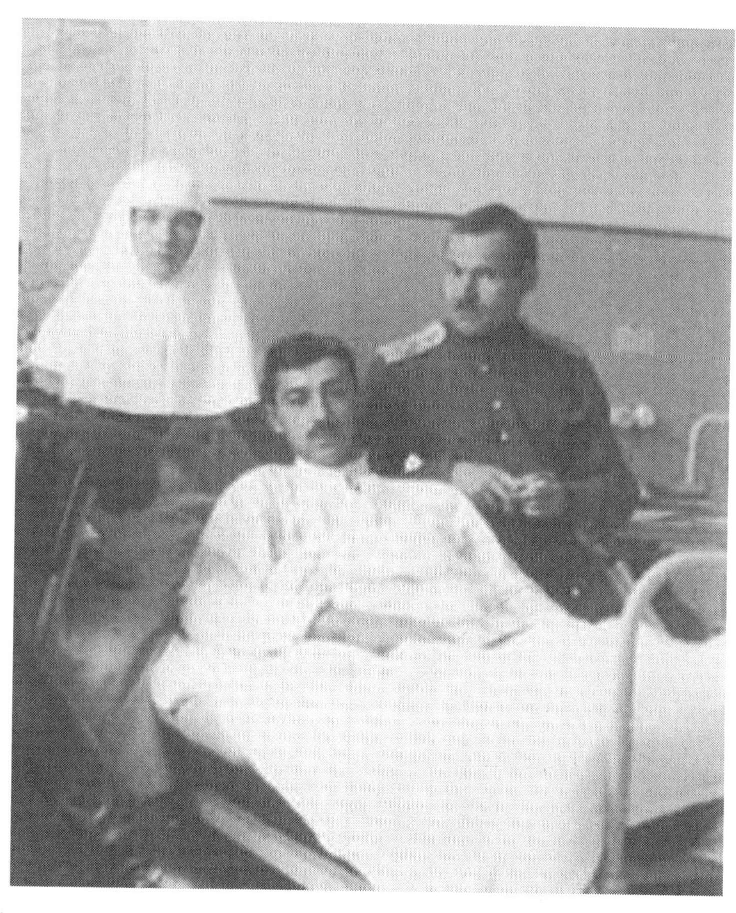

Olga at the infirmary. In bed is Dmitri "Mitya" Shakh-Bagov[81]

Anastasia to Nicholas Alexandrovich

9 June 1916. My dear Papa Darling. We just played ping pong with Maria and were bustling around and yelling so incredibly much that now my hands are shaking like someone with a head injury. I think that in a few days they will bring Viktor Erastovich to our

[81] Wounded officer, Olga's romantic interest

infirmary, he requested for another cornet from the Tekinsky Regiment to come with him, they will bring them from Poltava. Of course, this is pleasant.

Anastasia with Viktor Erastovich Zborovsky

We are now moving to a nearby infirmary, the one that looks out on to the Convoy gathering and the Sobor. We will have an infirmary there now, so very cozy. Maria and I went there a few times to look, and we were satisfied.

Anastasia and Tatiana exiting infirmary in Feodorovsky Gorodok

Today Mama, Olga and Tatiana are going to the city for the Executive Committee, and I don't envy them, while Maria and I are staying here. We keep swinging in the hammock. Well, when Vera and Georgiy[82] were here, they had breakfast [here] with their mother. So we picked them up and swung them, Vera was really happy, while Georgiy kept getting scared, and then Vera and Georgiy started fighting, and we were instigating them a little against each other and laughing. It will probably start raining now, but of

[82] Princess Vera Konstantinovna and Prince Georgiy Konstantinovich, the youngest children of Grand Duke Konstantin Konstantinovich

course I am not afraid of this as I am a brave little soldier. Well here it comes, congratulations!!! I wrote all the news and everything interesting, and the rest is as usual. Well, I will end my silly message now, masses of kisses to you and Alexei. May Christ be with you. Regards to all of yours. Miss [you]. Your loving loyal and faithful little Kaspiyitz. All the sisters kiss you.

From the 1916 diary of Tatiana Romanov

Monday, **13 June.** To *Znamenie* with Mama and to the infirmary. Colonel Zhuravsky of the 13th Belozersky Regiment—surgery. He was seriously wounded in the abdomen, chest and leg. Wrote, etc. Ate on the balcony. Wonderful weather. In the afternoon [we] lay out in the sun and picked flowers. At 6 o'clock rode around with Isa. Papa wrote. In the evening [went] to the infirmary without Mama. Sewed cushions until 11 o'clock. It is exactly a week that the little one left. May God save him. 9 [degrees] of heat.

Anastasia to Nicholas Alexandrovich

16 June. My dear Papa Darling! I am writing out of turn as I did not have a chance to write because we were going to our new infirmary a lot. We already moved and it is terribly cozy. On the very first day they brought 3 officers there and 10 lower ranks, four of them serious [wounded]. One boy, 16 years old, is also rather seriously wounded.

Anastasia with nurses outside infirmary

On 14 June we had a real housewarming. We went to our infirmary 3 times, alone in the morning. In the afternoon with Mama and the sisters, and in the evening again alone, to a concert. It was very cozy, masses of people and the wounded [were there]. But the funniest thing was when a 5-year-old boy Vitya (the son of our former patient, who is now our *banya*[83] attendant), he started to dance and everyone poked him and he got going, it was terribly funny, everyone

[83] Russian traditional sauna

was enjoying it and it was noisy and so forth, while he kept dancing calmly with his back to the public. When we were leaving, it was really cozy, as on the pink gangway they lit a lamp and there was pink light. [It was] awfully appetizing. Yesterday Count Grabbe came to [see] Vik. Erastovich and the Cossack who recently arrived wounded in his arm and hip, his name is something like Boyarkin. He is very merry and talks a lot. Now we feel sad passing by the old infirmary, the poor thing is just standing there, although there are 6 [wounded of the] lower ranks [there] who do not get dressings and they are waiting to depart for Finland, so Maria and I go there, there are masses of workers and a lot of scattered things.

Maria and Anastasia in Feodorovsky Gorodok

Right now, the weather is sunny and warm, [but I] don't know what it will be like in the afternoon. Well, I must end. I send [you] a terribly big kiss, Darling Papa and Alexei 100000000 times. May God keep you, your loving loyal and faithful *Kaspiyitz*.

Maria to Nicholas Alexandrovich

17 June, 1916. My dear Papa! Right now, I am sitting on the balcony with Mama and Anya. We just finished breakfast. The rain storm is everywhere, and the thunder is very loud. I don't know what we will do.

Alexandra and "Anya" Vyrubova on the balcony

Oh, pray, Holy Magdalene,

For their fate.

1916

Sergei Yesenin; Sisters of Mercy Olga and Tatiana Romanov

Nurses and wounded officers in front of Grand Duchess Olga Nikolaevna's Military-medical train #164.

Inside of Grand Duchess Anastasia Nikolaevna's imperial military-medical train #61

Anastasia to Nicholas Alexandrovich

24 June, 1916. Tsarskoe Selo. My dear Papa darling. Maria and I just rolled around in the grass in front of the balcony. It was terribly pleasant and now I am the color of raspberries.

We are waiting for Mama and the sisters for breakfast. Sashka will have breakfast with us today. Next to me on the table are your and Alexei's letters, which were just brought to us. I think that Maria wrote to you that we have a new officer at our infirmary from the 10th Sharpshooter regiment, he is wounded in the arm, his name is Zhilinsky, I think, he is sweet although we don't know him well yet. Vik. Erast. is fussing about when and how the 1st Hundred will arrive.

Anastasia with an infirmary patient

Yesterday we four started a bonfire and jumped over it. It was wonderful. We cut off old branches with dull knives and with our hands, and then swung in hammocks. Now there are two hammocks, as Marie has one too and they are hanging in a wake column[86]. Do you remember that yesterday was 3 years since we had the evening picnic in the Skerries[87] and we all danced and Artemov told [us] all kinds of stories. I read my diary and therefore was reminiscing about every little detail from beginning to end. It was so nice then!!! Everything is as always now. I had a cold and a cough, I was so embarrassed because it is not

[86] A nautical term referring to the deistance between ships following in the wake of each other

[87] In Finland

supposed to happen in the summer, but it's a bit better now. So, at this moment I just sneezed, you tell me "Bless you," I am very grateful to you for this. Well, I will end my letter with masses of kisses to you and Alexei 1000 times. May God be with you. Sleep well. Your loving. Your loyal and faithful little *Kaspiyitz.*

Tatiana in a hammock

From the 1916 diary of Maria Romanov

29 June. Went to *obednya* 4 with Mama at the Palace infirmary. Had breakfast 4 with Mama, Isa is on the balcony. Before that rode around with Shvybzik[88] and Trina. Went to the new infirmary of the Svodny

[88] One of Anastasia's nicknames, from the German word *beschwipst* meaning tipsy or merry

regiment No. 36 with A. Went to the new infirmary with A.

"Isa" Buxhoeveden

Sat with Shurik too. Had tea with Shvybz and the same [people] swung in a hammock. Rode around with A. and Isa. Had dinner 4 with Mama on the balcony. Went to the sisters' infirmary. Played croquet and Dobchinsky-Bobchinsky.

Playing croquet at the infirmary

Tatiana to Nicholas Alexandrovich

30 June. My dear Papa. Just said goodbye to the officers of the 4th Hundred, and tomorrow will go to *moleben* and see them off. It is so nice when every time we go out to the entrance and see all the wonderful Cossacks all bearing standards. Saw Alexander Konstantinovich from afar, he lost weight poor thing, after an illness. Uncle Georgiy had breakfast with us. Tomorrow [he] is going to You. I am very happy that maybe we will see each other soon. Old Aunt Olga[89] is going to Grandmama's in Kiev for about 10 days. Grandmama invited her. Then she

[89] Queen of Greece

said that Nicky and Andrei will come soon, so she is very happy. Did you walk a lot with Petrovsky? Who will be with You in his stead?... Today Baron Taube had surgery. His leg hurts terribly, poor thing. [There are] many new serious[ly] [wounded], who were brought in by Princess Gedroitz[90] from the positions, but these brave lads endure [well]. Must end as Mama is waiting to send the letters. Christ be with You. I embrace [you] both. Your *Voznesenetz.*

[90] Princess and physician Vera Ignatievna Gedroitz

From the 1916 diary of Maria Romanov

1 July. Had lessons. Rode around with Anastasia and Trina. Breakfast 4 with Mama and Isa on the balcony. In the afternoon went to our infirmary with A. Sat as usual. Went 4 to the farewell *molebna*. The 4th Hundred rode on *vetka*[91] and they passed by us, and we bid [our] farewells. Had tea 4 with Mama on the balcony. Rode around with A. and Trina. Had dinner 4 with Mama and Zhilik on the balcony. Went to the sisters' infirmary. Played croquet and D.[obchinsky]-B.[obchinsky].

[91] The train line

3 July. Went to *obednya* with Mama at the Pal. Infirmary. Rode around with A. and Trina. Had breakfast 4 with Mama and Anya on the balcony. Went to our infirmary with Anya. Sat as usual. Had tea and dinner 4 with Mama on the balcony. Rode around with A. and Shura. Went to the sisters' infirmary and played croquet and D.B.

Playing croquet at the infirmary

Tatiana to Alexei

Tsarskoe Selo. **14 July**, 1916. Alexei, my little sweet darling. We are so lonesome here without you and

Papa. It was so nice in Mogilev visiting you![92] The weather is warm. We are sitting on the balcony. I was just at the Grand Palace with Maria and Shvybz. Tell Papa that Nurse Mobushina is still cross-eyed. A lot of the wounded were there. Some old colonel, a Siberian, your Godfather, is sending his regards to you and wishes you good health etc. Of course, I don't remember his name. Tell V.N. that there are a lot of wounded. A total of 48. They brought in 11 men yesterday, and all are bedridden. All of them are from outside of Riga from Siberian regiments. Some of Grandmama's [too]. Ours are all fine. [They] ask about you a lot, and want to see you very much.

The porch at Olga's and Tatiana's infirmary

[92] The Grand Duchesses and Empress recently went to visit the Tsar and Alexei at the military headquarters

Thank P.V.P.[93] for his letters and tell him that he can write more. Well, goodbye. Darling Alexei, may God keep You. I kiss you and Papa very very affectionately. [I] squeeze You in my thoughts and love you very very much. Yours, Tatiana. I hug [you] tightly.

Maria to Nicholas Alexandrovich

20 July. My precious Papa, almost forgot to write to you today, I must be confused. We will go to the Grand Palace with Shvybzik now. The sisters are

[93] Pyotr Vasilievich Petrov, Russian language tutor to the imperial children

going to Petersburg, and after the Gr. Pal. we will go riding around with Mama and Anya. An ensign from my regiment, Shtyrev, is a patient at our infirmary, he was wounded in the leg by an explosive bullet, but he can walk on crutches. He told [us] a lot about the regiment. Today it is awfully cold and damp, but we still have breakfast on the balcony, albeit in our jackets. The motor was supposed to be here already, and it just arrived so I will run. I kiss you affectionately and warmly and squeeze you. May God keep you. Your *Kazanetz.*

From the 1916 diary of Tatiana Romanov

22 July. Went to *obednya* 4 with Mama. Breakfast on the balcony with same. 4 with Mama went to the n[ew] infirmary for a concert. Had tea 4 with Mama and Uncle Nicky. Wrote telegrams, had dinner 4 with Mama and Anya. And went with A[nastasia] to the n[ew] infirmary, there was a play "An Evening at the Mansion of the Noblewoman XVII." Went to the sisters' infirmary, played ruble.

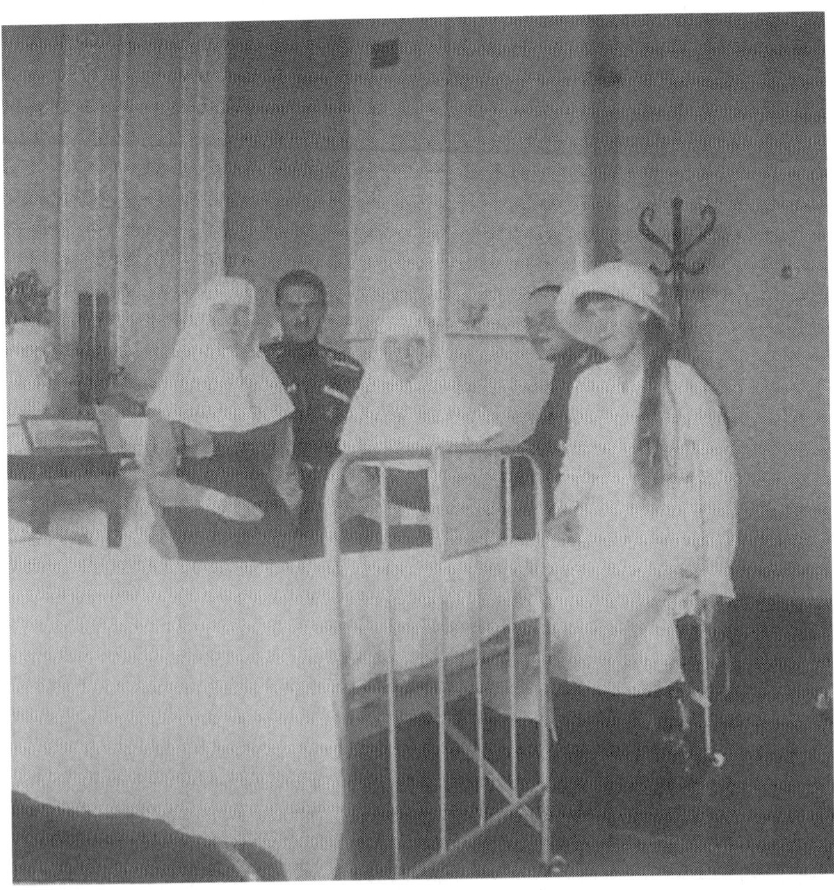

Maria to Nicholas Alexandrovich

25 July. My dear Papa, I am so terribly happy to visit you and Alexei, after all you are so missed here. I have not packed yet, although not taking a lot of things with me, only the most necessary. I got a letter from N.D.[94], will bring it with me and show it to you. [It] may be interesting for you. Yesterday we finally had a nice day, although not very hot but very pleasant, so a lot of wounded were lying outside. They brought three officers to us, 2 Keksumentzy and a Petrogradetz or a Muscovite. We saw them only for a few minutes as they just brought them in, and the doctor and Lazarev were with them. We had a very successful concert here at our infirmary on 22 July. Please thank P.V.P. for the letters. I will not have a chance to write to him. I kiss you and darling Alexei affectionately.

---

[94] Nikolai Demenkov

Maria and Anastasia with officers outside their infirmary

Anastasia to Nicholas Alexandrovich

16 August, 1916. My golden Papa darling! Thank you for the kisses in the letters. Today we got up rather late because no lessons. I already took Mama and the sisters to the infirmary. The weather is really rotten and it is raining now and rather cold, only 10 degrees, and now this [kind of] weather is every day. Yesterday Aunt Miechen[95] had tea with us, she returned recently and now lives in Tsarskoe.

[95] Grand Duchess Maria Pavlovna the Elder, wife of Grand Duke Vladimir

Maria and Anastasia in a carriage with Alexandra in front of their infirmary.[96]

Yesterday morning we were riding around and saw when the train from Mogilev arrived and saw Nilov and Voiekov—who came in a motor, it was very nice to see them. This afternoon we all and Mama, will go to the Grand Palace as we will take [photographs]—this is not so pleasant but that's the way it is. And in the morning Maria and I will go to our infirmary. [...]

[96] Courtesy of Igor Sikorsky Jr

From the 1916 diary of Alexei Romanov

19 August. Had 2 lessons in the morning. Wrote to Mama before breakfast and took a walk. Had breakfast with everyone in the tent. In the afternoon rode down the Dnieper. In the evening listened to Sig's[97] reading and studied with P.V.P. Went to bed early-ish.

Alexei with his tutors at Stavka

From the 1916 diary of Maria Romanov

21 August. Went to *obednya* with Mama. Then said goodbyes at our infirmary with Shvybz.

[97] Nickname of Sidney Gibbes, English tutor to the imperial children

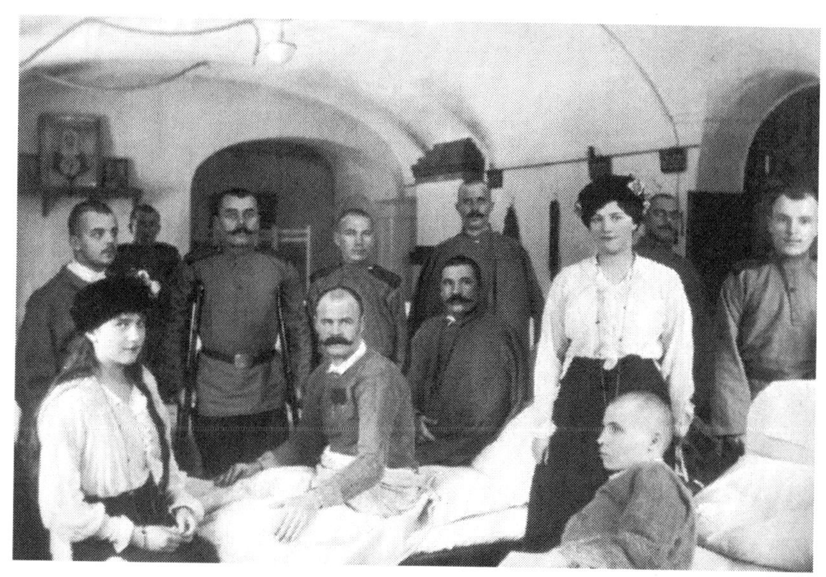

Maria and Anastasia at their infirmary

Boarded the train[98] and went to Smolensk. Had breakfast, tea and dinner 4 with Mama, Isa, Resin, Lavrov, Zhilik and 2 engineers. Zhilik read "Anand ee monde s'enuie" to us. Then went to see Mama on the balcony. Alexei was there too. Accompanied them to Anya's [room], then they read. Had tea and dinner with Papa, Mama, the Aunt. In the evening Papa read. 18 degrees, summer lightning far away at sea. In the afternoon there was a thunderstorm in the mountains. [It was] sunny here.

98 Again they were going to visit their father and brother at Stavka

Grand Duchessess on the train

Alexei to Alexandra Feodorovna

Mogilev. **5 September.** My dear Mama. It is so empty without you and boring. Today the sky is blue and it's 15° in the sun. The cat is lying on the couch, and Joy was searching for fleas on her and tickled her frightfully. If you need for Joy to look for fleas on you, I can send him, but that will cost you 1 r.[uble]. I will have 2 or 3 lessons. Will pray for you and the sisters. May God keep you! Yours, A. Romanov

Alexei with his spaniel Joy and a cat

Maria to Alexei

Tsarskoe Selo. **6 Sept**., 1916. My darling little soul, Alexei! You cannot even imagine how boring it is to be back at Tsarskoe. Today, when I just woke up, I was really surprised to be back in my room. I saw you in my dream, as if we never left you. The head of the infirmary, Baron Kaulbars, also wanted to be in the photo and sat on the little table which you [would normally] put near a bed. Of course, the table couldn't hold him, one leg broke, and he fell, it was all very funny. I kiss you and dear Papa affectionately. Your sister Maria. May God keep you.

Tatiana to Nicholas Alexandrovich

11 September. My dear darling Papa. Zhilik is writing the sequel to "The Mysterious Hand" for us, terribly interesting, and he is so good at storytelling. Last night after dinner we went with Mama to Petrograd to a *panikhida*[99] for Countess Hendrikova.[100] [I feel] terribly sorry for Nastenka, the poor thing is crying a lot. Our poor Batushka's[101] eldest and most favorite son was killed. He is in the Pavlovsky regiment. <...> When I look at photographs from Mogilev that we took there, I want so much to be back [there] with You. I imagine how you are all digging a hole and searching the excavations. Ravtopulo is still here. He comes to our infirmary. My one Ulan, cornet Ulyanov, is wounded and is a patient here. The weather is damp, drizzle in the morning, which is very tiresome. Well, good-bye, Papa darling. May God bless You. Big kisses to you and Alexei. Your *Voznesenetz.*

---

[99] Memorial service for the dead

[100] Nastenka's mother

[101] "Father" or priest

Olga and Tatiana outside of their infirmary

15 September. My dear darling Papa. I have a small request from You. These two officers - their names are written on the piece of paper – are now at the Pavlovsk school. They were promoted to officers last year, but they kept them as assistant officers. They have long been dreaming of getting into the Yerivan Regiment, they are familiar with the regiment since [their] childhood practically - and grew up in front of their eyes. And now on 1st October, they like all the others, are being sent to the reserve regiments, which means they did not get into the Yerivan Regiment. Could you somehow arrange for them to be allowed to go straight to the regiment! I would be very happy if it happens.

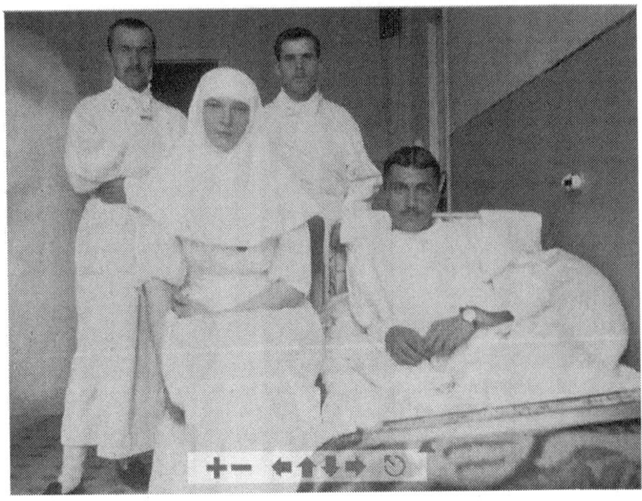

Well, today the Japanese[102] is here for breakfast. It is clear but cold, at night only 1 [degree], if not less. So I did not expect such joy, when Igor came here. Did You let him go for a long time? Went horseback riding again with the Shvybz. It was wonderful. Nikolai Pavlovich was with us – had dinner. I was glad to see Mordvinov and Zenoviy Ivanovich today. Our lessons are going fine. Not very much, since P.V.P., Mr S. and Zhilik are not here. Right now the hair dresser is curling Maria's hair. After that, will do mine - for the Japanese. In town everyone is saying that I am to marry him. They are forgetting that he has a wife, and

[102] Consul from Japan?

that he is a pagan. Pretty stupid. Well, goodbye for now. I apologize for the smear. Well, just got back from breakfast. Sat with Uncle Andrei and Nikolai Mikhailovich. [There were] a lot of people. The little messenger girl was there - very cute. Everyone talked for a bit after breakfast. Zinoviy Ivanovich came over to me, I wanted to talk to him, but Igor immediately approached him and led him away, the idiot. Well, goodbye. Big big kisses, [as big as the way] I love [you]. Your *Voznesenetz.*

Anastasia to Nicholas Alexandrovich

17 September, 1916. My good Papa Darling! This morning we had a light but nasty snow, and now it's sunny but cold. [...] We are as usual. The other day we played tennis with our wounded officers, they play rather well now as they practice every day.

Tatiana to Nicholas Alexandrovich

23 September. Papa, my dear. I am sitting now in the morning before lessons, while Maria and Anastasia are playing the gramophone and raising the flag. Playing the March of the Escort Guard. After that, our hymn and some march which was played on the yacht. They brought a wounded officer to us, a

Chernogoretz[103]. He was in the Kiev Corps for 7 years, and now is in 57th Maudlin Regiment. He does not know of course where his relatives are. He asks us, where King Nicholas and King Peter are, and where he is, we don't know and he is so anxious, since his brother is Peter's adjutant. He is seriously wounded, poor chap. An enormous wound on his back, his left arm is paralyzed, the right is wounded and the right hip. He is small and thin. I am glad that Nikolai Pavlovich is with you again. Today the grass is covered with frost and [there are] very few leaves [left]. Well, goodbye, Papa, my darling. I kiss you affectionately, and Alexei. May the Lord keep you both. Your much loving, Voznesenetz

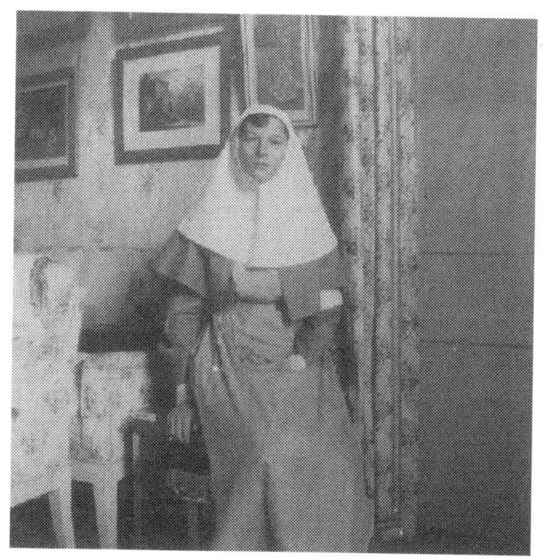

[103]Montenegrin

From the 1916 diary of Olga Romanov

Sunday. **2nd October**. [We] had our hair curled, went to *obednya* at the grotto church[104], after that—to the infirmary.

On the left are steps leading down to the grotto chapel (right)

Trina and Nastenka had breakfast. At 3 o'cl. stopped by *Znamenie* with Mama and [then] boarded the train. Rain, snow, nasty. Met Mitya's mama. Going with us are Shvedov, Anya, Isa, Botkin, Resin, and Kern. Papa wrote. Saturday.

15th October. With Mama to *Znamenie* and the infirmary. Freezing, overcast. Trina had breakfast. We 4 went to the Grand Palace, later took a ride in the

[104] Imperial family's private chapel in the cellar of Feodorovsky Cathedral, aka "lower chapel"

motor. Rode by Mitya's mama's [house] but she wasn't home, we did see her yesterday morning and today.

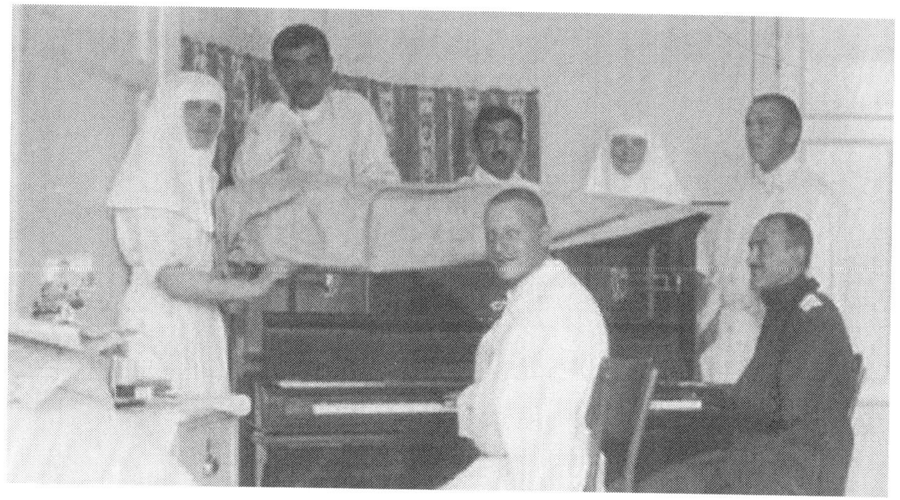

Olga and Tatiana with patients at their infirmary. Mitya Shakh Bagov is in the center next to Tatiana

Papa wrote. Anya had tea. Going to *vsenoshnaya* with Mama. We 4 went to the infirmary. Was talking in the front room with Kulnev when suddenly Mitya walked in. So awfully happy to see him with a part in his hair. Stood in the hallway and sat. [I] darned socks.

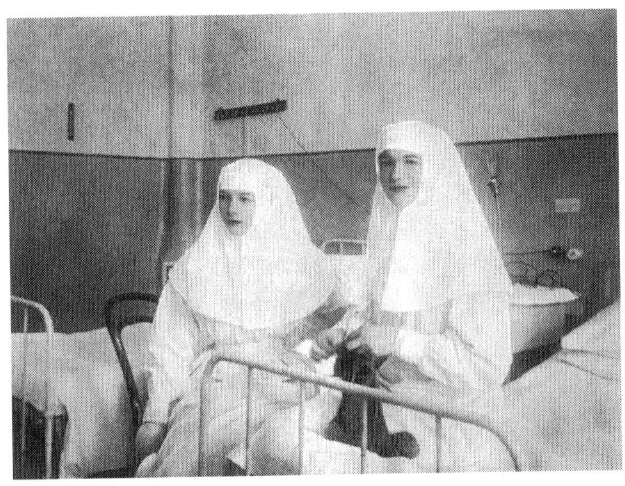

Anastasia to Nicholas Alexandrovich

17 October, 1916. Tsarskoe Selo. My golden Papa Darling! Just now I had arithmetic lesson and now I am free and have to write a lot and do homework. It's so nice that you are coming here! We are all awfully happy. There is snow on the ground today and it's kind of strange, but it is sunny, but 3 degrees of frost, the weather is fair. Yesterday I got a very sweet letter from Mordvinov. Do you know if he sneezed when he got my letter from Orsha[105]. It is so pleasant to remember how nice and fun the time in Mogilev was, and how we used to play hide-and-seek in the evenings. When we were returning it was very nice that Viktor Erastovich was there, otherwise it would

[105] Anastasia was known for pranks, this may have been one of them

have been terribly boring, and he sat with us for a little while in the afternoon and after dinner. It was cozy! Now we have lessons, we go to the infirmaries and all is the same there. We do not have any new wounded at our infirmary, only an officer from Maria's regiment, a *Kazanetz.*

Mama is going to her infirmary for dressing changes in the mornings for now. Yesterday afternoon we rode around with Mama, Anya and all four of us. Did not run into too many people, almost no one was out walking. Yesterday Mama received Countess Karlova and her daughter Merica, as she is planning to get married in November, so she returned, [she is] rather pretty. Maria just walked by here and sends you a big kiss. I think she now has a history lesson. Well, my Papa Darling it's time for me to end. I send you and

Alexei an awfully big kiss 1000 times. Regards to Mordvinov. May God keep you. Your loving loyal and faithful little 15-year-old *Kaspiyitz*.

From the 1916 diary of Maria Romanov

20 October. Went to Petrograd with Papa, Mama, O. and T. to the Fortress,[106] for the funeral *obednya* for Grandpapa.[107] Had breakfast 5 with Papa, Mama and Igor.[108]

[106] St Peter and Paul Fortress
[107] Emperor Alexander III
[108] Prince Igor Konstantinovich, son of Grand Duke Konstantin Konstantinovich

St Peter and Paul Cathedral in St Petersburg; mausoleum where Tsar Alexander III is interred

Walked 4 with Papa and Mama [rode] in a carriage. Had tea and went to *vsenoshnaya*, the same [people] confessed. Had dinner 4 with Papa, Mama and Igor.

From the 1916 diary of Tatiana Romanov

Saturday, **22 October**. In the morning [we] two went with Mama to *Znamenie*, from there—to the infirmary. Took photographs in two shifts in the sitting room, since last time the pictures did not come out. Later dressings for Syroboyarsky, Bogdanov. The others—Mama. Also took photographs on three other wards.

Olga, Tatiana, Nicholas and Alexandra with infirmary staff

Between that sat with Volodya in the hallway. Later played *bloshki*[109] with Volodya, Petrov and Lieutenant Girs. Later the lieutenant had gone and was replaced by—Prince Eristov. Then said goodbye to Volodya. It was so sad, he and seven more are going to the Crimea today, Bogdanov, Vinogradov, Galakhov, Pavlov, Jurgenson, Kamensky, Motsidarsky.

[109] Tiddlywinks

Breakfast with Papa, Mama and Gavriil[110]. Walked in the afternoon. Mama—in a small carriage. Read. Had tea with Papa and Mama. Went to *vsenoshnaya*. Met up with Yuzik's brother. Had dinner with the same [people] as breakfast. After, went to say goodbye to Alexei and little Makarovs, Zhenya and Lyolya. They came to visit Alexei yesterday. [They] spent the night with us and were together all day, and will spend another night again today. Sat at Mama's downstairs. Worked. Anya was here. Then Papa came.

[110] Prince Gavriil Konstantinovich, second son of Grand Duke Konstantin Konstantinovich

From the 1916 diary of Olga Romanov

Friday. **28th October.** We 4 had breakfast on the train with Mama on the way to the city. T. and I went to her committee, after which I received O. B. Stolypina.[111] The Little Ones[112] went around the infirmary at the Grand Palace with Mama. There are currently 358 people there. Tea on the train with Viktor Erastovich. It's drizzling and awfully dark, but warm. Now Mama is receiving. Papa telegraphed from Kiev. They went to Grandmama's for her fiftieth wedding anniversary. In the evening we 4—to the infirmary. Played the piano in the sitting room. Mitya came in toward the end. Returned after 11 o'clock. Rain.

[111] Widow of Prime Minister Pyotr Stolypin, who was assassinated 4 years prior in a theater in Kiev in front of Nicholas, Olga, and Tatiana

[112] Maria, Anastasia, and Alexei

Tatiana to Alexei

29 October, 1916. Tsarskoe Selo. Alexei, my little darling. So how are you? Are you happy to be with Papa again? You probably saw a lot of interesting things. We are fine, only missing you [both]. Yesterday it was cold, today is better. Our wounded are all fine, asked about you. After dressings we sat with them and played different games. It was very cozy and merry. It is so good that we were in Mogilev and now know how you live, because now when I think of you, I imagine the house and everything in general. P.V. asked me to pass on his letter. Well, goodbye, darling. May God keep you. I kiss you and Papa very very affectionately. Regards to Kolya and Dmitri. Your Tatiana.

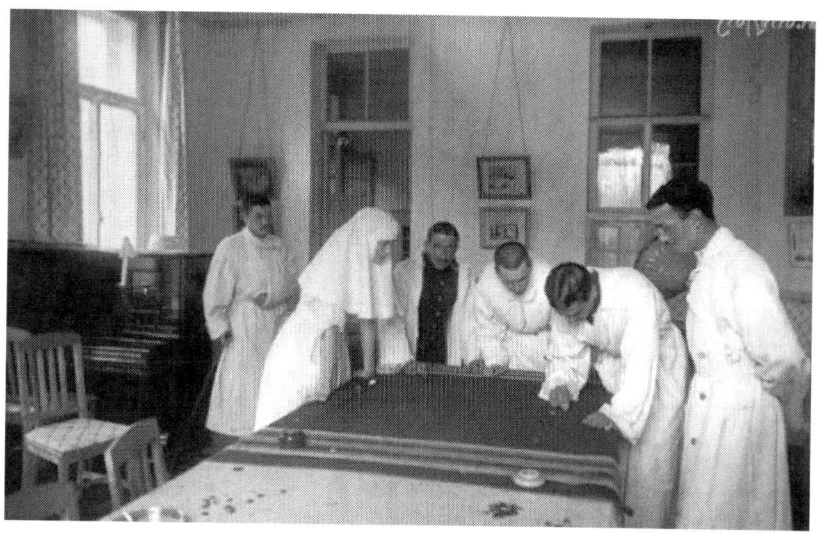

Sister T. Romanov playing a table game with her patients

Maria to Nicholas Alexandrovich

30 October. My dear Papa darling! Today is already two years that the dear Grand Palace infirmary exists, and therefore we must go to a concert there. Your friend Lersky will be there, I am happy to see him as he usually tells such nice funny stories.

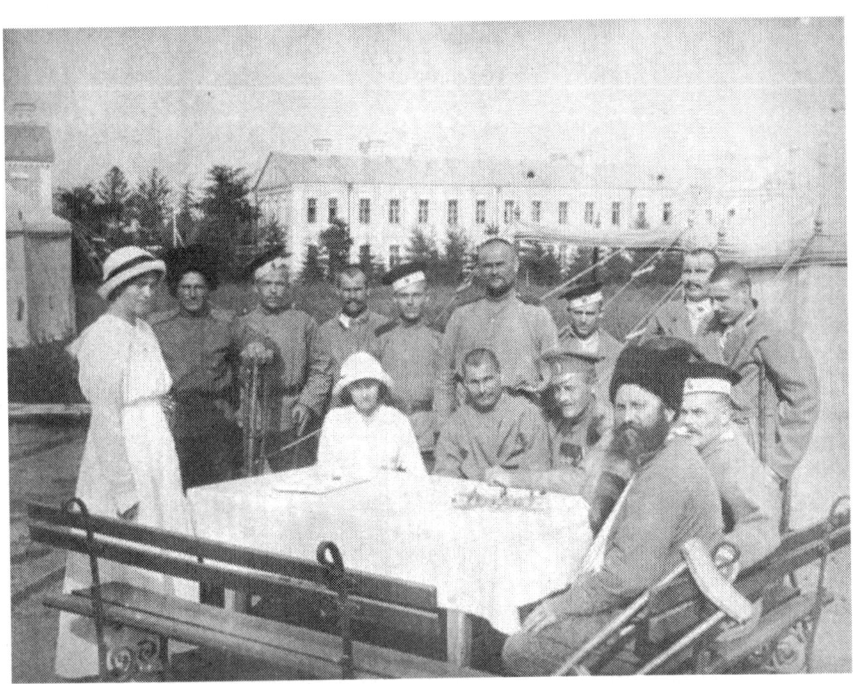

Maria and Anastasia with infirmary patients

I am now sitting at Mama's. In the morning we went to an early *Obednya* and after that to our infirmary. At first we went to [see] lower ranks then the officers. There we played billiards. I played like swine of course, because it is hard without practice. Yesterday Viktor Erastovich came to our infirmary. He wins against everyone in billiards.

Time to end as I have to complete [sewing] two shirts for the officers who are leaving our infirmary and are bidding their farewells to Mama at 6 o'clock. I kiss and squeeze you darlings affectionately. May God keep you both + . Your *Kazanetz.*

Maria in 1916

Anastasia to Nicholas Alexandrovich

31 October, 1916. Tsarskoe Selo. My dear Papa Darling! Well it is again my turn to write to you. Now I will have my last lesson with Pyotr Vasilievich as he is leaving today. I am very envious of him, he will see you tomorrow already! Forgive me that I'm writing so violently, but this quill scratches terribly and nothing comes out. Right now it is raining and rather nasty as it is windy and a bit cold - Tatiana Andreyevna Gromova wrote and described to us how you and Alexei came to their infirmary at Aunt Olga's. It was written in a very funny way and very detailed, even what you said, she was awfully happy to see you.

Yesterday we went to a concert at the Grand Palace. They were celebrating a two year anniversary of their infirmary. It was rather nice. Your friend Lersky was there and Mama saw him for the first time and she liked it. They sang and talked a lot etc., but generally everything is the same.

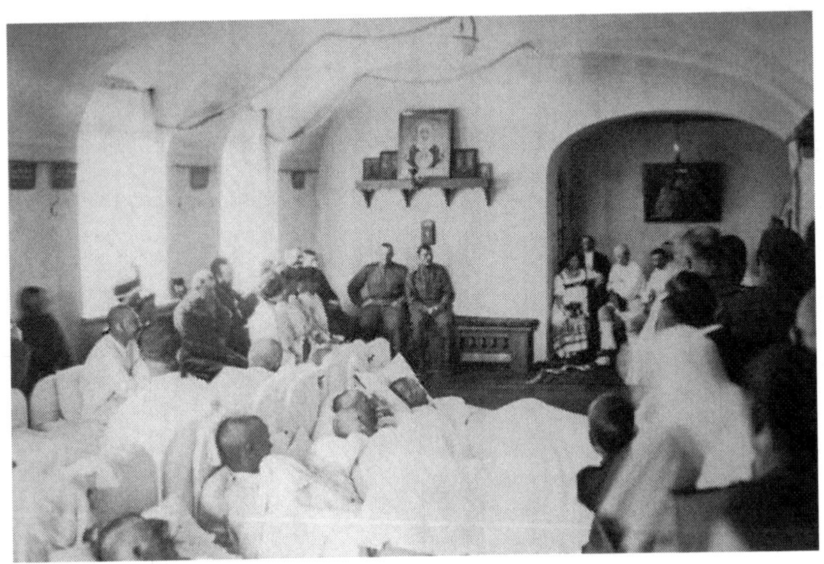

At an infirmary concert

We continue playing billiards a bit at our infirmary, sometimes it turns out well - and then I'm happy. Viktor Erastovich comes over and plays sometimes and of course better than anyone else.... Right now Olga's cat is running around here, I think she grew and is rather cute. I think Igor is coming to [see] you too with this letter, you are probably very happy about this! ... Well now, my dear Papa! I send you and Alexei 1000 awfully big kisses, may God be with you. Your loving loyal and faithful *Kaspiyetz* [sic].

Alexandra Feodorovna to Tatiana

5 November, 1916. My dear, Anya asked me to come to the laying of the foundation of the church[113] at 12:30 (Our Friend[114] will be there). Can at least one of you four come with me, otherwise I will be completely alone, as I do not have even one lady in waiting? Mama +

Anastasia to Nicholas Alexandrovich

5 November, 1916. My golden Papa! We just got up and now having had the morning milk I am alone at a lesson. I don't know where Maria is. Well, everything is as usual. The only thing [different] is that I don't have a lesson. I slept well and dreamed of you. It snowed very little, and the trees are covered with frost and it is rather cold. I don't think we did much yesterday, rode around and went to our infirmary – played billiards. And in the evening we went to Mama's infirmary – as usual. Ah, it has started snowing now! [...]

---

[113] At the site where Vyrubova's infirmary was to be built. Rasputin would be temporariy interred in this chapel after his murder in less than 2 months

[114] Rasputin.

Tatiana to Nicholas Alexandrovich

6 November, 1916. My dear Papa. I congratulate you with the Hussar holiday! Do you remember how you used have supper with them on this day - if we were not in the Crimea. And there you went to Uncle Nikolasha's. Today the weather is finally clear. The trees are covered with fine snow. We don't have very many wounded at the infirmary now. There is a very charming one, just a boy [who is] missing his left arm and right leg. [He is] so cheerful and undiscouraged.

He tells himself that at least he has the other leg and arm. He is 21 and was wounded before too. I hope that Alexei will get up soon – the poor darling. I feel so sorry for him, but it's good that his pain is not severe. I embrace you, Papa darling, and kiss you. May God bless You. Have not heard anything about my regiment. They say that [there were] heavy losses, is that true? Your *Voznesenetz*

Anastasia to Nicholas Alexandrovich

9 November, 1916. [...] Yesterday evening we four and Mama rode around, and then went to the infirmaries. Then we had lessons and in the evening, went to the infirmary again. Well, that was our whole day. [...]

Tatiana to Nicholas Alexandrovich

10 November. My dear Papa. I am sorry for bothering you again with papers. One is the request for the transfer of three military school cadets from Pavlovsky school directly to the Yerivan regiment, would you pass it on to Kondzerovsky, while the others, well, I will not explain, as You can read them yourself. And I enclose the copies of the order. Forgive me if these notes are printed poorly, but I printed them myself at the infirmary when I had free time. I rejoice so much that we will see each other soon. We don't have a lot of wounded at the infirmary, cornet Kasyanov was injured again, we told you that he was here this summer - handsome and plays the violin well. Mama showed us photos of Alexei, which were taken by the Englishman. [They are] very nice. Well, good-bye, Papa darling. May Christ be with You. Big kisses to you, as much [as I] love [you]. Your *Voznesenetz.*

Maria to Nicholas Alexandrovich

10 November. Papa my dear! Such joy to be going to [see] you. I was afraid that we would not get to you before winter. Just now I walked Mama, Olga and Tatiana to the infirmary. I will have a lesson with Batushka, and then I am thinking of taking a walk or else riding around with Shura. In the afternoon we will go to the medical train named after Mama. They will have *moleben* there and tea with the Metropolit. Of course Loman[115] arranged this. Yesterday we went to our infirmary with Shvybz. Viktor Erastovich was there too, and we played billiards with him and one [other] wounded [patient].

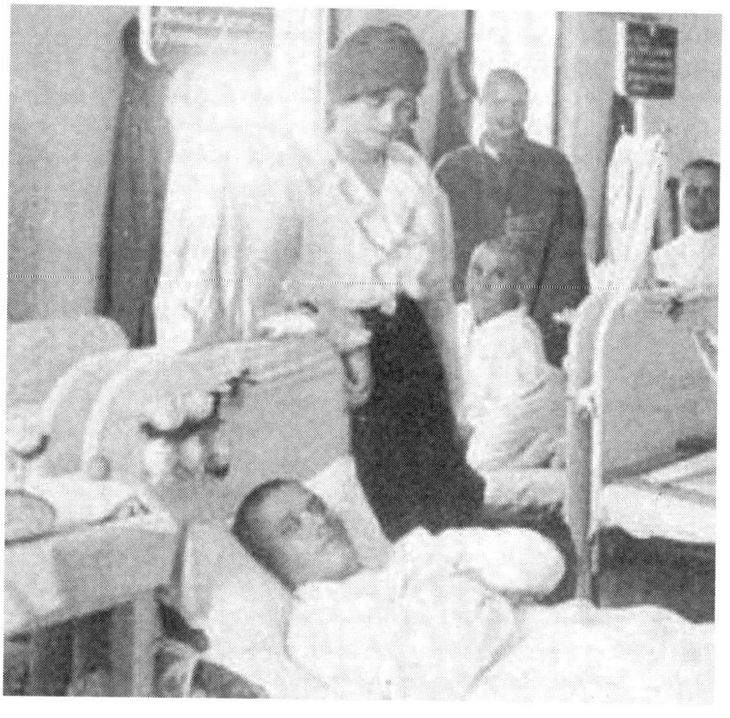

It is terribly nice to see chests in the hallway, gives one the feeling that we are going soon. This time Nastenka is coming with us. I don't think Isa is too

[115] D.N. Loman, colonel of the Life-Guard Pavlovsky Regiment, churchwarden of Feodorovsky Cathedral

happy, but I don't care as I like Nastenka more, she is after all more simple than Isa. Time to end. I will also write to Alexei's P.V.P., and I kiss you Papa my darling very very affectionately. May Christ be with you.
+ Your very own *Kazanetz*. The pictures which A. is in – [give] to Alexei, the rest are for you, the ones you wanted.

19 November. My darling Papa! Today I am the one writing to you, as Olga and Tatiana just went to Petrograd to the charities. I had lessons in the morning. Mama rode in the train with Olga, Alexei and Anastasia. Yesterday I was at the Grand Palace with Mama and the sisters, to see the wounded officers and saw that young officer who had a big bed sore on his back. He has a very sweet face. We signed his cards, and now he is waiting for you to return and maybe sign for him too. Right now it is two o'clock. Mama is lying on the couch and writing you a letter, while Anastasia – to Aunt Olga. At 2.30 Anastasia and I will go to our infirmary. Probably new [patients] also arrived there. At tea I always sit in your chair. Mama got a letter from you before breakfast. Later she will go to the Grand Palace for dressings of two officers.

Alexei is upstairs resting after breakfast. Tomorrow Chakhov is going back to the front. I am so happy that it's a holiday on Friday, so that we will not have lessons, and this is very pleasant. Today during the arithmetic lesson the teacher bent down to see if I wrote something correctly, and broke the chair leg with his weight, and almost fell on me. Well so long, goodbye my Darling. I kiss you affectionately and love you. Your *Kazanetz.* May God keep you + Regards to Sasha and Kolya and tell the latter to behave.

22 November. My very own darling Papa! Mama left with the sisters last night at 9 o'clock. Malama had tea with us as he is returning to the regiment. Iedigarov left the infirmary yesterday [he went] to Petrograd for a couple of days to [see] his wife, and then to the regiment. Mama will arrive tomorrow morning at 9 o'clock, and her train with Loman will already be at the station. So Anastasia, Alexei and I will go meet her and go directly to the train with the wounded.

Colonel Loman and his son in front of Feodorovsky Cathedral

We are getting 3 new officers at our infirmary. Now I will stop by Isa's, who has fever and stomach ache, which was why she did not go with Mama. Well so long, goodbye, my darling. May God keep you. + Your always loving *Kazanetz*. Regards to your companions.

26 November. My sweet and dear Papa! The other day I wrote you a letter, but tore it up, as the courier already left. I have been going to my infirmary every day. The last train brought some rather seriously wounded [patients]. One of them came to us with a torn lip. Aunt Ella is now here with us, she tells us a lot of interesting things about her journey. May God keep you. Your very own *Kazanetz.*

30 November. My golden Papa! Mama is now lying on the sofa and resting. This morning all of us, 5 with Mama went to *obednya* and then to change dressings, and Alexei also watched and counted how many he was present at. After breakfast we took [photographs] with the wounded officers at the Grand Palace. From there we went to the Invalid House, and there Mama gave out St George's medals to several lower ranks.

Mama is very tired, and therefore she will not write to you today. We will now have tea with Uncle Pavel. Yesterday at *vsenoshnaya* I saw my darling Demenkov, while Shvedov was at the meeting. So both Olga and I were very happy. Yesterday afternoon we went to the local infirmary, where Mama also awarded medals. Today after tea Mama will receive the officers, her two Crimeans, one from my regiment and the other from Olga's. I kiss you affectionately, your always loving *Kazanetz*. May God keep you.+ Regards to Kolya and Sasha.

From the 1916 diary of Olga Romanov

Saturday. **3rd December**. To *Znamenie* and to the infirmary. Mama and Alexei came at 11 o'clock for Colonel Dzerzhinsky's surgery. Excised (with Novocain) some fatty tumors from his shoulders. Al.[exei] stood in the door the entire time. Later he played "ruble" with everyone. Ate all together. During the day at 2 ¾ took a walk with Papa and Mama like yesterday. Very dark and slippery. Will all go to *vsenoshnaya*. In the evening Papa pasted [photos into] an album, Tatiana read "Gdye apelsini zreyut" [Where the Oranges Blossom].

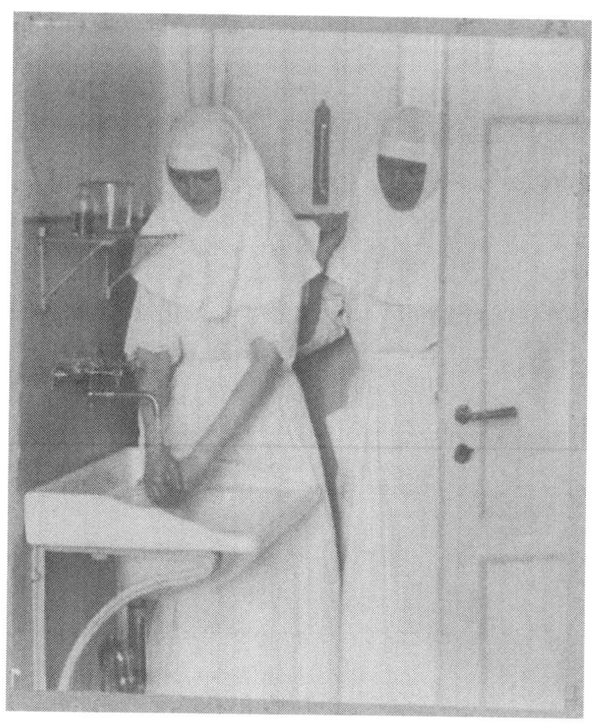

From the 1916 diary of Maria Romanov

4 December. Went to *obednya* 5 with Papa and Mama and the same had breakfast with Toto. Showed Toto our rooms. Walked 5 with Papa. Saw off Papa and Alexei (they went to Mogilev). Went 4 to a concert at the G.P. Had tea 4 with Mama and Anya. Went to the old infirmary with A., played checkers. Stopped by Nastenka's and Isa's. Had dinner 4 with Mama, the same went to the sisters' infirmary. Played checkers with Shareiko.

Maria and Anastasia in front of their infirmary

Tatiana to Nicholas Alexandrovich

8 December. Papa my darling dear, I am writing to You from the infirmary, as will not have time [to write] at home. Aunt Mavra with the lovely Vera will be having breakfast with us. Later I will have a lesson, and then probably go riding around with Mama, so I will not have time. Yesterday Olga received a very nice telegram from Count Grabbe and from the Convoy. They wrote that the Convoy welcomes and congratulates the young Cossack Scout with a thunder of "Hurrahs". She was terribly pleased. It is such a pity that you did not see Olga's face when Your telegram arrived. It became dark crimson and immediately she could not say a word, and just smiled foolishly while showing the telegram. Now that You are not here, we ride with Mama in a sleigh. She and Anya in one, while we 4 in others. Quite a lot of snow, but in some places [it] sometimes touches the sand. It was nice to talk with Alexei on the telephone, though [I] could not hear very well. Well, how are the Romanians? Still running or better? Well, goodbye, Papa darling. May Christ be with you both. Big kisses, [as many as] I love [you]. Your *Voznesenetz.*

From the 1916 diary of Maria Romanov

12 December. Arrived at Tsarskoe Selo[116]. Went to the old and new infirmaries with A. Had breakfast and tea 4 with Mama. Rode in a *troika* with Isa. Sat and read. There was music. Had dinner 4 with Mama and

[116] Returned from Stavka

Grigori at Anya's. Went to the infirmary 4 with the sisters. Played ruble, then checkers with Shareiko.

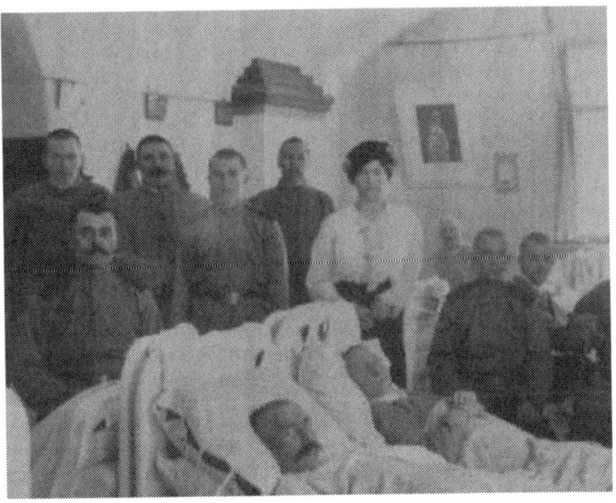

Tatiana to Nicholas Alexandrovich

13 December. My dear darling Papa. I will not describe our train journey, as you already received long letters from Mama, Olga and Anya. It was very nice, but it was a shame that on the way back from Chodov station we could not ride through Bologoye and further. It was awfully cozy to sleep on the train. Yesterday a lot of snow fell, and all the trees are bent as there is so much snow on them. I really hope that soon you will come to us again. Such lovely things Igor does - still pesters us charmingly. Mordvinov wrote a nice letter to Shvybz, and Mr. Gillard to me about "Mysterious Hand." Very interesting. I have the great pleasure to go to the Petrograd Committee[117] today. Oh! Not wanting to [go] at all. Well, may Christ be with You. Big kisses to You and Alexei. Your very loving *Voznesenetz.*

Tatiana and Olga at a Committee meeting

Anastasia to Nicholas Alexandrovich

15 December, 1916. Tsarskoe Selo. My Dear Papa Darling! You already know well about our trip to Novgorod as I think Olga wrote to you a lot about it. In my opinion it went very well! It was so cozy to sleep on the train and the feeling was a little like we were

[117] Charity committees both Tatiana and Olga sat on

going to see you in Mogilev. Maria just came over and is sending you a big kiss. Well Christmas is so soon! We are all waiting for you! This Tuesday I was remembering and imagining how you were going to the theater. Right this minute I got a letter from Zhilik and the continuation of the "Mysterious Hand." I have not yet read it so we will read it aloud all together, more interesting that way!

I think that today Igor is leaving you, on 15 December? We just had breakfast with Kozhevnikov, who arrived in Petrograd a few days ago, but soon he is leaving again. He told us masses of interesting things—how their transfer went and etc. He remains the same. Well now, Papa my Darling it's time for me to end. May Christ be with you. I send you and little Alexei an awfully big kiss. Your loving loyal and faithful little 15-year-old *Kaspiyitz.*

From the 1916 diary of Olga Romanov

Saturday. **17th December**. We 2 to *Znamenie.* Did everything as usual, made up beds, etc. Sokolov is gloomier than dark night. Played *bloshki* with Kasyanov against T.[atiana] and Ulan. Ate with Mama. Anya had tea, had dinner. Sat all day with Mama. Father Grigori is missing since last night[118]. They are looking for him everywhere—awfully hard. Attended *vsenoshnaya* here at the house. In the evening, Mama, Anya, confessed. Lili Dehn was here. Papa wrote. Sat almost until 12 o'clock. Everyone was waiting for a telephone [call] from Kalinin, etc.[119] Slept all 4 together. Lord help us.

From the memoirs of V.I. Chebotareva[120]

In the evening at about five o'clock, we learned that [Rasputin was] missing, tears, despair. On Sunday,

---

[118] Rasputin had been murdered the night before

[119] Presumably for news about Rasputin

[120] Nurse who worked with the Grand Duchesses

[Alexandra] and Tatiana had communion. On Sunday, the children did not come at all, [they] came on Monday, tearful, staring at everyone suspiciously. Tatiana came out in the middle of dressings, spoke with Varvara Afanasievna, burst into tears, returned to the operating room, barely restraining herself [from crying]. What anxiety we experienced since the 17th! I stopped by the infirmary at around 7 o'clock, the nurse on duty ran over to me: "They told us on the telephone that Grigori was killed." The Stock Exchange News arrived - a confirmation. The children [then] called: " We cannot be there this evening, we have a duty, we need to stay with Mama." At eleven in the evening Elizaveta Nikolaevna called, her husband was told by the Commandant - Yusupov did the killing, the body was not found. It is interesting that they already knew about the incident at 2 o'clock. On the 20th the Emperor returned, [we] went to meet them, remained in the train for a long time; [he] came out confused, forgot to greet those who were meeting him, went to his chambers, then remembered, came back, silently shook hands.

From the 1916 diary of Olga Romanov

Monday. **19th December.** As usual, to *Znamenie* and to the infirmary. Almost nothing to do. Went with Kasyanov to the drawing room and behind closed doors, without anyone present, I played and he sang various new beautiful things. Ate with Mama. Found out that Grigori was killed, likely by Dmitri and thrown from a bridge by Khrestovsky. They found him in the water. It's so terrible, should not even write. Sat and drank tea with Lili and Anya and the entire time felt Father Grigori with us...

Rasputin's body was found under ice near Petrovsky bridge, where it was disposed of by his murderers

At 6 o'clock met Papa and Alexei[121]. Such joy. Had dinner together. After 10 o'clock Papa and Mama received Kalinin, then Uncle Pavel. We were in Anya's rooms.[122] At 12 o'clock to bed.

---

[121] Who arrived from Stavka

[122] After Rasputin's murder, Anya moved to the Alexander Palace for safety

From the memoirs of Anna Vyrubova

When the capitol learned of Rasputin's murder, everyone went mad from joy, the society's glee was boundless, everyone congratulated each other: "the beast has been crushed" – as they put it – "the evil genius is no more". They were hysterical with delight. [It was] decided to temporarily bury [Rasputin] in Tsarskoe Selo, and bring him to [his] hometown in the spring. They prayed for him at Chesmensky Monastery, and at 9 o'clock in the morning, on the same day, 21st December, one of the nurses delivered Rasputin's coffin in a motor. He was buried in the park, on the land where I was planning on building a refuge for invalids. Their Majesties and the Grand Duchesses arrived, myself and two or three others. The casket was already lowered into the grave when we arrived; Their Majesties' priest did a short *panikhida* service and we left.

Pathway leading to the construction site of Anna Vyrubova's infirmary and chapel where Rasputin was initially interred; the imperial family would have walked through this path to attend his burial

Construction site of Anna Vyrubova's church where Rasputin was interred. The infirmary and church were never completed

From the 1916 diary of Maria Romanov

21 December. Went to Grigori's funeral 4 with Papa and Mama and others. He was buried at Anya's construction. Had lessons, history and Batushka. Had breakfast 4 with Papa and Mama. Went to the old infirmary with A. Walked with Papa. Went to the new infirmary with A, and Vikt. Er. was there. Had tea 4 with Papa and Mama near Alexei, he has worms in his belly. There was [a] music [lesson]. Went to Anya's, saw Matryona[123], Varya[124] and Akulina.[125] Had dinner 4 with Papa, Mama and Sandro. Anya was here. Papa read.

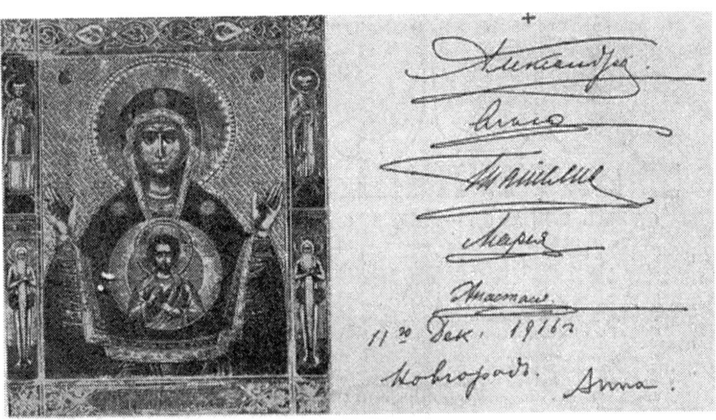

Icon signed in the back by the Empress, the imperial children and Anna Vyrubova on 11th December, 1916 in Novgorod, which was enclosed in Rasputin's casket

123 Maria Rasputina, eldest daughter of Grigori Rasputin

124 Varvara Rasputina, Grigori's younger daughter. Both daughters lived with him on Gorokhovaya Street at the time of his murder

125 Rasputin's housekeeper at Gorokhovaya apartment

From the 1916 diary of Nicholas Alexandrovich

21st December. Wednesday. At 9 o'cl. The entire family drove past the photography building and to the right towards the field, where we were present for a sad scene: the casket with the body of the unforgettable Grigori, murdered on the night of 17th December by the monsters at F. Yusupov's house, was already lowered into the grave. F[ather] Al[exander] Vasiliev conducted litia, after which we returned home. The weather was grey with 12° of frost. Took a walk before the reports. Received Shakhovskoy and Ignatiev. In the afternoon I took a walk with the children. At 4 ½ received our Velepolsky, and at 6 o'cl. Grigorovich. Read.

Rare photo of the Grand Duchesses and Empress originally identified as the funeral of Grigori Rasputin. It is unclear if this is correct, however it was taken at roughly the right time

Original location of burial of Rasputin's body

22 December. Thursday. Sandro was here to see me in the morning. At 12 ½ went to the itinerant church in honor of Anastasia's name day. Mordvinov had breakfast and dinner. Walked with him and the daughters around the park. At 4 o'cl received Protopopov, and after tea—Pokrovsky. Studied in the evening.

Nicholas's study at the Alexander Palace

Tatiana to Alexandra Feodorovna[126]

My own precious Mama darling. I pray that God may help you now through this horribly difficult time + that he may bless and protect you from all bad. – Believe that the soul of our beloved Friend is always with us + is praying for you my sweet angel Mama. Tender kisses fr yr loving own girl. Tatiana **Xmas** 1916

From the 1916 diary of Olga Romanov

Christmas Day. At 10 ½ with Papa to *obednya*. Mama and Al. later. Ate all together. Beautiful bright sun, sky, 7 [degrees] of frost. At 2 everyone went to the

[126] In English

arena for Convoy Christmas party. All the dear ones were there. Looking at them is so comforting. Went for a walk with Papa for a half hour—after that he and Mama received Kalinin. At 6 we 2 with Mama to our infirmary, a Christmas tree was set up in the drawing room. Everyone except Sokolov was gathered there—Mama gave out gifts to all. Left at 7. Mama received Prince Golitzyn. After dinner [I] played, at Papa's request, religious things [music] and everyone went to Anya's where Father Grigori's entire family was present: Paraskovia[127], Mitya[128], Matryona, and Varya. They are leaving for Pokrovskoe[129] on Tuesday. Went to [see] Al.[exei] and Zhenya. At 11 to bed. Mama doesn't feel too well, but she is so brave. Save her, Lord.

From the 1916 diary of Nicholas Alexandrovich

27 December. Tuesday. In the morning heard reports—from Shuvaev and Bulygin. After breakfast went to the riding hall for the third and last Christmas party. The Railroad regiment choir played beautifully again. Took a walk with Tatiana and Maria. The

[127] Rasputin's wife
[128] Rasputin's son Dmitri
[129] Their home village in Siberia

weather was excellent, sunny and frosty—8 deg [...]. After tea [we] saw cinematograph—the same theme as in Mogilev. Alexei's right arm started to hurt from a bruise; poor thing, he suffered a lot at night. Studied for a long time after dinner.

From the 1916 diary of Maria Romanov

28 December. Went to the old infirmary with A. The Metropolitan came over to praise Christ. Had breakfast 4 with Papa and Mama, Anya and Groten. Went 4 to the G.[rand] P.[alace]. Walked 4 with Papa. Went to a concert at the new infirmary with T. and A. Plevitskaya was there and Vaganova danced. Had tea 4 with Papa and Mama, dinner with same. Anya was here, [I] pasted in the album with her and Shvybz—Alexei was in bed all day, his arm hurts and [he] slept badly.

With infirmary fir tree

31 December. Went to the old and new infirmaries with A., played billiards with Kotov and Tolstov. Had breakfast and dinner with Papa, Mama and Nicky. Walked with Papa, O. and T. Went to the nanny school[130] *yolka*[131] with T., A. and Nastenka.

[130] Nanny School of Tsarskoe Selo, also an orphanage patronized by Alexandra Feodorovna

[131] Literally "fir tree" in Russian, refers to Christmas or New Year parties

Nanny School of Tsarskoe Selo

Had tea 4 with Papa and Mama. Went to *Vsenoshnaya* with Papa. Read fortunes with Anya, sharpened wax and peeled the shells. Had tea. Went to *moleben* 3 with Papa and Mama at the house church.

From the 1916 diary of Olga Romanov

Saturday. **31st December**. We 2 to *Znamenie* and to the infirmary. Rita was helping replace Val.[entina] Iv.[anovna][132] in the operating room, and I was [helping] a little on the ward. Distributed medicines, etc. Wrote.

---

[132] Chebotareva

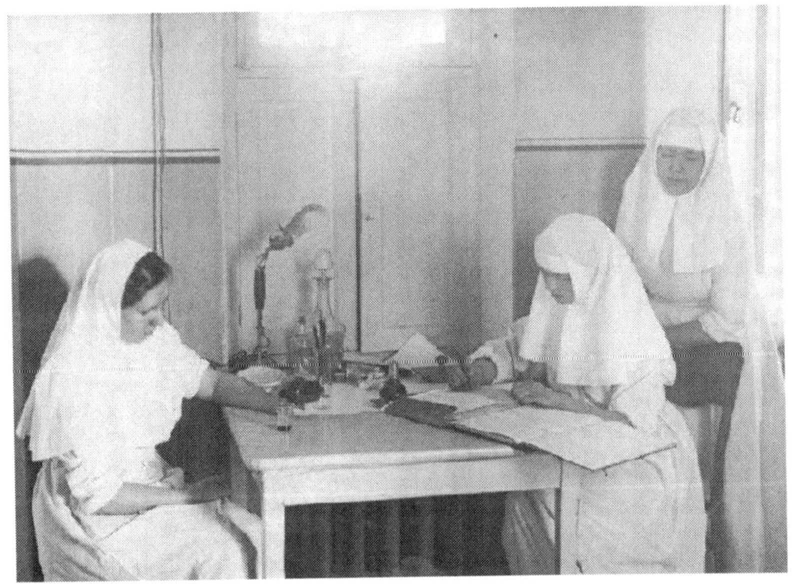

In general, not much to do, only during dressing changes. Around 3 went home to get dressed and go to a *yolka* at the School for Nannies, but I and Papa walked a little more. Mama and Anya were at Al.'s He feels better, but doesn't get up yet. At 6 1/2 we 4 with Papa went to *vsenoshnaya.* Will stop by [to see] Al.[exei] to say good night. In the evening [we] will gather for prayers. Read [our] fortunes with Anya using wax and paper. Lord, save us and have mercy on us in 1917, the new year.

* * *

YEAR 1917:
Abdication and arrest

From the 1917 diary of Nicholas Alexandrovich

1st January. Sunday. The day remained greyish, quiet and warm. At 10 ½ went to *obednya* with the daughters. After breakfast took a walk around the park. Alexei got up and also went outdoors. Around 3 o'cl. Misha[133] arrived, with wh[om] I headed to the Grand Palace to receive the ministers, suite, heads of the chapters and diplomats. All that ended at 5.10. I wore the Plastun *cherkesska.*[134] After tea [I] studied and responded to telegrams. In the evening read out loud.

---

[133] Grand Duke Michael Alexandrovich, the Tsar's younger brother

[134] Uniform of infantry Cossack

From the 1917 diary of Michael Alexandrovich

1 January. Sunday. Gatchina. ... I took an extra train to Tsarskoe [Selo]. From the Alexander Palace, went to the Grand Palace with Nicky, where they conducted greetings, - the ministers, the suite, the diplomatic corpus. At 4 o'cl. I went to see Boris; Kirill, Andrei were there. Stayed there until 5 ½ then went to Gatchina.

<...>

From the 1917 diary of Nicholas Alexandrovich

2nd January. Monday. The freeze increased again. Took a short walk. Received Grigorovich, Rittikh and Voinovky-Kriger, the new Controller of the Railway Ministry. Walked around the entire park with the daughters. At 6 o'cl. Protopov came to see me, and then Taneyev. Studied in the evening after saying goodnight to Alexei.

From the 1917 diary of Olga Romanov

Minevich. Tuesday. **3rd January**. We 2 to *Znamenie* and to the infirmary. Abashidze had surgery. Removed shrapnel from his neck. Made a lot of beds, changed dressings, set up, etc. There was enough to do. Fed Merkuriev. Voskanov and D[illegible] were transferred. Ate all together. We 4 went to the Grand

Palace—at about 4 o'clock we 3 took a walk with Papa. Very cold, 16 deg. of frost, bright in the evening. At 6 o'clock went to Anya's and sat with the Cossacks. Aleks.[ei] K.[onstantinovich], Vikt.[or] and Yuzik, like last time in front of the fireplace. After that, only one lamp was lit on the floor, [we] took turns sitting in the comfortable chair, fought with Vikt. with pillows and pushed each other hard for the best chair. It was so cozy and nice.

Inside Anya's house

Alex.[ei]'s voice is somewhat better. Lishevich had dinner. [He] spoke nicely with Mama. Her voice is also hoarse. Papa read Chekhov to us, "The Teacher." After that [I] wrote the words and notes of

Father Grigori to Anya's dictation. After 11o'clock to bed. Al. is [doing] fine, [he] took a walk.

From the 1917 diary of Nicholas Alexandrovich

4th January. Wednesday. In the morning Alec[135] came over for the occasion of triple portrait award. Took a walk. At 11 o'cl. received Dobrovolsky and then Prince Golitzyn-Muravlin. After breakfast spent an hour and a half at Kostritsky's[136]. Took a walk in semi-darkness. At 6 o'cl. Scheglovitov came to see me. Studied. In the evening read aloud.

Dr Kostritsky, who treated the imperial family in Tsarskoe Selo, Crimea and also followed them to Tobolsk

[135] Alexander Petrovich, Prince of Oldenburg

[136] Imperial dentist Sergei Sergeyevich Kostritsky

5th January. Thursday. In the morning received Prince Golitzyn. At 11 o'cl. Went to *obednya* with blessings of the waters. After the service Father Alexander sprinkled all our rooms. After breakfast again sat at the dentist and took a walk with Tatiana and Maria. Before tea received general Shilder, director of the Lyceum. Before dinner received Gruko, who arrived from Mogilev for 3-4 days. Studied for a short time.

6th January. Epiphany. Went to *obednya*, which was conducted by Metr.[opolitan] Pitirim, quickly and magnificently. After breakfast went to Kostritsky for a long while. Took a walk with Tatiana and Maria. It was sunny and frosty - 10°. Before tea received A.S. Botkin[137], and at 6 o'cl. Prince Shirinsky. Read a lot and finished everything. Vilkitsky (on duty) had dinner. In the evening read aloud.

7th January. Saturday. Belyaev did his first report as the military minister. After him received Rodzyanko[138]. From 2 until 3 ½ sat at Kostritsky's. Took a walk with Maria. Fredericks had tea with us. Went to *vsenoshnaya*. In the evening received Protopopov.

---

[137] Alexander Botkin, brother of Dr Evgeny Botkin (who was later the intended recipient of the latter's last letter from Ekaterinburg)

[138] Mikhail Rodzyanko, President of the Duma

8th January. Sunday. After *obednya* went to meet Carol – the heir of Romania - and brought him home. He had breakfast with us. [We] received his suite; then talked a lot with him and with the Chairman of the Council of Ministers Bratiano. Took a walk with Maria and Anastasia. Slight frost. Studied until 8 o'cl. N.P. had dinner (on duty).

9th January. Monday. Took a short walk. After Grigorovich's report received Shuvayev and Count Ignatiev. From 2 until 3 o'cl. sat at Kostritsky's. Took a nice walk. Before tea received Gen. Mrozovsky from Moscow. Studied until 7 ½ o'cl. [They] served dinner to Carol and all the Romanians. Misha also came over. Talked until 9 ½. Was free in the evening.

Tatiana to Nicholas Alexandrovich

10 January. My dear Papa darling! I am writing to you now before *obednya*. It is snowing mixed with rain because it is one degree of warmth, we have had this weather for three days already. We saw Nik.[olai] Pav.[lovich], he alone came over two or three times, and yesterday he left for Helsingfors[139]. One of these days N.N. Rodionov is supposed to arrive, and I am

[139] Modern day Helsinki

very happy. We have not seen him for almost a year. Alexei and Anastasia are both moving their beds into the playroom, where they lie next to each other all day. During the day we all have tea up there. The [Christmas] tree still stands, so cozy. It will be sad to take it down, but for now it is not dropping its needles, so it is fine.

Alexander Palace Christmas tree

So tiresome that Mama still does not feel well, but she still gets up during the day and lies on the sofa a little there. We take turns going to Anya's so that she doesn't get too bored lying in bed. The other day

Emelyanov had surgery, remember him? He was at the Christmas party at the Arena. They removed a bullet fragment from his bone. Now he is in a lot of pain, but the rest are fine. Well, goodbye, Papa my darling dear. We have to go to church. May God bless you, I kiss You very very firmly same as I love you. Your faithful *Voznesenetz.*

View from Olga's and Tatiana's room into Maria's and Anastasia's room at the Alexander Palace

From the 1917 diary of Nicholas Alexandrovich

11th January. Wednesday. In the morning Voiekov and Botkin stopped by to see me. Took a short walk.

Received Boitzovsky-Kriger, Yagmin, com[mander] of the Nizhegorodtzy, and senator Krivtzov. After breakfast both [of us] received Kulnev's wife with their little son, my godson. Took a walk with Olga. At 4 o'cl. received Scheglovitov, and at 6 o'cl. Shturmer. Did paperwork. Dinner: Lili Dehn with her husband, who arrived with The Varyag[140] from Murman, Anya and N.P. In the evening read aloud.

From the 1917 diary of Olga Romanov

Count Zamoisky. Thursday. **12th January**. We 2 to the infirmary. Wrote, distributed medicine and made beds on the 2nd ward with Nurse Shevchuk. Volga is leaving. Changed dressings on Abashev's neck, etc. Volodya,[141] Motzidarsky, Fedya Baroshkov, Lieutenant [illegible] came by to congratulate T.[atiana][142]. At 12 ½ [they] left. D[illegible] [was] at the church for prayers. Uncle Mimi[143] had breakfast. M.[aria] and I walked with Papa. Around 5 deg. frost, nice, quiet. After tea 6 o'clock cinematograph. "Tayinstvenaya Ruka"[144], etc. Mama wasn't there. In the evening

---

[140] Name of a ship
[141] Vladimir Kiknadze, one of Tatiana's favorite soldiers
[142] The celebration of Grand Duchess Tatiana's name day was on 12 January
[143] Grand Duke Mikhail Alexandrovich
[144] Early moving picture "Mysterious Hand"

Papa, as usual, read after 10 o'clock, Chekh[ov]'s "Myslitel", "Doch Albiona", "Na Chuzhbine", "Kuharka Zhenit'sya" and "Drama." After 11 o'clock to bed.

From the 1917 diary of Michael Alexandrovich

12. January. Thursday. Gatchina... At 12 o'cl everyone went to Petrograd, and I got off at the Alexandrovskaya and went to Nicky and Alix's, where had breakfast, and then had a talk with Nicky. At 2 3/4 saw Yuzefovich there at the Alexander Palace, then in an auto (From the Imperial garage) drove to Petrograd... The weather was dark, 5°

Tatiana to Lili Dehn

Tsarskoe Selo 12/I [**12 January**], 1917. Lili, darling, thank you so much for the sweet letter and wonderful little vase, which I liked an awful lot. I was awfully glad to see you both yesterday and happy for you that it is nice for you there. <...>

Lili Dehn

From the 1917 diary of Olga Romanov

Stefanovich. Saturday, **14th January**. Zborovosky. We 2 to Znamenie and to the infirmary. Rita[145] got Ward II for Volga, her substitute is S. Freidlikh, while Alice — [substitutes for] Olga Porf. Mikhalsky had surgery, [they] removed shrapnel from his shoulder. Everything is fine. Wrote, distributed medicine, etc. as always. Count Fredericks had breakfast. M.[aria] and I walked with Papa. 4 deg. [of] frost. It is snowing. Lyolya Makarov came to see Al.[exei] before breakfast. We 4 and Papa [went] to *vsenoshnaya*. Stefanovich

[145] Margarita Sergeyevna Khitrovo, lady-in-waiting and friend of Olga Nikolaevna

had dinner. In the evening Papa read "Captain's Uniform" and "Living Chronology" to us.

Vilkitsky. Monday. **16th January**. To *Znamenie* and to the infirmary, we 2. Did the same as always, made the beds, wrote, fed Pop[ov], etc. Zaremba tried to walk with the help of his 2 nurses. Vilkitsky had breakfast. At 3 o'clock M.[aria] and I walked with Papa. As always, the sun came out. Papa is in a good mood, Mama still tired — [we] did nothing unusual. Vilkitsky had dinner. After 10 ¼ Papa came over and read "The Exclamation Point," "Well, Public," "He Over-salted," "He Poured" and "Chameleon".

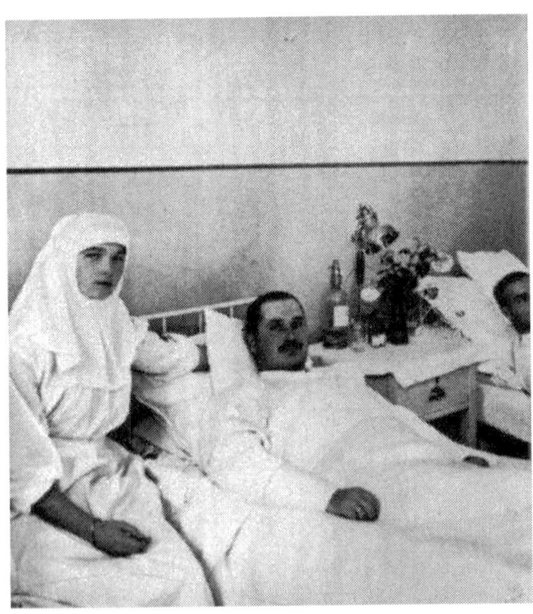

Michael Alexandrovich to Nicholas Alexandrovich

19/I [**19 February**] - 1917. Gatchina. Dear Nicky, Regrettably 3 days ago I completely forgot to tell you that Colonel Tolstoy, who was the cavalier guard under Dmitri's command, asked that you allow him to visit Dmitri in Persia. Tolstoy feels very burdened by the circumstances he is in and would like to visit him. Please notify me via a telegram about your decision. I would also like to remind you about the old man Klopov, whom you agreed to receive. I am imploring you to do this within the next few days, i.e. prior to his departure to Stavka. I gave Kira Naryshkin his address. I can add that I'm convinced and based on general consensus, the old man Klopov is loyal and deeply devoted to you. I am leaving for Kiev this evening via Moscow, and farther to the front. On the way back in will see you at Stavka. I hug you firmly. Your Misha *

From the 1917 diary of Olga Romanov

N.P. Sablin. Friday. **20th January**. Directly to the infirmary, there were a lot of dressings [to do]. Wrote [notes] on both wards, distributed medicines, made the beds, etc. Fed Kamenetsky. [...]. Had not seen him for

2 years. The British millionaires had breakfast, N.P. and Valya Dolgorukov.[146] During the day walked with Papa, we 2 and Shvybz.[147] Sunny, very cold. 18 of frost. After tea cinematograph at Al.'s. In the evening 37.7°. N.P. had dinner. Nothing unusual happened in the evening. Mama is more or less fine. At 11 o'clock to bed.

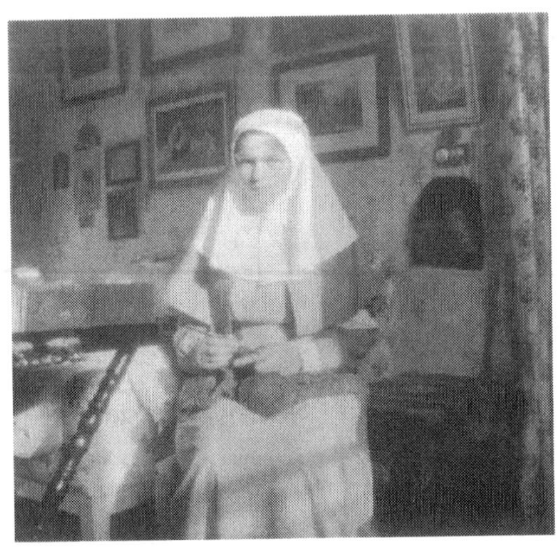

Count Kutaisov. Mordvinov. Saturday. **21st Jan**. Kolesnikov. Directly to the infirmary, we 2. Kasyanov finally returned. Distributed medicines, made the beds, set up some [patients], and wrote. Nikolaev did not feel well, then it passed. [I] changed the dressings on Ponomarev's hand. Mordvinov and Count

[146] Prince Vasily Alexandrovich Dolgorukov.

[147] Aka "Shvybzik" one of Anastasia's nicknames

Fredericks had breakfast. [It is] sunny and very cold. In the morning 25 of frost. Stayed home. With Mama saw two Englishwomen, Sybil Grey and another one. Then [saw] Anya, Alya and Seryozha. Had tea, as always and then cinematograph at Al.[exei]'s. About 7 o'clock, we 4 with Mama to *vsenoshnaya*. Papa received. He had dinner with a mass of foreigners, while we [ate] with Mama. She plans on receiving Strashikh just now. He came after 10 o'clock. Early to bed.

Thursday, **22 January**. At 9.30 [we] 4 went with Papa and Mama to church for *moleben*. At 10 o'clock Papa departed. So sad. [We] two went to the infirmary. Bandaged Krat, Gordinsky, Belitsky, Otmarshteyn and Gumanyuk. Took photographs in each ward. Breakfast and lunch with Mama. At 2 o'clock Gogoberidze came to say goodbye at Mama's. Then [we] walked. Sat a little with Alexei, who is in bed as [his] leg and arm ache. Went to the Grand Palace. Had tea with Mama upstairs at Alexei's. Had lessons. After lunch we went to [see] ours. Sat with the Nizhegorodtzy. Put together a puzzle with Navruzov and Vachnadze, then worked. Returned, sat with Mama.

Monday. **23rd January**. Directly to the infirmary. Wrote a lot, arranged flowers, then the medicines. Fed Pop[ov]. Everyone is fine. The little nurse, Kotenovskaya was there. Prince Ernestov and Prince Kastelno, [and] the French had breakfast. At 2 ½ at [illegible]. Papa was receiving [illegible] 200 officers who graduated from the higher military academy. Mama gave out the [holy] images. We just stood there. It lasted two hours and of course they were tired. Papa [is] "plastun."[148] After tea cinematograph at Al.'s. 20 [degrees] of frost. Sunny. [I] did the pulverization of Shareiko's throat. Prince Ernestov and Anya had dinner. In the evening Papa read an interesting report

[148] Infantry Cossack

from the commander of the battleship "Chezma" and the report from Captain Tr. Schultz of the English Navy. After that, Chekhov's "Anyuta." "In Moscow on Trubnaya Plaza" and "Horse Family Name." Count Sheremetiev.

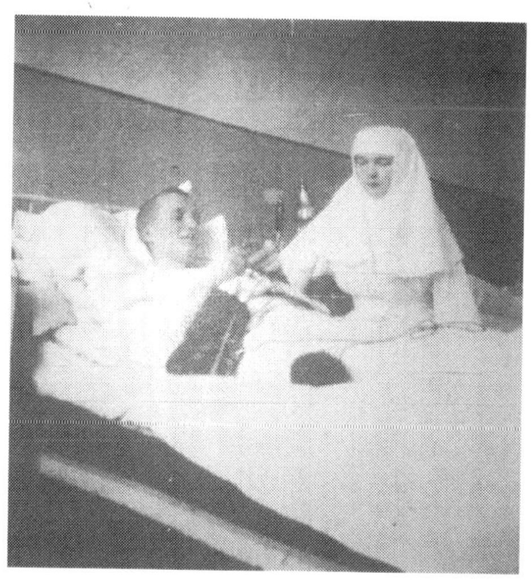

Tuesday. **24th January.** Directly to the infirmary. Not much to do—wrote, fixed beds, etc. Talked to Kasyanov. He played 2 new things on the piano and sang along. He is signing up for ambulatory treatment, like Biserov. Carol of Romania[149] had breakfast. At 3 [I] went for a walk with Papa. 12-13 [degrees] of frost. Walked around the garden. After tea cinematograph at Al.[exei]'s. T.[atiana] and I had

---

[149] Prince Carol of Romania was once considered as a dynastic match for Olga

[our] hair washed and curled. In the evening [did] nothing unusual. Papa wrote in his album. At 11 o'clock to bed as usual.

Prince Carol of Romania

Mordvinov. Friday. **27 January**. To *Znamenie* and we 2 to the infirmary. Bleshenkov had surgery. Removed shrapnel and sutured the hips with wire. Wrote quite a lot. Ritka[150] too. Hauled breakfasts and helped make the beds. Golitzyn came by. He is ill. Mordvinov had breakfast and will have dinner. We 2 with Mama received three Americans, from the inactive

[150] Margarita Khitrovo also worked as a nurse

automobile-medical regiments. After that, she was lying down on the balcony.

Olga, Tatiana and Rita Khitrovo with their patients

We walked a little, with Papa, and he went to work on the fortress. Wonderfully sunny, warm—virtually a spring day. In the evening when it got dark, 1 [degree] of frost. After tea, cinematograph. [We] teased and tormented Mordvinov in the halls. Early to bed.

Nicholas working on the snow fortress

Count Zamoisky. Saturday. **28th January**. Directly to the infirmary, we 2. Wrote, made the beds and distributed medications, etc. Popov will be getting weight extensions. Unexpectedly, came over: Irakliy Vachnadze, Kiknadze, Kasyanov, Chernyatsov (from Evpatoria) and Adamka. As usual noisy, charming and cheerful. Bibi wrote to Mitya with him. Ate altogether. Walked with Papa, 2 [degrees] of frost. Later he dug at the fortress, while we 4 came to the ruins with skis and raced around the garden. Tumbled down constantly, of course.

After tea at Al.[exei]'s, cinematograph, and after that with Papa to *vsenoshnaya.* Mama [came] later. Count Zamoisky had dinner. After that, Shvybz and I rode in a sleigh [...]. Papa assembled a puzzle. After 11 o'clock to bed. Yesterday before dinner we rode in the *troika* with Shura.

The Grand Duchesses riding in a *troika* in Tsarskoe Selo

Count Zamoisky. Wednesday. **1st Feb.** In the morning, we 2 to the infirmary. Pop[ov] had surgery on his finger and clavicle. Strong pain, also Popov with [illegible] and Poturev. [I] changed their ice, distributed medicine, fixed beds, set up Nikolaev, etc., wrote. Dzhenkovich is fine, coughing. Koraikozov stopped by. Ate altogether. 2 [degrees] of frost. Alternately sunny with snow and storm. Went to the Grand Palace, after that to the ruins. In sleds and skis raced around across the park. Met up with Papa and M. who were walking, and we switched with her. [I] walked with Papa, he was going to a reception, and the four of us walked on. After tea, cinematograph at

Al.[exei]'s. At about 7 o'clock, drove with Papa to *vsenoshnaya.* Mama later. AleksKonst[151] [sic] from the escort was there. In the evening, pasted in my album with M. Papa read Chekhov's "Tragic," "The Martyred Ones" and "The Eve Before Lent." At 11 o'clock to bed. Right now, it is 8 degrees of frost and a heavy snow storm.

Mordvinov. Thursday. **2nd February**. All of us [went] with Papa to *obednya.* Mama [came] later. Dear Aleksei Konst.[antinovich]. Met up with [illegible] of the escort. Mordvinov had breakfast. After '*tomleniye*'[152] [did] a puzzle and the deputation of 1st Grebensky

---

[151] Alexander Konstantinovich Shvedov, an officer in the tsar's Escort Guard
[152] A languid rest

Kislyar. Papa's regiment. He was the hetman of Cherkessky, blue *beshmet.*[153] Sunny, 12 deg. frost. Walked on skis for about 2 ½ hrs, and around 4 o'clock went to Feodorovsky Sobor,[154] where 2 Sidorovsky Cossachkas[155] arrived, Nina and Ludmila. And we came down with them sitting and standing [...]

Feodorovsky Cathedral and its imperial entrance

Lots of fun, returned by 5 o'clock. Al.[exei] does not [feel] badly. In the evening horsed around with Mordvinov in the halls. Early to bed. Mama went to Anya's infirmary at *vsenoshnaya.*

[153] Overcoat with no buttons.
[154] Feodorovsky Cathedral.
[155] Wives of Cossacks

Olga, Tatiana, Maria and Anastasia getting ready to get into an automobile with Alexandra

Monday. **6th Feb.** We 2 to the infirmary. Everything is fine there. Wrote, distributed medicines, fed Pop[ov], etc. Kiknadze and B[illegible] came by. Biserov went to Odessa, while Cherepahov is planning [to go] to Chelyabinsk. Dzhurkovich is not bad. Kutaisov had breakfast. We 2 sat home with Al.[exei] in the playroom with Mama and Anya. [Illegible]. Uncle Mimi had tea. Very cold, bright and Papa [is] in a Plastun *cherkesska*. Kutaisov had dinner and stayed rather long, putting together a puzzle. Papa read "Avgusteishiye Kadetsvo," "Pro-Dedushku." Very charming. At 11 o'clock to bed.

Playroom at the Alexander Palace

From the 1917 diary of Michael Alexandrovich

6 February. Monday. Gatchina... At 4.25 I went to Tsarskoe to Nicky's, where had tea. At 6 ½ I went to the Alexandrovskaya [train station] where I joined Natasha[156], who was going to Gatchina with Maria V and Fanny M...

From the 1917 diary of Nicholas Alexandrovich

7th February. Tuesday. Frosty day. From 10 ½ received: Gurko, Belyaev, the new Japanese—after that Ushid with the embassy and Pokrovsky. Svechin

[156] Michael Alexandrovich's wife

(dut.) had breakfast. Took a walk alone. At 6 o'cl. Uncle Pavel came over with the report. Read and wrote. Spent the evening all together.

From the 1917 diary of Michael Alexandrovich

10 February. Friday. Gatchina. Walked in the garden before breakfast. Tata and Miss Nim went to Tsarskoe at 10 ½ to [see] the Tolstoys. After breakfast Natasha, Baby and I headed to Tsarskoe in a sleigh- automobile. Rode for an hour. N went to the Tolstoys', and I received Yuzefovich on business at the Alexander Palace. Then had tea at Nicky's, after which had a talk with him. At 6 ½ picked up Natasha, stayed at the Tolstoys' ¼ of an hour, then went to Gatchina...

From the 1917 diary of Olga Romanov

Petrovsky. Saturday. **11th February**. Te° 37,2 – 37,6 – 38,0. – Until 12 o'clock [I was] lying down in daybed. Mama came by while Polyakov[157] was examining me. Until after dinner [was] lying down in the Crimson Room. During the day, Ritka sat with me and had tea. Al.[exei] came in [his] bed for breakfast. Such a

[157] One of the imperial physicians

darling. [...] Ear hurts. Mama and Papa came by in the evening.

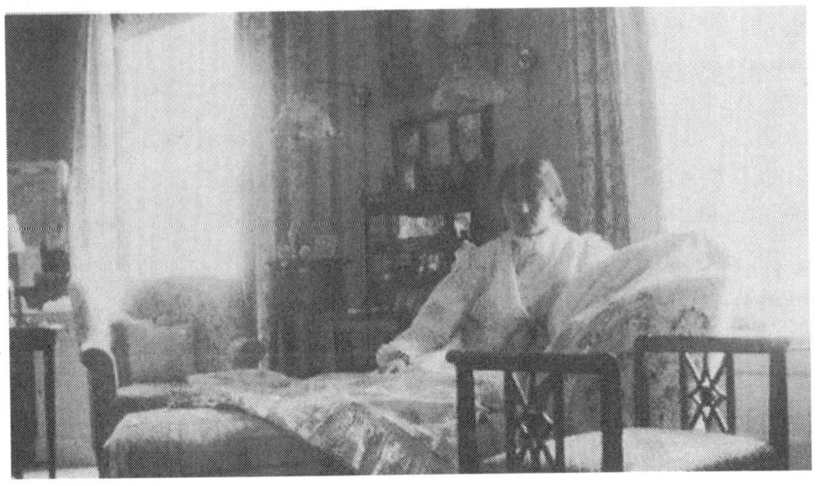

Olga convalescing at the Alexander Palace

Sunday. **12th February.** In bed until 12 o'clock. Then Polyakov and to the Crimson Room. 37,5 – 37,7 – 37,7 – 37,6. Al., Lyolya and Zhenya had breakfast with me and were here during the day. [They were] cheerful. Mama sat for a long time and Anya. Papa stopped by. In the evening they came again before Gulesov. Nyuta[158] read to me.

[158] Anna Stepanovna Demidova, a maid in the service of the Empress. Followed the family to Siberia and the Urals and was ultimately murdered along with them.

Crimson Room at the Alexander Palace

Mordvinov. Tuesday. **14 Feb.** Slept well. Polyakov was here, and [made] a warm compress. [I] was lying down on the sofa all day. Mama sat during the day and Anya. Papa stopped by. After tea, Bibi sat with me, then N.P.—Nyuta read. T° – 37,1 – 37,2 ½ – 37,2 – 37,4 – In the evening Mama, Papa, N.P. and Mordvinov came by.

Tatiana and Maria keeping Olga company during her illness

From the 1917 diary of Nicholas Alexandrovich

16th February. Thursday. From 10 o'cl. received: Ilyin, Kochubei and Mosolov. At 11 ½ went to the clock [?]. N.P. had breakfast and dinner. Sat at Olga's, Maria's and Alexei's. Took a walk with Tatiana and Anastasia. It was 5° of frost and quiet. At 9 ½ received Protopopov.

Olga to V.I. Chebotareva

18-II **[18 February]** 1917. Dear Valentina Ivanovna! I am thinking of You today and kiss [you] very

affectionately. May the Lord keep Your Grisha.[159]
Sister O. Romanova

Olga on the second floor of the Alexander Palace, circa 1917

From the 1917 diary of Olga Romanov

Petrovsky. Tuesday. **21st February**. Was lying down until after 12 o'clock, had breakfast in bed; until after dinner [stayed] in the Crimson Room, around 2 o'clock Elena came over and sat for a bit. She was in Elizavetgrad, Voznesensk and Odessa. [She] saw Serbian refugees and the division. After that, Polyakov. Papa stopped by before his walk. Mama sat until 4 o'clock when AlekKonst. and Viktor came over.

159 V.I. Chebotareva's son, Grigori

We sat together until 5 ½ o'clock, so nice and cozy. Talked a lot. Shurik[160] is going to Mogilev with Papa tomorrow. T° 36,3- 37,1 – 36,9 ¾ – Bibi received a lovely, nice letter from Mitya.[161] Tat.[iana] does not go to the infirmary, we are quarantined this week due to measles, which Lyolya Makarov was ill with. In the evening Mama and Papa came by. Anya too.

From the 1917 diary of Michael Alexandrovich

22 February. Wednesday. Gatchina... At 12 o'cl J[ohnson] and I went to Tsarskoe. J went to see Boris, then to Petrograd, while I had breakfast with Nicky and Alix. At 2 o'cl Nicky left for Mogilev, and I took the extra train to Gatchina at 2 ½ ...

Mikhail Rodzyanko to Nicholas II

[Telegram. **26 February**, 1917] The situation is [getting] serious. The capital is in a state of anarchy. The government is paralyzed; the transport service has broken down; the food and fuel supplies are in complete disarray. Discontent is widespread and on the increase. There is disorganized shooting in the streets; troops are firing at each other. It is urgent that

---

160 Possibly Alexander Shvedov

161 Dmitri Shakh-Bagov, a wounded soldier and Olga's romantic interest during the war years

someone who enjoys confidence of the country be entrusted with formation of a new government. There must be no delay. Hesitation is fatal.

From the 1917 diary of Nicholas Alexandrovich

27th February. Monday. Riots began in Petrograd a few days ago; unfortunately, the military started to take part in them. What an awful feeling to be so far away and receive only snippets of bad news! Stayed for the report for a while. During the day took a walk on the highway to Orsha. The weather was sunny. After dinner decided to leave for T.[sarskoe] S.[elo] as soon as possible and moved into the train at one in the morning.

Mikhail Rodzyanko to Nicholas II

[Telegram. **27 February**, 1917]. The situation is growing worse. Measures should be taken immediately, as tomorrow will be too late. The final hour has struck when the fate of the country and the dynasty is being decided. The government is powerless to stop the disorders. The troops of the garrison cannot be relied upon. The reserve battalions of the Guard regiments are in grips of rebellion, their officers are being killed. Having joined the mobs and the people's revolt, they are marching on the offices of the Ministry of the Interior and the Imperial Duma. Your Majesty, do not delay. Should the agitation reach the Army, Germany will triumph and destruction of Russia along with the dynasty is inevitable.

Alexandra Feodorovna to Nicholas Alexandrovich

[Telegrams. **27 February**, 1917]. 11.20am. Yesterday the revolution took on terrifying proportions. I know that other squads joined in. The news is worse than ever. Alix. 1.03pm. Compromise is necessary. Strikes continue. Many troops switched to the side of revolution. Alix. 9.50pm. Lili spent the day and night with us – there were no carriages or motors. Regional Court is burning. Alix.

From the 1917 diary of Michael Alexandrovich

1 March [Petrograd]. In the morning Preobrazhensky [regiment troops] were going around the apartments of the building, did not come into ours[162], Prince Putyatin was very nervous. At 12 ½ a deputation consisting of several officers and sworn attorney Ivanov arrived. They asked me to sign the manifest project, where

---

[162] Michael Alexandrovich at this time was staying at Prince Putyatin's apartment in Petrograd, on Millionnaya Street, near the Winter Palace

there were already signatures of Uncle Pavel and Kirill. In this manifest the Sovereign granted a full constitution. In the afternoon the Vorontsovs and Vrangel came over. In the evening Klopov was here, who stayed until 3 ½ in the morning. I wrote a letter to Rodzyanko. In the streets [things were] same as yesterday, the same driving of automobiles, shooting. Preobrazhensky passed by with music. We heard about several killings nearby, by the soldiers of Count Shtakelberg, by the way. Nicky was supposed to return from Stavka today, but never arrived, and it was unknown where his train was, rumors had it that it was outside of Bologov. All power was concentrated in the hands of the Provisional Committee, who finds it very difficult, in light of strong pressure on them from the Soyuz [sic: Soviet] of the workers and soldier deputies. Rodzyanko was supposed to come see me, but was unable to do it...

From the 1917 diary of Nicholas Alexandrovich

1st March. Wednesday. During the night [we] turned back from M.Vishera, as Luban and Tosno turned out to be rioting. Went towards Valdai, Dno and Pskov, where [we] stopped for the night. Saw Ruzsky. He, Danilov and Savvich had dinner. Gatchina and Luga also turned out to be too preoccupied [with riots]. Shame and disgrace! Was not able to reach Tsarskoe. But thoughts and feelings are constantly over there! How hard it must be for poor Alix to live through all these events alone! May the Lord help us!

Nicholas Alexandrovich to Alexandra Feodorovna

[Telegram. **2 March**, 1917]. Departed this morning at 5. In thoughts always together. Weather is wonderful. I hope you are feeling well and calm. Many troops sent from the front. Loving affectionately Nicky.

From the 1917 diary of Nicholas Alexandrovich

2nd March. Thursday. Ruzsky came over in the morning and read [the transcript of] his very long telephone conversation with Rodzyanko. According to him, the situation in Petrograd is such that the Duma ministers are helpless to do anything since the soc.[ial]-dem[ocrat] party, in the form of the worker's committee, is fighting against them. They want my abdication. Ruzsky passed on this conversation to Stavka, and [General] Alexeyev to all the military commanders. At 2 ½ responses[163] arrived from all. The

[163] All were calling for abdication

bottom line is that in order to save Russia and keep the army at the front in tranquility, [I] must decide on this step. I agreed. They sent the draft of manifesto from Stavka. At one in the morning I left Pskov with a heavy feeling about all I had experienced. All around is treason and cowardice and deceit!

Nicholas Alexandrovich to Michael Alexandrovich

[Telegram. **2 March**, 1917]. [To] His Imperial Majesty Michael. Petrograd. The events of last few days have forced me to irrevocably decide on this extreme action. Forgive me if I upset you and that did not get the chance to warn you. I will always remain your loyal and faithful brother. Returning to Stavka and from there hope to get to Tsarskoe Selo in a few days. I fiercely pray God to help you and your Motherland. Nicky.

From the 1917 diary of Nicholas Alexandrovich

3rd March, Friday. Slept long and deeply. Woke up far outside of Dvinsk. The day remained sunny and frosty. Talked with my [people] about yesterday's [events]. Read a lot about Julius Caesar. At 8.20 arrived in Mogilev. All ranks of staff were [standing] on the platform. Received Alexeyev in the train car. At 9 ½ transferred to the house. Alexeyev arrived with the latest news from Rodzyanko. It turned out that Misha abdicated. His manifesto ends with a four-tail election in two months (Universal, direct, equal, and secret suffrage. There was no definite time set for the Constituent Assembly) for the election of a constituent assembly within 6 months after the Constituent Assembly. God only knows who put it into his head to sign such filth! In Petrograd the disturbances have stopped - if it would only remain that way.

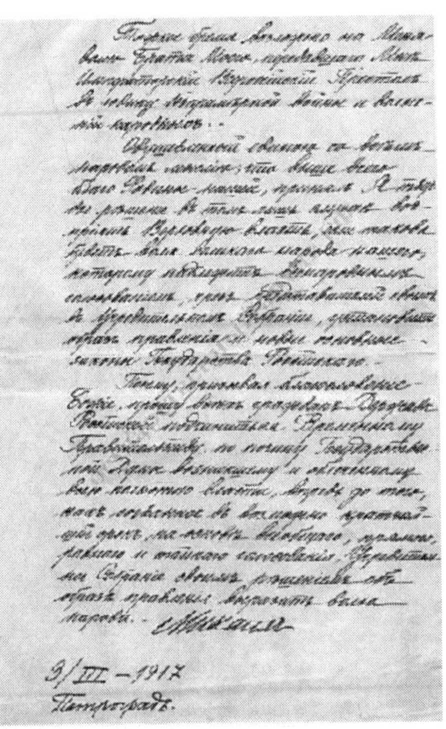

3/III – 1917
Петроградъ.

Michael Alexandrovich's abdication dated **3 March**, 1917

From the 1917 diary of Nicholas Alexandrovich

4th March, Saturday. Slept well. At 10 o'cl. the good Alec came over. Then [I] went to hear the report. At 12 o'cl. [I] drove to the platform, to meet dear Mama who arrived from Kiev. I took her to my [quarters] and had breakfast with her and our [people]. [We] sat for a long time and talked. Today I finally received two telegrams from dear Alix. Took a walk. The weather was revolting – cold with snowstorm. After tea received Alexeyev and Fredericks. At 8 o'cl. Went to have dinner with Mama and sat with her until 11 o'cl.

Dowager Empress Maria Feodorovna, Nicholas's mother

5th March. Sunday. The wind was very strong during the night. The day was clear and cold. At 10 o'cl. went to *obednya*, Mama came over later. She had breakfast and stayed with me until 3 o'cl. Took a walk in the little garden. After tea received N.I. Ivanov who returned from a business trip. He was at Tsarskoe Selo and saw Alix. Said goodbye to poor Count Fredericks and Voiekov, whose presence here annoys everyone for some reason; they went to his estate in Penzenkaya County. At 8 o'cl. went to Mama's for dinner.

6th March. Monday. In the morning I was very happy to receive two letters from dear Alix and two letters from Maria. The wife of Captain Golovkin of the Finland regiment brought them. Took a walk in the little garden. Mama came for breakfast. We sat together until 3 o'cl. Took a walk; a snowstorm started again. After tea received Williams. At 8 o'cl. went to Mama's train.

7th March. Tuesday. Received two more letters from dear Alix, which were delivered by two convoy officers. At 11 o'cl received Williams, Janin, Rychel; everyone is treating me warmly and with consideration. Mama had breakfast and [I] sat with her until 2 ½. Received Coanda, Romei, Marcengo and Lontkevich. Took a walk for about an hour. The weather was mild, but it snowed all day. After tea started to pack [my] things. Had dinner with Mama and played bezique with her.

8th March. Wednesday. Last day in Mogilev. At 10 o'cl. signed the farewell command to the armies. At 10 ½ o'cl. went to the guard duty house where [I] said goodbye to all the ranks of staff and commands. At home said goodbye to the officers and regiment Cossacks and Svodny regiment– my heart almost broke! At 12 o'cl. went to Mama's train compartment, had breakfast with her and her suite and remained with her until 4 ½ o'cl. Said goodbye to her, Sandro, Sergei, Boris and Alec. Poor Nilov was not allowed to go with me. At 4.45 departed Mogilev, a crowd of people saw me off emotionally. 4 members of the Duma are escorting me in my train! Headed to Orsha and Vitebsk. The weather is frosty and windy. Difficult, painful and lonesome.

UNDER ARREST IN TSARSKOE SELO

From the 1917 diary of Nicholas Alexandrovich

9th March. Thursday. Arrived at Tsarskoe Selo quickly and safely – at 11 o'cl. But Lord, what a difference, outside and around the palace, in the park are the guards, and inside, at the entrance are some kind of ensigns!

Imperial train station at Tsarskoe Selo where Nicholas arrived from Mogilev for the last time

Went upstairs and there saw darling Alix and the dear children. She looked healthy and vigorous, but they all were in beds in a dark room. But everyone feels well, except Maria who just caught measles recently. Had breakfast and dinner in Alexei's playroom.

Playroom at the Alexander Palace

Saw the good Benkendorf[164]. Took a walk with Valya Dolg.[orukov] and worked with him in the little garden for a bit, since we were not allowed to go any farther! After tea unpacked some things. In the evening went to see all the residents on the other side[165], and found them there all together.

From the 1917 diary of Michael Alexandrovich

9 March. Thursday. Gatchina… Today Nicky arrived from Mogilev. They brought him to Tsarskoe and Alexander Palace, where he is under arrest with his family.

---

[164] Count Alexander Konstantinovich Benkendorf, a diplomat, embassador and friend to the imperial family

[165] Some members of the suite resided in the right wing of the Alexander Palace

From the 1917 diary of Nicholas Alexandrovich

11th March. Saturday. Received Benkendorf in the morning, found out from him that we will remain for a rather long time. This is a pleasant idea. Continued to burn letters and papers. Anastasia got an earache – the same as with the others. From 3 o'cl. until 4 ½ o'cl. walked in the garden with Valya D. and worked in the garden. The weather was unpleasant, windy, 2° of frost. At 6.45 went to *vsenoshnaya* at the camp church. Alexei took his first bath. Stopped by Anya's and Lili D.[ehn]'s and then [went to see] all the rest.

12th March. Sunday. It started to get warmer. In the morning Benkendorf and Apraksin[166] were here; the latter is leaving Alix and said goodbye to us. At 11 o'cl. went to *obednya.* Alexei got up today. Olga and Tatiana feel a lot better, while Maria and Anastasia are worse, headache and earache and vomiting. Took a walk and worked in the garden with Valya D. After tea, continued to put papers in order. In the evening made rounds of the house residents.

[166] Count Pyotr Nikolaevich Apraksin was the secretary of Empress Alexandra

Nicholas and Valya Dolgorukov (far right) and two guards "working" – clearing snow off paths in Alexander Park

13th March. Monday. It continues getting warmer, the day was semi-grey. Took a walk in the morning for about half an hour. Kept busy with old business. Maria continues to have high temp. 40.6, and Anastasia has earache. The rest felt well. Took a walk during the day and worked. In the evening sat at Anya's with Lili D.[ehn].

14th March. Tuesday. A grey and warm day. In the morning took a walk with Valya D. for three quarters of an hour. Now – [I have] a lot of time to read for pleasure, although I spend a lot of time sitting upstairs with the children. Maria continues having high fever – 40.6. Anastasia is having complications with her ears, even though yesterday they drained her right ear. During the day took a walk around the entire park.

15th March. Wednesday. Lovely sunny frosty day. Took a nice walk with Valya D., and as is usual now, escorted by one of the guards. Maria and Anastasia's condition is the same as yesterday; slept badly and Maria's fever reached a record [high], as during the day it was 40.9. The rest are completely recovered. Walked and worked a lot during the day. Read before dinner, and sat with the children in the evening until 10 o'cl., and the two of us had tea alone.

16th March. Friday. Clear frosty day. Walked in the morning. Maria's and Anastasia's condition is the same, in bed in a dark room and cough a lot; they have bronchitis. Walked and worked during the day. In the evening sat at Anya's and then at the Benkendorfs'.

17th March. Wednesday. The same [kind of] sunny day. Walked from 11 o'cl. until 11 ½ o'cl. Maria and Anastasia's temp. went up and down alternatively, and also vomiting. Took a long walk during the day and worked; finished [clearing] the path by the old gazebo with Valya D. In the evening stopped by Anya's and Lili Dehn's.

18th March. Saturday. A grey day and a warm spell; in the morning during my walk, there was some wet snow. During the day Maria had [temperature] 40.9 and occasional delirium, in the evening it went down to 39.3; Anastasia's during the day – 37.8, in the evening – 39.3. Worked for a bit during the day. At 6 ½ went to *vsenoshnaya* with Olga and Tatiana. Spent the evening with the family and [we] separated early to rest.

Alexander Palace dinner menu

18 March, 1917: Consommé borscht; Buckwheat and pirozhki; Pike-perch in Hollandaise sauce; Turkey stew; Salad; Semolina pudding.

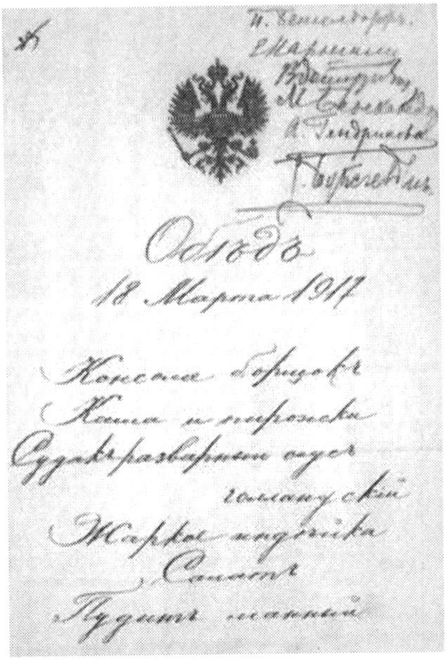
Обѣдъ
18 Марта 1917
Консоме борщокъ
Каша и пирожки
Судакъ разварной соусъ голландскій
Жаркое индѣйка
Салатъ
Пудингъ манный

Dinner menu translated above

19th March. Tuesday. Bright day. At 11 o'cl. went to *obednya* with Olga, Tatiana and Alexei. Maria's and Anastasia's temp. went down to normal, and only in the evening Maria's went up a little. Went out for a walk at 2 o'clock, strolled, worked and enjoyed the weather. Returned home at 4 ½. Sat with the children for a long time, and in the evening [we] went to Anya's and the other residents'.

From the 1917 diary of Nicholas Alexandrovich

20th March. Monday. Apparently Maria's and Anastasia's illness broke, the temp. remained normal; they are weak and slept all day, of course with breaks. Walked from 11 o'cl. Lots of [snow is] thawing. Worked a little during the day. Sat at Anya's in the evening.

Nicholas in the "sick room" with convalescing Maria. March 1917

21st March. Monday. Kerensky[167], the current Minister of Justice, showed up unexpectently today,

[167] Alexander Kerensky, head of the Provisional Government.

walked through all the rooms, wanted to see us, spoke with me for about five minutes, introduced the new commandant of the palace and then left. He ordered the arrest of poor Anya and for her to be taken to the city along with Lili Dehn. This happened between 3 and 4 o'cl. while I was taking a walk. The weather was awful and [it] matched our mood! Maria and Anastasia slept almost the entire day. After dinner the four of us, with O. and T., spent a quiet evening.

Alexander Kerensky

22nd March. Wednesday. There was a snowstorm during the night and masses of snow fell. The day remained sunny and quiet. Olga and Tatiana went outside for the first time and sat on the round balcony while I was taking a walk. After breakfast I worked a lot. The youngest ones slept and felt well. Spent the entire time together.

23rd March. Thursday. A bright day after 2 o'cl and a warm spell. Took a short walk in the morning. Took inventory of my things and books and started to put aside everything that I want to bring with me if we have to go to England[168]. After breakfast walked with Olga and Tatiana and worked in the garden. Spent the evening as usual.

24th March. Friday. A nice quiet day. Took a walk in the morning. During the day Maria and Anastasia were transferred to the playroom. Successfully worked with Valya D.; now almost all the paths are cleared [of snow]. At 6 ½ went to *vsenoshnaya* with O. and T. In the evening read Chekhov aloud.

25th March. Annunciation. Spent this holiday in strange circumstances – arrested in our own home and without even a remote possibility of contact with Mama and with our [people]! At 11 o'cl. went

---

[168] At this time some negotiations were going on by Provisional Government for England to offer asylum to Russia's former imperial family, which never panned out

to *obednya* with O. and T. After breakfast walked and worked with them on the little island. The weather was overcast. At 6 ½ went to *vsenoshnaya* and returned with pussy willows. Anastasia got up and walked around the rooms upstairs.

26th March. Pussywillow Sunday.[169] It was foggy all day. Took a walk and worked on the island. Tatiana just went out. Put away books and clothes. In the evening we stopped by the residents' of the other side.[170]

27th March. Monday. Started *govet'*[171] but it did not bring any joy. After *obednya* Kerensky arrived and asked us to limit our contact with the children during meals and to sit separately; supposedly this is necessary in order to calm down the infamous deputies of the Soviet of Workers and Soldiers! We had to submit in order to avoid any violence. Took a walk with Tatiana. Olga got ill again with a sore throat. The rest feel well. At 9.45 went down to my rooms, Tatiana sat with me until 10 ½ o'cl. Then I read, had some tea, took a bath and went to bed on my cot!

[169] Equivalent to Palm Sunday in the west

[170] He is referring to the right wing of Alexander Palace

[171] Fast and attend divine services

28th March. Tuesday. Slept very well. The weather was warm, roads became even worse because of that; took a walk. At 11 o'cl. went to *obednya*. Olga's throat continues to hurt, temp. rose up to 39.4, how tiresome – she only recently recovered from measles. Walked and worked on the little island with T. At 6 ½ o'cl. Anastasia went to the service with us. Spent the evening with Tatiana again and slept at night in my room.

29th March. Wednesday. A nice warm day. Got up at 9 ½ o'cl., as did not sleep well. Took a walk before *obednya*. The services are conducted in the camp church by Father Afanasy Belyaev, due to the illness of our priest Father Vasiliev, the deacon, lector and four choristers are excellent at their duties. Such pity that not all the children are able to go to church with us! Took a walk with T. and worked for a long time with her on the little island; two of the guard officers also helped us. After dinner, spent the evening together until 10 o'cl., and then Tatiana sat with me for a while. Went to bed early.

30 March, Thursday. During the day it got very windy and blew away the clouds. At 10 o'cl. went to *obednya*, where a lot of our people took the holy communion.

Took a short walk with Tatiana; today they had a funeral of the "victims of the revolution" in our park across the center of the Alexander Palace, not far from the Chinese [pavilion].

Funeral of victims of revolution. Alexander Park. **30 March**, 1917

One could hear the sounds of funeral march and the *Marseillaise.* It all ended by 5 ½ o'cl. At 6 o'cl. [we] went to the service of the 12 Gospels, Father Belyaev was a sport and read them all himself. Spent the evening the same way as all other [evenings] lately.

31st March. Friday. A nice sunny day. Took a walk with Tatiana until 11 o'cl. At 2 o'cl. There was a Procession of the Shroud. Walked and worked near the ferry. At 6 ½ went to the service. In the evening confessed to Father Belyaev.

Nicholas clearing snow in Alexander Park

1st April. Saturday. Forgot to mention that yesterday we said goodbye to 46 of our staff who were finally released from the Alexander Palace to [go to] their families in Petrograd. The weather was nice with a strong southern wind. Walked until breakfast. During the day started to break ice as usual by the bridge over a stream; [with us] worked Tatiana, Valya and Nagorny.

Took a nap until dinner. Gifted each other [Easter] eggs and photographs. At 11 ½ went to the start of the *polunoshnitza.*[172]

2nd April. Holy Easter Sunday. Morning service and *obednya* ended at one o'clock 40 [minutes]. *Govet'* with everyone, 16 people in total. Did not go back to sleep right away as I ate a lot. Got up around 10 o'cl. The day was bright, really festive. Took a walk in the morning. Before breakfast exchanged triple kisses with

[172] Midnight service

all the servants, and Alix gave them porcelain eggs which we had in stock. Altogether there were 135 people. During the day started to work by the bridge, but soon a large crowd of onlookers gathered behind the lattice fence – we were forced to leave and spend the rest of time bored in the garden. Alexei and Anastasia went outside for the first time. At 7 o'cl. there was an evening service in the playroom. After dinner [we] disbanded at 10 o'cl.; [I] read to Tatiana aloud in my room. Went to bed early.

Olga to Nicholas

Christ is risen! My Golden priceless Papa. May the Lord let You peacefully and happily greet this holy day. I send you an enormously affectionate kiss, my very own dear Papa. Your loyal *Plastun*. **2nd April**, 1917.

+

Nicholas, Olga, V. Dolgorukov and a guard outside of Alexander Palace. April, 1917

From the 1917 diary of Nicholas Alexandrovich

3rd April. Monday. An excellent spring day. At 10 o'cl. took a walk with Valya Dolgorukov. At 11 o'cl. went to *obednya* with Tatiana and Anastasia. After breakfast went outside to the park with them and Alexei and broke ice the entire time by our summer docks; a crowd of onlookers again stood by the lattices and stared at us from beginning to end. The sun warmed [us] nicely. After tea went through masses of postcards received previously. In the evening played "Windmill" with Alix upstairs, then read aloud to Tatiana in my [room].

Alexandra to Lili Dehn

3rd April, 1917. Ts. Selo. Aunt Baby kisses you firmly and greets you with the holy day. All day [illeg] to all hearts and ears. The sun is shining softly but one feels sadness and anguish... We took the Holy Communion on Saturday, Olga, Maria and Alexei are upstairs. Do you have any news of Trina and family? How is my little godson adjusting; I can imagine the happiness that [you are] finally together, kiss him many times for me. Have you seen Rita? Hard to write. I remember you with affection and humbly [and] fiercely pray for you, dear one. May God keep you. [illeg] and not allowed to write. Will write the rest to you next time.

From the 1917 diary of Nicholas Alexandrovich

4th April. Tuesday. A marvelous spring day: 12° in the shade. In the morning took a walk for almost an hour. In the afternoon continued to break ice, and a crowd still stared through the lattices from the street. Started to read "History of the Byzantine Empire" by Uspensky; a very interesting book. Spent the evening the same as the last ones.

5th April. Wednesday. It rained during the night from which the snow almost disappeared. The day remained grey and cool. Slept badly and got up late. Took a walk in the morning. In the afternoon worked with Alexei at both spots. A few people were staring at us. There was a lot of water, it overflowed through the stone tiles. Before dinner read my book, and in the evening aloud to Tatiana.

6th April. Thursday. It got really cold, and the weather remained overcast. Took a walk simultaneously with Alexei, and broke ice during the day in the gateway under the bridge and then by the creek, all this time for some reason 6 shooters, besides an officer, escorted us everywhere! Spent the evening as usual.

7th April. Friday. The weather improved and it got warmer. Took a long walk in the morning, as it was nice [outside]. In the afternoon worked with Tatiana and Alexei. The soldiers' faces and their rude bearing made a disgusting impression on everyone. Read a lot. From 10 o'cl. in the evening in my [room] downstairs.

8th April. Saturday. Quietly celebrated the 23rd anniversary of our engagement. The weather was spring-like and warm. In the morning took a long walk with Alexei. Found out why yesterday's guard was so disagreeable: it was made up of the soldiers' deputies.

At least a good guard replaced them from the reserve battalion of the 4th Sharpshooter regiment. Worked at the dock because of the crowd, and enjoyed the warm sunshine. At 6 ½ went to *vsenoshnaya* with T., An. and Al. Spent the evening as usual.

9th April. Sunday. Wonderful spring day. Took a half hour walk. Went to *obednya*. From 2 o'cl. until 4 ½ o'cl. worked and broke ice between two bridges across the center of the house. Read a lot after tea. In the evening it got cloudy, it was very warm; they removed winter frames from Alix's [windows].

10th April. Monday. The day remained cool. Alexei got a bit of a sore throat and was put to bed. Olga is still in bed, while Maria gets up for a few hours. During the day worked with Tatiana between the bridges. Spent the evening as usual.

Anastasia to Lili Dehn

Thank you so much for the postcard, dear Tili[173]. Maria is also very grateful. I now take walks with Papa, Tatiana and Alexei when it is warm out, And how are you? I send you good wishes. I kiss you and the little

[173] Their nickname for Lili

one affectionately. Your loving Anastasia. **10th April**, 1917. T.S.

From the 1917 diary of Nicholas Alexandrovich

11th April. Tuesday. Once again a wonderful quiet day. Took a walk from 11 until 12 o'cl. During the day Alix finally came outside with us for a stroll. Nagorny pushed her in a wheelchair. She watched as we worked on the ice. The sun warmed [us] wonderfully. Read before dinner. Alix requested *vsenoshnaya* upstairs for the children. Sat downstairs in my [room] with Tatiana until 11 o'cl.

Alexandra in Alexander Park. April, 1917

12th April. Wednesday. Cold windy day. Took a half hour walk and then sat with the children while Alix was at *obednya.* Kerensky came by during the day and distracted me from my work on the ice. At first he spoke with Alix, then with me. Read after tea. In the evening we sat upstairs, had tea together and also slept all together.

13th April. Thursday. Freeze during the night down to 3° and the day remained cold with an unpleasant wind. As usual took an hour walk with Valya D. in the morning. In the afternoon with Tatiana and Alexei's state (?) but without him. Read before dinner, and aloud to the daughters in the evening until 11 o'cl.

14th April. Friday. The air temperature is wintery, instead of rain there was occasional wet snow. Took a ½ hour walk. None of the daughters went out for a walk in the afternoon, afraid of catching a cold. After tea checked my boots and picked out the old and worthless ones. In the evening read aloud to the daughters, C. Doyle's book "The Valley of Fear".

15th April. Saturday. Cold day, but a bit better and without snow. Took a walk and read a lot. In the afternoon went outside with Tatiana. At the end of our work the free sharpshooters from the guard room walked over to us and stared with curiosity at how we pulled out ice floes! At 6 ½ went to *vsenoshnaya*. In the evening read aloud the same book.

16th April. Sunday. During the night the freeze came down to 3°. Besides that, there was cold wind. At 11 o'cl. [we] went to *obednya*. Took a walk with Tatiana. Read until dinner time in my [room] and in the evening to the children.

17th April. Monday. Could not help remembering the feast of the 1st and 2nd infantry regiments; but today neither human nor trumpet voices were heard at the walls of the Grand Palace. During the morning walk I thought about this. From 12 o'cl. until breakfast [I] gave Alexei a geography lesson. Took a walk and worked with Tatiana, the weather was clear and warmer. Spent the evening like yesterday.

18th April. Tuesday. Today is the 1st of May abroad, therefore our blockheads decided to celebrate this day by parading in the streets with choirs of music and red flags. Apparently they entered our park to place wreaths on the grave! But by the time of this ceremony – it started to snow dense and wet! I went outside for a walk at 3 ½ when everything was over, and the sun peeped out. Worked for an hour and a half with Tatiana. In the evening started to read "A Millionaire Girl" aloud to the children.

19th April. Wednesday. The weather was the same as yesterday but a little warmer. From 12 o'cl. until breakfast sat with Alexei at his Russian history lesson. Took a walk with him and Tatiana during the day. For the first time the entire family had dinner at the same table – Olga and Maria recovered at last.

20th April. Thursday. Unusual autumn weather continues: the sun appears, then dense snow falls while very strong wind blows. In the morning from 10 o'cl.

until 11 o'cl. I gave a geography lesson to Alexei. Then took a walk. In the afternoon [we] worked on the ice. Saw a sleeping guard, who was sitting on a bench, wrapped in his sheepskin coat! Read for a long time before and after dinner.

Alexei on a walk in Alexander Park. Spring 1917

21st April. Friday. The weather got a bit warmer and stayed [that way] with no rain. Took a walk with Alexei on the "children's island" and then studied Russian history with him. In the afternoon Anastasia also went outside for an hour and half; worked on the ice between the bridges strenuously. Before dinner read "History of the Byzantium Empire" and aloud in the evening upstairs.

Olga to Alexandra Feodorovna

"For suffering of others, you are full of anguish,

And no one's grief bypasses you.

Only to yourself are you relentless

Always merciless and forever cold!

But if your loving soul could see

Just once with someone else's eyes your sorrow –

Oh, how you would pity you.

And how you would weep so sadly for yourself!"[174]

To my beloved Mama [**23 April**, 1917]

Tatiana to relatives in Crimea

25 April, 1917. Tsarskoe Selo. [...] With sadness and joy I remember the two wondrous days spent by us last year where you are now enjoying the delightful beach. [...]

[174] Poem by Aleksei Konstantinovich Tolstoy, penned in 1859. Grand Duchess Olga copied it down and dedicated it to her mother, Empress Alexandra Feodorovna, on 23 April, 1917.

Tatina and Alexei in Alexander Park

From the 1917 diary of Nicholas Alexandrovich

27th April. Thursday. Birthday of dear Georgiy[175]. The weather improved a bit. In the morning took a longer walk after the geography lesson with Alexei. E.A. Naryshkina had breakfast. From 2 ½ until 4 ½ [we] took a walk and broke the last of the ice floes in the same spot. Before dinner read in my [room], and in the evening upstairs aloud.

[175] Nicholas's brother who died in 1899

28th April. Friday. The day remained nice, sunny. Took a walk between 11 o'cl. and 12 o'cl. and had a history lesson with Alexei. In the afternoon took a walk and began work devising the kitchen garden in the park across from the windows of the house. T., M., Anast. and Valya energetically dug the earth, while the commandant and the officers of the guard watched and occasionally gave advice. In the evening finished [reading] "A Millionnaire Girl".

29th April. Saturday. The same nice clear weather. Took a walk. In the afternoon the entire family went out into the garden; Alix [sat] in wheelchair on the lawn [and] watched us work on digging the soil. At 6 ½ [we] went to *vsenoshnaya.* These last few days we eat dinner without electric lighting upstairs, as of yesterday the evenings became bright. Started [reading] aloud S. Holmes book "The Hound of the Baskervilles".

30th April. Sunday. Excellent weather. Took a walk before *obednya.* At 2 o'clock we went out into the garden with many of our people who wanted to work. Everyone was digging the soil with a lot of enthusiasm and even joy, and worked until 5 o'cl. without even noticing [the time]. The weather was pleasant. Read before and after dinner.

Anastasia, Tatiana and others digging the vegetable garden

Olga and Tatiana to Lili Dehn

[Tatiana]: **30 April**, 1917. Thank you, my cherished one, for your darling letter .. Please pass this postcard on to Lizochka and tell her what we are up to. Well, that's all my dear. [cut off...] better, hence Maria and the Little One take walks. Just now we returned from working for 3 hours, it is wonderful. Our people also worked hard with us. Mama sat while [illeg] and Trina worked. May the Lord keep you. I kiss you as strongly as I love you. Your Tatiana. [Olga]: I kiss you very affectionately and thank you my dear, darling darling Tili. I apologize for this silly letter but for some reason yours arrived much later than Rita's, where she wrote that she went to see you. And we were a little surprised that you did not write along with her (to pass on to us). But having received your letters we were very happy + Your Olga.

From the 1917 diary of Nicholas Alexandrovich

1st May. Monday. Wonderful, warm day. In the morning took a nice walk. From 12 o'cl. I gave Alexei a geography lesson. During the day worked again in our vegetable garden. The sun was scorching hot, but work is progressing well. Read before dinner, and aloud in the evening. Yesterday we found out that General Kornilov left his post as Commander-in-Chief of the Petrograd Military District, and this evening about Guchkov's resignation, both for the same reason: the irresponsible interference in the military authority by the Soviet of Workers' Deputies, and some other organizations that are far more on the left. What does providence have in store for poor Russia? May God's will be done to us! +

2nd May. Tuesday. Grey warm day. Took a walk. Finished reading Kasso's book "Russia on the Danube" and started a multi-volume composition by Kuropatkin "The challenges of the Russian Army". In the afternoon worked in the vegetable garden, completed around half. By the end it started to drizzle. Spent the evening as usual.

3rd May. Wednesday. Alexei's arm was hurting, and he stayed in bed all day. From morning until night, it was pouring rain, which was very beneficial for the emerging vegetation. Took a short walk in the morning and afternoon with Maria and Anastasia. Read a lot. In the evening finished [reading] an English book aloud.

Olga's letter dated **3 May**, 1917, translated below

Olga to Lili Dehn

3rd May, 1917. T.S. My sweet dear Tili – we are staying at home as it is raining. But himself: healthy: will go out walking. [illeg] little hand is hurting again – this is from dampness and work. But it is always very difficult to watch. How is Titi's cough, so this is not necessary and probably should not bother you. Would you be able to write to dear Zina[176], she is probably awfully sad, not having news from anyone. Tell her I kiss her affectionately and Mama always remembers her with fondness. Does her society for the wounded still exist? We remember when we saw her in Smolensk last year… Rita found out about [illeg] and saw her mother

[176] Countess Zinaida Tolstaya

yesterday – just think - but of course this meeting is difficult... Trina is working with the others in the garden, Nastenka too. Not much interesting to write about myself. I think about you a lot with affection, my dear one, and humbly pray. I embrace you and dear little godson + May God keep you.

Maria to Lili Dehn

"Indeed He Is Risen! Darling Tili, I thank you immensely for your greetings, and also send you wishes. I am still in bed as [I have] inflammation in [my] left lung, [it] still has not gone away. Every day they put a compress on my side, and spread iodine so my skin is peeling. [I] tried to walk but [my] legs are like rags and I am swaying awfully, looking so foolish. At one point I had ear ache but [it was] not too bad, now we all talk loudly. I kiss you affectionately three times. **Easter**. 1917. Maria

From the 1917 diary of Nicholas Alexandrovich

4th May. Thursday. The weather remained clear but cool. Alexei's arm did not hurt, there were no lessons as he stayed in bed. After the morning walk [I] read a lot. In the afternoon everyone came out into the garden where once again there was a major joint effort in the kitchen garden. In the evening started to read "Le Mystere de la Chambre Jaune" aloud.

5th May. Friday. After the morning walk taught history to Alexei. His arm stopped [hurting] and he got up after breakfast. Continued our work in the garden; Alix came outside for an hour. At 6 ½ [we] went to *vsenoshnaya.* Before dinner received gifts. Read aloud to the daughters.

6th May. Saturday. I turned 49 years old. Not far from a half a century! In my thoughts I was especially longing for dear Mama. So hard not to even be able to correspond. I know nothing of her except some foolish and horrid articles in the papers. The day felt like a

Sunday: *obednya*, breakfast upstairs, puzzle! Friendly work in the garden; started to dig vegetable beds, after tea [was] *vsenoshanaya*, dinner and evening reading – [spent] a lot more time with [my] darling family than usual in the past years.

Making garden beds. On the left is the physician Dr V.N. Derevenko. The Tsar is right-center

7th May. Sunday. Cold windy weather with snow squalls. At 11 o'cl. went to *obednya.* Took a walk with Tatiana, Maria and Anastasia, while Alexei was playing on the island. Before and after tea, enjoyed lots of reading. In the evening the weather became completely wintery – it snowed with 2° of frost.

8th May. Monday. In the morning everything was covered in snow. Cold wind was blowing, and it was not pleasant to walk outside. From 12 o'cl. taught geography to Alexei. At 2 o'clock the sun came out, it got warmer and milder. Took a walk with the children and sat with them on the island. Saw the commandant of T.[sarskoe] Selo, Colonel Kobylinsky[177], who was walking with the palace commander Lieutenant Colonel Korovichenko. The evening passed as usual.

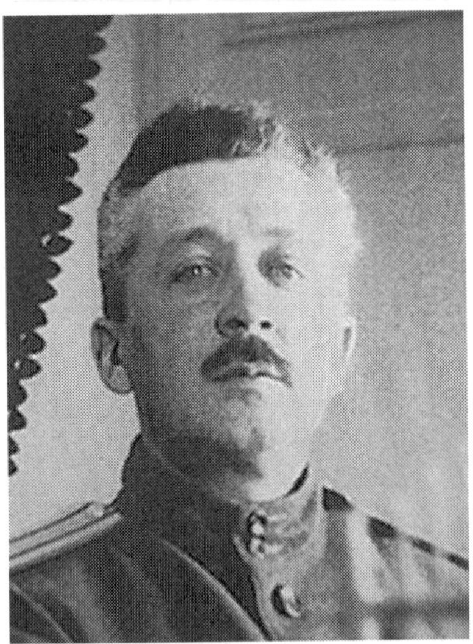

Colonel E.S. Kobyinsky

[177] Colonel Evgeny Kobylinsky, commander of the special detachment who oversaw the imprisonment of the imperial family.

Olga to Lili Dehn

9th May, 1917. Dear Tili darling! I kiss you firmly and also thank you for the last letter. Today the weather is revolting and we stayed at home with Mama. The garden is working out well. We remember you very often, sweet one. Your Olga

L-r: Nastenka, unknown man, Olga, Alexei, Anastasia and Tatiana resting after work in the garden. Anastasia is holding her little dog Jimmy, who will be killed with his owner in Ekaterinburg

From the 1917 diary of Nicholas Alexandrovich

9th May. Tuesday. A very nice sunny day. Took a walk for almost an hour with Alexei. In the afternoon [we] vigorously worked on the vegetable garden; it was hard digging the vegetable beds due to dampness of the earth after snow. Read the Kurapatkin book with interest before dinner, and in the evening a French one aloud.

10th May. Wednesday. Excellent warm day. Spent an hour in the fresh air with Alexei, and then taught him history. In the afternoon went to the park, worked in the garden and started to plant some vegetables. At 6 ½ went to *vsenoshnaya.* In the evening finished the French book.

11th May. Ascension of the Lord. Wonderful summer day. Took a short walk with Valya before *obednya.* After breakfast stopped with Alix to [see] E.A. Naryshkina, who is ill, apparently pneumonia. Worked in the garden and sweated profusely. Read until 7 o'cl. and then rode bicycles for the first time with the daughters. It was also very pleasant to breathe the evening air.

12th May. Friday. Took a walk with Alexei on this wonderful morning. Went to see the ongoing work on the planks "ground" for our tennis [court] at its former spot. Before breakfast, taught history to Alexei. At 1 ½ o'cl. went out to the garden. Helped others to dig vegetable beds in two of our people's kitchen garden in front of the 1st and 4th entrances, then returned to the park and continued to work on our kitchen garden. The weather got overcast and cool. In the morning E.A. Naryshkina was transferred to the Grand Palace in the medical motor, at her request, in order to see her relatives more often.

13th May. Saturday. Sunny day with a cool breeze. Went for an hour walk with Alexei. In the afternoon worked nicely in the garden. Saw when they brought canoes and boats to our pond. Tatiana and Alexei took advantage and boated around. At 6 ½ o'cl. went to *vsenoshnaya*. In the evening read aloud the book "Le Parfum de la Dame en Noir", which [I] started on 11th May.

Tatiana and Alexei in the park with guards

14th May. Sunday. Spent the 21st anniversary of the coronation in a rather different atmosphere! The weather was excellent; 15° in the shade. Took a walk with Alexei before *obednya*. Spent the afternoon in the garden from 2 o'cl. until 4 ½ o'cl.; canoed and boated, worked in the kitchen garden where the new vegetable beds were being prepared, and also on the island. Read after tea and also in the evening.

15th May. Monday. A clear and very warm day. After the walk had a geography lesson with Alexei. Went out into the garden at 2 o'cl. and worked the entire time with the others on the vegetable garden; Alix and the daughters planted various vegetables in the prepared beds. At 5 o'cl. returned home in sweat. After tea did some reading. At 7 ½ went out with Tatiana, Maria and Anastasia and rode bicycles until 7.45. spent the evening as usual.

Tatiana, Nastenka Hendrikova, Nicholas and others working in the garden

16th May. Tuesday. Wonderful summer day; after noon it was 20° in the shade. Took an hour walk in the morning, while Alexei was playing on the island. Finished the first volume of "Challenges of the Russian Army" by Kuropatkin and started the second. From 2 until 5 o'cl. worked with sweat literally pouring down [our] faces in the vegetable garden. The guards from the 2nd reserve battalion of the Tsarskoe Selo regiment (ensign Belyakovsky) acted properly, not one sharpshooter was just hanging around the park and the guards' bearing was decent. Before dinner [we] rode our bicycles with pleasure.

Olga riding a bicycle with Anastasia walking in Alexander Park

17th May. Wednesday. Gorgeous hot day: 20° in the shade, 33° in the sun, with light southern wind. Took a walk for over an hour with Alexei, then taught him history. In the afternoon [we] strolled, worked, boated on the pond and sat on its bank. Before dinner rode kick scooters with the daughters. Around 1½ it got cloudy and the much needed life-giving fluid was shed onto earth.

Tatiana and Anastasia hauling water for the garden. May 1917

18th May. Thursday. The same wonderful day, a little cooler after yesterday's rain. Everything got very green in the park. The air was magnificent during [our] walk after the geography lesson. In the afternoon we once again worked strenuously on cleaning the turf and setting up new vegetable beds. Before dinner [we] rode bicycles. The evening got rather cool - 9°.

Tatiana riding a bicycle by the Alexander Palace

19th May. Friday. It was very cloudy in the morning but by 11 o'cl. the sun came out and the weather immediately got warm. After a walk taught Alexei history. In the afternoon diligently dug the vegetable beds with the others, we now have 65 of them. The guards from 2nd sharpshooter regiment once again were dissolute and the officers inferior. Before dinner [we] rode bicycles.

Maria, Olga, Anastasia and Tatiana resting near vegetable garden

20th May. Saturday. Ideally hot day, but without the humidity. Took a walk for an hour with the four and Alexei in the morning. In the afternoon worked with the others in the kitchen garden and rested by sailing in a row boat. At 6 ½ went to *vsenoshnaya*. The aroma from the garden is amazing, when one sits by the window. Yesterday started to read "Le Fauteuil Hante" aloud.

Tatiana and a guard carrying fertilizer for the garden. On the left may be Leonid Sednev, later the kitchen boy and only human survivor from the Ipatiev House

21st May. Pentecost. Wonderful weather without even one cloud in the sky. Took a walk with Alexei until 10 o'cl. At 10 ½ *obednya* started, and then *vechernya*[178], which ended at 12 o'cl. In the afternoon stayed in the garden for three hours. Sawed a fallen tree for fire wood in the garden, row boated and rode a bicycle. Read until 7½ and walked for a bit with the daughters before dinner.

---

[178] Vespers

22nd May. Day of the Holy Spirit.[179] Warm grey day. Went for a walk until 11 o'cl. with Olga, Anastasia and Alexei. Had breakfast at 12 o'cl. In the afternoon spent three hours in the garden, on the island and on the pond. Towards the end it started to rain, which continued until 8 o'cl. The aroma wafting through the windows was remarkable. Today is the anniversary of the beginning of the army's offense of the south-western front! What mood it was back then and what it is now!

Olga, Maria, Anastasia and Alexei resting by the garden

[179] Whit Monday

23rd May. Tuesday. Another grey day. The sun came out only towards the evening. In the afternoon sawed down three dead trees with my people– a birch on the island and two large spruce trees a bit farther in the park. Before dinner [we] rode bicycles with the daughters. The evening was wonderful.

Nicholas in Alexander Park on a wooden bench he made

24th May. Wednesday. Warm day with passing rain. Took a walk with Alexei in the morning. Before breakfast taught him history. Cut into pieces one of yesterday's spruce trees. Returned home a bit earlier due to rain. At 6 ½ went to *vsenoshnaya*. Before dinner Alix got our modest gifts.

25th May. Thursday. Birthday of my dear Alix. May the Lord give her health and peace of mind! Before *obednya* all the house residents came with their greetings. Had breakfast upstairs as usual. In the afternoon Alix came out into the garden with us. Chopped and sawed [wood] in the park. At 7 ½ rode bicycles with the daughters. The weather was nice. In the evening read "Le Comte de Monte Cristo" aloud.

Olga riding a bicycle by Alexander Palace

26th May. Friday. The newly arrived commander of the Petrograd district, Gen. Polovtzev delayed mine and Alexei's walk in the garden by 20 min. The weather was wonderful. At 3 o'cl. we all headed for a walk; sawed down two more trees with bark beetles. Sailed in a row boat, and rode a bicycle in the evening.

Nicholas riding a bicycle by the Alexander Palace

27th May. Saturday. Forgot to mention yesterday that after our dinner Korovichenko asked to stop by in order to say goodbye, and brought with him his successor - Commandant of Tsarskoe Selo garrison regiment Kobylinsky. None of us regrets his departure, but on the contrary everyone is happy about the appointment of the other. The day remained wonderful. In the morning took a walk farther out in the park, was looking for more dead trees. In the afternoon chopped a lot and sawed. Sailed in boats with the children. At 6 ½ went to *vsenoshnaya.* In the evening read aloud.

28th May. Sunday. Before *obednya* took a walk with Tatiana, Maria and Anastasia; the weather was wonderful. In the afternoon went outside at 2 o'cl. Headed to work in the woods with the same daughters. Alix sat by the water as usual, across from "children's island", where Alexei was playing. After 4 o'cl. returned here and boated. At 7 ½ rode bicycles. Before dinner Tatiana got gifts.

29th May. Monday. Dear Tatiana turned 20 years old. In the morning took a long stroll with all the children. At 12 o'cl. had *moleben*. In the afternoon spent three hours in the garden, out of which I worked for two hours in the woods. Then sailed in a row boat. The day was magnificent. Before dinner took a walk and also went to the kitchen garden. In the evening read aloud as usual.

Tatiana and Anastasia with Nicholas and a guard

Tatiana to Lili Dehn

29 May, 1917. Tsarskoe Selo. Tili my dear, darling, thank you so much for the congratulations and the transfer sticker. I kiss you both firmly. I am so embarrassed that I have not written to you for so long and did not thank you for the postcards...

Tatiana across canal from the Children's Island. Spring, 1917

From the 1917 diary of Nicholas Alexandrovich

30th May. Tuesday. The day remained excellent, but a bit cooler. Took a walk from 11 until 12 o'cl. while Alexei played on the island. After breakfast [we] went out into the garden at 2 o'cl. The following worked with me, sawed and chopped wood, the usual: Valya D., Volkov – Alix's valet, Teteryatnikov, Martyshkin, Korneyev, and today an additional fireman. The following were present and moved the wood: T., M., An., two officers and four sharpshooters of the 1st battalion. Returned home for tea at 5 o'cl. Before dinner took another walk for a half hour inside the "circle".

Nicholas with guards, working in the garden

31st May. Wednesday. Yet another nice day - cloudless and warm. Took a walk with Alexei and then taught him geography. In the afternoon successfully worked near the path past the tennis [court]; fell five dead spruce trees and cut them up for firewood. After tea, unsealed a small cupboard in Papa's study with Benkendorf, and looked through all the papers and things that were inside. Before dinner took a walk with the daughters. In the evening started [reading] the second volume of "Le Comte de Monte-Cristo".

Tatiana with her dog Ortipo and Nicholas. Spring 1917

From the 1917 diary of Nicholas Alexandrovich

1st June. Thursday. A beautiful very warm day. From 10 o'cl. taught Alexei history, then took a nice walk around the park. After breakfast [we] sawed down a huge spruce tree near yesterday's spot. It was very hot to work and the flies were very annoying. Before dinner we also took a walk.

2nd June. Friday. In the morning took a walk inside the park again, where it was so nice and dense. Before breakfast had a lesson with Alexei. In the afternoon Alix was present at our work at yesterday's spot; [we] finished sawing the entire tree. Sailed in row boat. After reading for an hour and a half, took a walk in the garden with O., Mar. and An. The weather was marvellous.

L-r: Anastasia, Olga, Alexei, Maria and Tatiana. Their hair was shaved off around this time because it started falling out as they recovered from measles

3rd June. Saturday. After morning tea, Kerensky arrived unexpectedly in a motor from the city. He did not stay here very long: asked me to send to the investigation commission any papers or letters related to internal politics. After a walk and until breakfast, helped Korovichenko to sort out these papers. In the afternoon he continued it together with Kobylinsky.

Kerensky and colleagues posing in front of the imperial Lyceum

Finished sawing the tree trunks from the first spot. At this time the incident with Alexei's rifle occurred; he was playing with it on the island; the sharpshooters who were walking in the garden saw it and requested the officer to allow them to take it away, and they took it to the guard-house. Later, it turned out that the rifle was sent over to town hall for some reason! Such fine officers who do not dare deny requests of the lower ranks! Went to *vsenoshnaya.* The evening - as usual.

Olga and Anastasia kayaking by the Children's Island

4th June. Sunday. Marvelous hot day with wind. Before *obednya* took a walk with the daughters. The 3rd sharpshooter reserve battalion came on guard for the first time. The difference was vast compared to the others. In the afternoon finished sawing the already downed trees. Boated in rowboat. Before dinner took the usual short stroll.

Olga and Alexei by the pond

5th June. Monday. Today darling Anastasia turned 16 years old. Took a walk with all the children until 12 o'cl. Went to *molebna.*

Anastasia and Nicholas

In the afternoon cut down two large spruce trees at the crossing of three roads near the Arsenal. The heat was tremendous, the sun looked reddish, there was a burning smell in the air – probably from peat being burned somewhere. Sailed in a boat for a bit. In the evening took a walk until 8 o'cl. Started the 3rd volume of "Le Comte de Monte-Cristo".

The Arsenal in Alexander Park

Olga to Lili Dehn

5 June, 1917. My darling Tili! Tatiana and I are very grateful for the beautiful postcard. What wonderful weather is here all the time. We planted roses along the edges of the path and have to water them daily. Today we ate our radishes for the first time and they are truly so delicious. I kiss you and Titi affectionately. May God keep you, my darling. Your Olga.

Olga and Anastasia in Alexander Park. Summer 1917

Anastasia to Lili Dehn

T.[sarskoe] S.[elo]. **5th June**, 1917. My dear good Tili, thank you so much for the greetings and the English birdy! I would like to kiss and squeeze you in person. Last night they pierced my ears and I put on earrings. I must write a lot more [letters], therefore will end. I mentally kiss sweet Tili and the little one affectionately. Please write. Your A.

Tatiana to Lili Dehn

6th June, 1917. My dear Tili! I apologize terribly that I have not written to you for so long, and did not even thank you for the card. So how are you all dear and your little one? I am so happy that D[illeg] is helping him and he will be completely well. I am writing to you from the red room, Olga is sitting by the window and reading, the others are on the [... incomplete...]

From the 1917 diary of Nicholas Alexandrovich

6th June. Tuesday. Today Kerensky reviewed all the reserve sharpshooter battalions. [He] did not come to see us. In the afternoon [we] cut down a large dead spruce tree near yesterday's spot, and another on the "children's island". The weather was ideal.

Anastasia and Nicholas with guards in Alexander Park

7th June. Wednesday. A very hot day and very strong burning smell. In the morning took a walk in the park. After breakfast sawed down three dead trees in the same spots near the arsenal. Canoed while some people were swimming on the far side of the pond. The head of the guards was the generally unpopular ensign Shumovich of the 2nd sharpshooter regiment.

8th June. Thursday. The hottest day so far: 24° in the shade. Before the morning walk taught history to Alexei. In the afternoon, despite the tropical heat, [we] sawed down two more spruces. Once again there is excellent guard from the 3rd sharpshooter regiment. Drank a great deal of tea after working. As usual, read before the evening walk, and aloud in the evening.

Suite members who remained at the Alexander Palace with the imperial family. L-r: Prince V.A. Dolgorukov, P. Gilliard, A.Hendrikova, S. Buxhoeveden, C. Schneider, Count P. Benkendorf, Dr V. Derevenko, seated is Countess Benkendorf

9th June. Friday. Exactly three months since I returned from Mogilev and here we are confined as prisoners. It is hard not to have news from dear Mama, but as for other matters, I feel indifferent. Today is even hotter; 25° in the shade, and 36° in the sun. Again a strong burning smell. After a walk, I taught

Alexei history in my new study, where it is cooler. We worked nicely at the same spot. Alix did not go outside. Before dinner five of us took a walk.

10th June. Saturday. During the night and during the day until 3 o'cl. it continued to be swelteringly hot and muggy. Took a long walk in the morning. Had breakfast like yesterday, in the children's dining room. During the day worked in the same spot. A rain storm passed in the distance, there were a few drops of rain. Fortunately, it got cooler. At 6 ½ went to *vsenoshnaya.*

Nicholas, Maria with guards and members of the suite

In the evening, around 11 o'cl. we heard a shot from the garden, after a ¼ hour the chief guard asked [permission] to come in and explained that a guard did shoot, as he thought he saw a red light signal from one of the children's bedroom windows. Having checked the location of the electric light and seeing the movement of Anastasia's head, [who was] sitting by the window, one of the unter-of.[ficers] who came in with him, realized what happened and they left, having apologized.

Anastasia

Alexandra Feodorovna to Lili Dehn

Sending you both the most heartfelt regards. May the Lord God comfort and strengthen you. I pray… pray… Remember… God will reward for everything, for everything – we must upovat'* in Him – I kiss you all affectionately, the big and the small.

May God keep you.

10th June, 1917. T.S.

======================

*upovat' in God (trust in God)

Шлю Вамъ обоимъ самый сердечный привѣтъ. Да утѣшитъ и подкрѣпитъ Васъ Господь Богъ. Молюсь, молюсь... Вспоминаю.... Богъ наградитъ за все, за все! на Него да крѣпко уповаемъ(+) — Всѣхъ Вашихъ большихъ и маленькихъ нѣжно цѣлую.

Храни Васъ Богъ

10го Іюня 1917г. Ц.С.

+уповать на Бга (trust in God)

Alexandra's letter dated **10 June**, 1917, translated above

From the 1917 diary of Nicholas Alexandrovich

14th June. Wednesday. Dear Maria turned 18 years old today! In the morning took a walk with all the children around the entire park. The weather was wonderful. At 12 o'cl. went to *molebna*. In the afternoon Alix came outside with us. Worked nearby in the park; cut down three large trees. After tea finished reading Kuropatkin's work "The Challenges of Russian Army", which I found really interesting. Started a French book "La Maison des Hommes Vivants".

Maria and Nicholas

15th June. Thursday. A hot clear day. Took a long morning walk. Studied geography with Alexei. Alix stayed home. Sawed and chopped at the same spot, fell a large fir tree by the little path. Took a refreshing bath before tea. Took a walk before dinner. In the evening started to read aloud the 5th chapter of "Comte de Monte-Cristo". Benkendorf, Valya D. and both ladies-in-waiting received a notice of their dismissal from service.

Nicholas's bathroom at the Alexander Palace

19th June. Monday. The weather was relatively cool. The day passed as usual. Right before dinner we got good news about the offensive at the south-western front. In Zolochinskliy direction, after two days of artillery fire, our troops broke through the enemy positions and captured about 170 officers and 10,000 men, 6 rifles and 24 machine guns. Thank the Lord! God willing, we shall have good luck! Feeling rather different after such joyful news.

20th June. Tuesday. Yesterday's battle was successful: in just two days our troops have taken 18,600 prisoners. Before breakfast there was a thanksgiving service in the camp church. In the afternoon [we] cut down four dead trees behind the tennis [court] and then worked in the vegetable garden for a little while until 4½. All day the weather was overcast, and from 4 o'cl. beneficial rain fell.

Tatiana to Zinaida Tolstaya

Tsarskoe Selo, **23 June** 1917. Dearest Z.S., I am terribly ashamed that I still have not thanked you for your letter on the 29th of May and the lovely embroidered bags. I kept the bluish one with multicolored flowers, Olga—the light blue one with yellow roses, Anastasia—the pink, and Maria—the all yellow. They are very useful to us and they always remind us of you. Mama always takes her bag to the garden with a book or something else. The weather here is warm all the time, then comes heavy rain and it becomes much refreshed. But we needed the rain as it was very dry. How are you all? And what does your husband read aloud to you while you work? In the evenings after we have our dinner, we all work too while Papa reads to us. We are now finishing Volume VI of the book "Le Comte de Monte Cristo" by Alexandre Dumae [sic]. Do you know it? It is extremely interesting. Earlier we read about various detectives; which were also interesting. Well, goodbye, dear Z.S. I will wait for your letters. I kiss you affectionately and also Dalechka[180]. Greetings to your husband and Seryozha. Take a photo all together and send it to me please. I will be very glad to have it. Tatiana+

Tatiana with her dog Ortipo and Anastasia

From the 1917 diary of Nicholas Alexandrovich

26 June/July 9, Monday. It was a glorious day. Our good commandant, Colonel Kobylinsky, has asked me not to shake hands with the officers in the presence of outsiders, and not to greet the soldiers. There have already been several occasions when they refused to answer. Worked with Alexei on geography. We sawed

---

[180] Countess Zinaida Tolstaya's daughter, Dalya

up an enormous pine not far from the green-houses. The soldiers themselves volunteered to help. The evening ended with reading.

Olga to Lili Dehn

30 VI [**30 June**], 1917. Dear Tili darling! How are you? Finally good weather again and the soil is better. We are clearing off the straw, spread it around and put in a pile. While the weather is good we have a good amount of work. I kiss you very affectionately, darling, may God keep you. Your O.

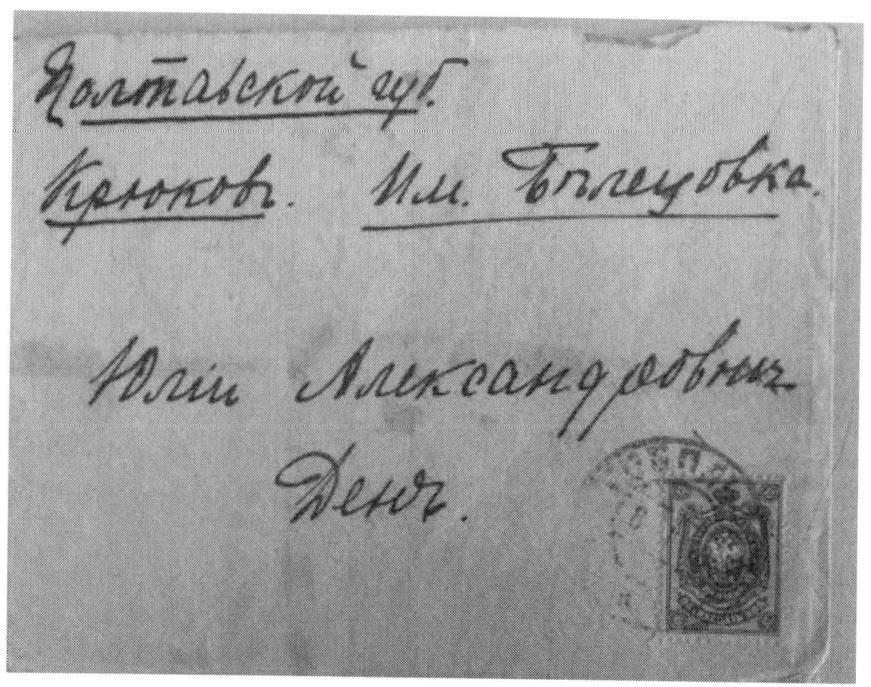

Envelope addressed to Yulia ('Lili") Alexandrovna Dehn in Olga's hand

From the diary of Pierre Gilliard

Now that we were done with work in the garden, in order to fill free time we asked for permission to cut down dead trees in the park. We move from place to place with the guards. We are becoming rather skilled lumberjacks and this way we prepare a lot of wood for next winter.

Gilliard and his student Alexei by the Alexander Park pond

From the 1917 diary of Nicholas Alexandrovich

5/18 **July**,[181] Wednesday. It rained all morning; by 2 o'clock the weather improved; and toward evening it grew cooler. Spent the day as usual. In Petrograd there are disorders these days, accompanied by shooting. Many soldiers and sailors arrived there

[181] Nicholas started temporarily using old/new style calendar format

yesterday from Kronshtadt to oppose the Provisional Government. Absolute chaos. Where are the people who could take this movement in hand and put a stop to strife and bloodshed? The root of all this evil is in Petrograd and not everywhere in Russia.

6/19 **July**. Thursday. Fortunately, overwhelming majority of troops in Petrograd remained loyal to their duty and order is again restored in the streets. The weather has been wonderful. Took a nice walk with Tatiana and Valya. During the day we worked successfully in the forest grove chopping down and sawing up four trees. In the evening I began...[sic]

Tatiana and Nicholas taking a walk by the garden

10th July. Monday. ... [took a] morning walk around the entire park. During the day cut down four dry pine trees and cut them up right there for firewood. Returned home exactly at 5 o'cl. Read a lot. Before dinner Olga received gifts[182]...

Olga to Lili Dehn

12th July, 1917. Tsarskoe Selo. My dear Tili! I kiss you affectionately for the flowers and greetings. I am happy for you that you mostly live in Finland. It must be very unpleasant in this city these days. We are, thank God, fine. Hopefully the weather will not get worse, it got rather Autumn-like, although we still take walks as before. This afternoon we cut down trees in the park, then we sawed wood, etc. In other words, the usual. Mama was there too, she sat on the grass and weaved a cane basket like old times in Belovezh, at a hunt. Isa and Nastenka also [illeg], but of course little and slow, cannot work for some reason. But Trina toils for everyone, you can say she breaks through walls, busy in the garden... I got a postcard from Olya Tikhabr. I don't know where she wrote from. Darling, pass this card to Shurik. And where are the others, do you ever

[182] For Olga's name day on the 12th of July

see them? ... I kiss you and Titi awfully hard, May God keep you + Olga

Olga looks on while Nicholas and Dolgorukov work on a tree

Baroness Sophie "Isa" Buxhoeveden and Countess Anastasia "Nastenka" Hendrikova in Alexander Park. Summer 1917

From the 1917 diary of Nicholas Alexandrovich

13th July. Thursday. In the last few days bad news has been coming from the south-western front. After our offense at Galich, a lot of regiments infected by the ignoble defeatist preaching, not only refused to move forward but in some areas retreated without even any pressure from the enemy. Taking advantage of this circumstance, beneficial to them, the Germans and the Austrians broke through southern Galitzia despite low army strength, which may force the entire south-western front to retreat east. Complete disgrace and despair! Today the Provisional Government finally announced that capital punishment has been instated against those on the military arena who are convicted of treason. I hope that these measures are not too late. The day stayed warm and overcast. Worked on the same spot on the side of the glade. Cut down three and cut up two felled timber logs. Slowly starting to pack clothes and books.

19th July. Wednesday. Three years ago, Germany declared war on us; it seems like a whole lifetime ago, these three years! Lord, help and save Russia! + It was very hot. Took a walk with T., M. and A. Once again, [with] the entire convoy of guards from the 3rd regiment. Worked on the same spot. Felled four trees and finished the pine trees which were downed yesterday. Now I am reading Merezhkovsky's novel "Alexander I."

22nd July, Saturday. Name Day of dear Mama and our Maria. The weather was lovely and hot. We worked in the afternoon, cut down three small trees and sawed them into pieces, as well as two other old ones, which were sitting for a while. Sweated awfully. At 6 o'cl. we went to *moleben* and *vsenoshnaya.* Read aloud as usual. Last night, Kerensky suddenly arrived from the city and stayed at the Lyceum. It turns out that the entire government fell apart, he himself had resigned and is awaiting the decision which various parties are supposed to come to after a meeting taking place at the Winter Palace.

Maria and a guard in Alexander Park

25th July. Tuesday. The new Provisional Government was formed with Kerensky at the head. We shall see whether he will do better going forward? The first issue consists of strengthening the discipline in the army and raising its morale, as well as bringing internal situation in Russia to some kind of order! Worked in the same spot; cut down four firs and sawed apart as many. Finished reading “Alexander I” by Merezhkovsky. The last few guards were good, owing to being sent from the front of 300 men from each sharpshooter regiment and the departure of many reserve marching companies.

28th July. Friday. Wonderful day; took a walk with pleasure. After breakfast found out from Count Benkendorf that we are not being sent to the Crimea, but to one of the far away governing cities three to four days of travel to the east! But where exactly, they are not telling us, even the commandant does not know. And we were hoping so much for a long stay in Livadia! Cut down a huge fir at the clearing near the path. A short warm rain came and went. In the evening I am reading aloud "A Study in Scarlet" [by] Conan Doyle.

Nicholas and his children with guards on Chidren's Island

29th July. Saturday. The same beautiful weather. During the morning walk, while passing by the gates on the way to the orangery, we noticed a guard sleeping in the grass. Unter-officer who was escorting us came over and took away his rifle. During the day we cut down 9 trees and sawed up one pine tree—all right by the road. It was humid and cloudy, and thunder was heard, but the sky cleared up towards the evening. After *vsenoshnaya* Alexei got gifts. Cleaned up and packed my things, so now the rooms look so empty.

30th July. Sunday. Today dear Alexei turned 13 years old. May the Lord grant him health, patience, strength of character and body in these difficult times! Went to *obednya*, and after breakfast to *moleben*, where we brought the *Znamenie* Holy Virgin icon[183]. It felt especially nice to pray to her holy image with all our people. The marksmen of the 3rd regiment brought it and carried it away across the park...

31st July. Monday. The last day of our stay at Tsarskoe Selo. The weather was beautiful. Worked in the same spot during the day; cut down three trees and sawed up yesterday's. After dinner waited for the appointed hour of departure, which kept being delayed. Unexpectedly Kerensky arrived and

[183] Our Lady of The Sign (*Znamenie*) icon was brought to them from the nearby *Znamenie* church where the family used to worship regularly.

announced that Misha will be coming soon. And in fact, around 10½ dear Misha came in, escorted by Ker.[ensky] and the chief of guards. It was so nice to see each other, but it was awkward to talk in front of outsiders. When he left, the sentry marksmen started to drag our luggage to the [semi] circular hall. The Benkendorfs, ladies-in-waiting, chambermaids and our people were there too.

Semi-circular hall: the last room the imperial family occupied at the Alexander Palace before they left Tsarskoe Selo forever

We paced back and forth, waiting for the trucks to arrive. The secret about our departure was kept to the point where the motors and the train were ordered after our appointed departure time... Alexei wanted to sleep; he lay down then got up. A few times there was a false alarm, we put on our coats, came out on the balcony and returned to the halls. It got light [outside]. We had tea and finally at 5 o'cl. Kerensky appeared and said that we can go now. We climbed into two motors and went to the Alexander station.

Handmade cards the imperial family gave to suite members who stayed behind

Boarded the train at the crossing. Some kind of a Calvary team rode on horseback near us, all the way from the park. We were met by: I. Tatischev and two commissars from the government in order to escort us to Tobolsk. The sunrise was beautiful, at which point we started the trip towards Petrograd and via connecting path came out onto the Northern line. Departed T.[sarskoe] S.[elo] at 6.10 in the morning.

From the 1917 diary of Michael Alexandrovich

31 July. Monday... At 10 o'cl went to Boris's in Tsarskoe. At 12 o'cl the palace commandant Kobylinsky came for me, and we drove to Alexander Palace. Got out by the kitchens and through the cellar [tunnel] went into the palace to the fourth entrance and to Nicky's reception room, where [present] were: count Benkendorf, Kerensky, Valya Dolgorukov and two young officers. From there I walked to the study, where I saw Nicky in the presence of Kerensky and the head of staff guard's ensign.

Nicholas II's study at the Alexander Palace

I found that Nicky looked rather well. Stayed with him around 10 minutes and went back to Boris's, and then to Gatchina. Kerensky arranged this meeting for me and it was called for due to the fact that today, completely by accident I found out this afternoon about Nicky's and family's departure to Tobolsk, which will take place this night...

Grand Duke Michael Alexandrovich

JOURNEY TO SIBERIA

From the 1917 diary of Nicholas Alexandrovich

1st August. [We] arranged ourselves in a nice sleeping compartment in an international society [train]. Went to bed at 7.45 and slept until 9.15 o'cl. It was very stuffy and dusty; 26° in the car. Took a walk during the day with our marksmen, gathered flowers and berries. [We] eat in the train restaurant, the kitchen feeds us very well, Eastern-Chinese food and etc.

2nd August. Took a walk before Vyatka, same weather and dust. By commandant's request had to close window shades at all stations; tiresome and foolish!

3rd August. Passed Perm at 4 o'cl. and walked in the Kungur suburbs along the Sylva river, in a very beautiful valley.

Contemporary photograph of Ekaterinburg

4th August. Having passed the Ural, felt significant coolness. Passed Ekaterinburg very early in the morning. All these days the second train with marksmen would catch up to us—we greeted [each other] like old acquaintances. Rode incredibly slowly, in order to arrive in Tyumen late, at 11½ o'cl. There, the train arrived almost next to the wharf, so we only had to walk down to the ship. Ours is called "Rus." They started to load our things, which continued through the night. Poor Alexei went to bed God knows when again! Banging and pounding lasted all night and did not let me sleep. Departed from Tyumen around 6 o'cl.

Wharf in Tyumen as it looked when the Romanov family boarded the steamer "Rus" on **4 August**, 1917

5th August. Cruising down the river Tur. Slept a lot. Alix, Alexei and I each have a cabin with no facilities, all the daughters are together in a five bed [cabin], the suite is close by in the hallway; farther towards the bow is a nice cafeteria and a small cabin with a piano. The II class is under us, and all the marksmen of the 1st regiment who were on the train with us are downstairs in the back. Walked around upstairs all day, enjoying the air. The weather was overcast, but mild and warm. In front of us is a ship and behind is another ship with the marksmen of the 2nd and 4th regiment and with the rest of the luggage. Stopped twice to load firewood. At night it got cold. Our kitchen is right here on the ship. Everyone went to bed early.

From the memoirs of N.D. Talberg[184]

[Pierre] Gillard told me something rather incredible. One day, when the imperial family was aboard the steamer on the way to Tobolsk, he was not feeling well and was lying down in his cabin. Suddenly he heard the voice of one of the elder Grand Duchesses (cannot remember which one exactly): “Zhilik, Zhilik, hurry to the window”. – Approaching the window and opening the curtain, Gilliard saw a vast village on the bank. – “This - is the hometown of Grigori Yefimovich, Pokrovskoe village”, – the Grand Duchess exclaimed, - “He told us that we will see it”.

Pokrovskoe village - photo taken by Gilliard from aboard steamer

[184] Monarchist Russian émigré

From the memoirs of P.Z. Ermakov[185]

In **August** 1917, they sailed in a steamer to Tobolsk, down Tobol River. On the way was the village of Pokrovskoe – hometown of the Friend of the Imperial Family, Grigori Rasputin. The *staretz's*[186] house, in its size as well as furnishing … stood out among common village *izbas*[187] and could be clearly seen from the river. Passing by it, the Imperial Family gathered on deck of the steamer and, in an animated way, were sharing memories of their late Friend.

From the 1917 diary of Nicholas Alexandrovich

6th August. Cruising down Tobol. Got up late, as I slept badly due to the general noise, whistles, stops, etc. During the night, entered Tobol from Tur. The river is wider, and the bank is higher. The morning was cool, and during the day it got really warm, when the sun came out. Forgot to mention that yesterday before dinner we passed by Pokrovskoe village, - Grigori's hometown. Walked and sat all day on the deck. At 6 ½ arrived in Tobolsk, although saw it an hour and ¼ earlier. There was a big crowd gathered

[185] Pyotr Ermakov: Ural Bolshevik, one of the murderers of the imperial family
[186] Elder
[187] Log cabins of peasants

on the shore, - this means that they know about our arrival. I remembered the view of the cathedral and the house on the mountain.

Contemporary photo of Tobolsk, seen from the river Tobol

As soon as the ship docked, they started to unload the luggage. Valya, the commissar and the commandant went off to look over the houses appointed for us and our suite.

View of Tobolsk circa 1917

When they returned we found out that the buildings are empty, without any furniture, dirty and we cannot move in. Therefore [we stayed] on the ship and started waiting for them to bring back the luggage needed for sleeping. Had supper, joked about the incredible incompetency of these people who cannot even arrange a dwelling and went to bed early.

7th August. Monday. Slept very well; woke up to rain and cold. Decided to remain on the ship. Some storms passed, but the weather got better by one o'clock. The crowds were still standing at the docks, their feet in the water, and [they] only ran under shelter when it rained. In both houses they are hastily cleaning and getting the rooms into presentable shape. All of us, including the marksmen, wanted to go somewhere farther down the river. Had breakfast at one, dinner at 8 o'cl., the kitchen staff is already cooking in the house, and someone brings our food from there. Walked about our cabins with the children all evening. The weather was cold due to N-W wind.

8th August. Tuesday. Slept very well and got up at 9 o'cl. The morning was bright, later got windy, and again got hit with several storms. After breakfast went up the river Irtysh, about 10 *versts*[188]. Docked on the right shore and went out to walk. Walked by some hedges and having crossed the creek, we went up a high bank from where a beautiful view opened up. The ship came to pick us up and we headed back to Tobolsk. Arrived at 6 o'cl., to a different wharf. Took a bath before dinner, for the first time since July 31st. Thanks to that [I] slept wonderfully.

9th August. Wednesday. The weather still wonderfully warm. The suite spent the morning in town as usual. Maria had fever, Alexei had some pains in his left arm. Before breakfast I remained upstairs the entire time, enjoying the sun. At 2½ our steamer moved to the other side and they started loading coal, while we went for a walk. Joy was bitten by a snake. It was too hot to walk. Came back to the steamer at 4½ and returned to the old spot. The residents were boating and passed by us. The marksmen from our convoy "Kormiletz" moved into their town residences.

---

[188] A verst is an obsolete unit of length, equal to 3,500 feet or just over 1 kilometer.

This postcard is marked "The Freedom House. Tobolsk 9 VIII [9 August] 1917"

10th August. Thursday. Woke up to rotten weather – rainy and windy. Maria was in bed with fever, and Alexei got an earache in addition to pains in the arm! The day was most boring, without a walk or anything to do. At 5 o'cl. the weather got brighter.

Anastasia to V. G. Maltseva[189]. 10 August, 1917

Dearest Vera Georgievna, We arrived here safely. For now we are living on the steamer as the house is not ready. As I write, it is wet with rain. M is lying down as she caught a cold, but she is already better now. Send our regards to [your] sister and Evg. Aleks. I hope you

[189] Vera Georgievna Maltseva was a nurse at the Feodorovsky infirmary

are all well. All the best. We kiss you. Don't forget us. Excuse the smudges.

From the 1917 diary of Nicholas Alexandrovich

11th August. Friday. Alexei slept very little, he moved to Alix's room for the night. His ear got better, the arm still hurts a bit. Maria is better. The day was calm. Walked around upstairs all morning. During the day went up the river Tobol. Docked on the left bank, walked down the road and returned along the river with all sorts of difficulties, of the amusing sort. At 6 o'cl. arrived in Tobolsk and with a loud crack approached the ship 'Tovarpar", breaking our side plating on it. During the day it was really hot.

12th August. Saturday. Again an excellent day without sun, but very warm. In the morning walked around the deck and read there too until breakfast. Maria and Alexei got up and went outside for fresh air during the day. At 3 o'clock went down Irtysh and docked at the base of a high bank, which we have been wanting to get to. Immediately climbed up there with the marksmen and then sat for a long time on a plain low stool, a wonderful view. Returned to Tobolsk during tea time.

13th August. Sunday. Got up early, and packed our last things immediately. At 10 ½, I and the children went down to the shore with the commandant and the officers and walked to our new residence. Looked around the entire house, from the top to the attic.

Governor's mansion during preparations for the Romanov family

Occupied the second floor, the dining room is downstairs. At 12 o'cl. [had a] *moleben* service, and the priest blessed all the rooms with holy water. Had breakfast and dinner with our people. Went to see the house where the suite will be staying. Many rooms are still not ready and look unattractive.

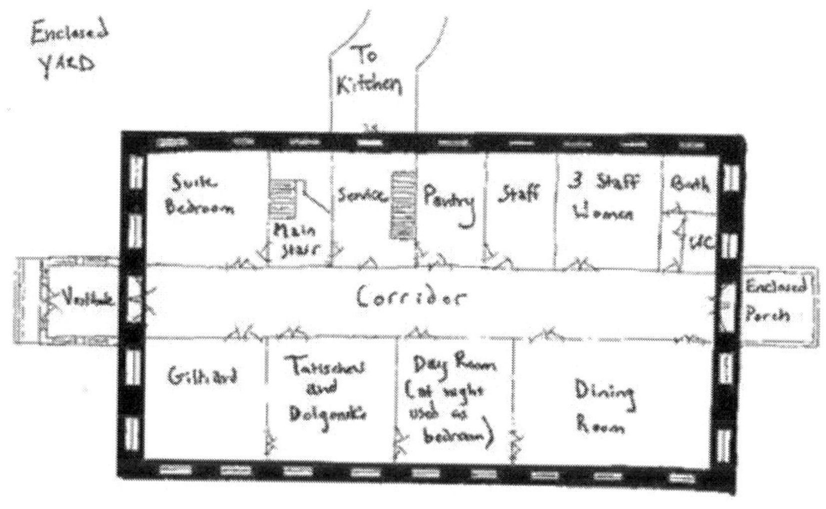

The Governor's House Tobolsk 1st Floor Plan

Then went to the so-called garden – terrible kitchen garden, looked over the kitchen and the guard room. Everything looks old and dilapidated. Unpacked my things in the study and bathroom, which is half mine and half Alexei's. Spent the evening together, played bezique with Nastenka.

Pencil sketch of Pyatnitskaya Street and Governor's mansion, thought to have been made by one of the Grand Duchesses (most likely Maria)

14th August. Monday. After yesterday's rain storm, the weather was cold and rainy before dinner, with a strong wind. Organized photographs from sailing trips 1890/1891 all day. I purposely brought them with us, in order to organize them at leisure. Said goodbye to Makarov – the commissar who was leaving for Moscow. Took a walk in the little garden, the children played on the new swings. Spent the evening with everyone.

Olga and Anastasia in the yard, with Alexei on the swing

Valya Dolgorukov to his mother[190]

Tobolsk 14 VIII [14 August], 1917. My very dear Mother, you will see here the houses where we live. The 1st is reserved exclusively for the family, the 2nd [belonging to] the Merchant Kornilov has 7 rooms above containing Hendrikova, Schneider, Ilyusha[191], me, two ladies-in-waiting, and two domestics. One room is destined for the TsIK (?).

[190] Translated from French by Nicholas B.A. Nicholson

[191] Ilya Tatischev

Governor's mansion (left) and Kornilov house (right)

Below, the Commandant, Botkin and a room for his daughter, one for the Doctor, Derevenko, and two officers. For meals one crosses the main street to the house. The sick ones, Alexis and Marie, are getting better. In general, my dear, it is filthy and barely civilized -- it's frightening! Thank God I'm doing well at present. It is too hot. I asked Makarov to have the permission to switch as needed, with a right to return. Makarov promised to petition for us. I embrace you to my heart warmly, and kiss your hands. How God has protected us until this lodging! Your Valya

Тобольскъ. 19 14/VIII 17 г.

Ma bien chère Maman,

Tu verras ci-dessus les maisons, que ns habitons. La 1re est reservée exclusivement pour la famille. La 2de, au marchand Корниловъ, contient en haut 7 chambres, la Hendrikoff, Schneider, [illegible], moi, 2 femmes de chambre et 2 domestiques. Une chambre est destiné pour la [illegible]. En bas — le commandant, Botkine et une chambre p. sa fille, une pour le docteur Derevenko et 2 officiers. Pour les repas on traverse la rue. Demain on déménage dans la maison. Les malades Alexis et Marie vont mieux. En générale, chère, quelle saleté et peu de culture — c'est effrayant! Dieu merci je vais bien jusqu'à présent. Il fait assez chaud. J'ai parlé à Макаровъ pour avoir la permission [illegible] [illegible] [illegible]. Je t'embrasse de coeur bien chaleureusement et je te baise les mains. Que Dieu te soigne. [illegible] comment arrivez vous avec le logement? Ton Valia [illegible]

Letter written by Dolgorukov to his mother from Tobolsk

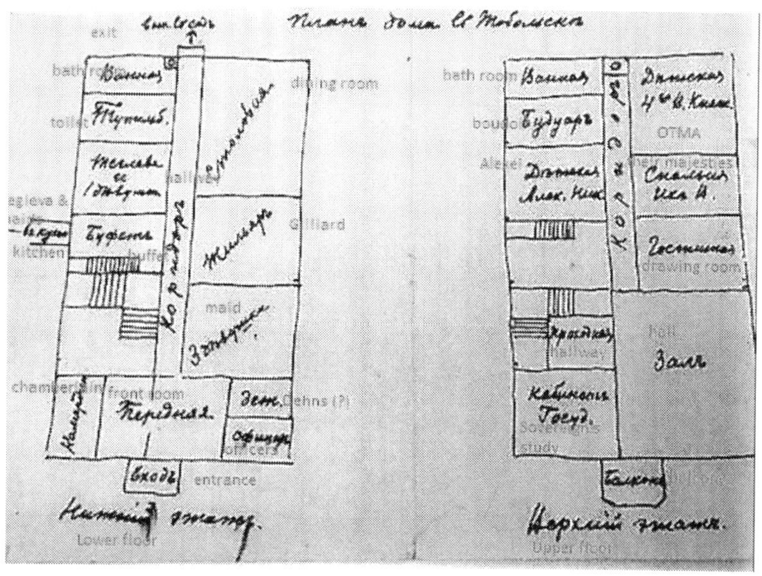

Plan of the Governor's mansion drawn by Dolgorukov was attached to the letter above

From the memoirs of Tatiana Botkin[192]

The Kornilov house was a rather large two story awkward construction, with marble staircases and decorations on wooden painted ceilings with fake moldings.

Kornilov house

On the upper floor resided: General Tatischev, Catherine Adolphovna Schneider, Countess Hendrikova, Mister Gibbs, Prince Dolgorukov, Doctor Derevenko with his family and three maids. Downstairs was the officer's dining area and buffet, the room where Regimental Committee meetings took place, and the room where resided: my father, commissar Pankratov, his assistant Nikolsky and ensign Zima.

[192] Daughter of Dr Botkin

Tatiana Botkin

In the cellar room lived the servants and 8 sharpshooter guardsmen. My father got two rooms, one of which was large, bright, with a window looking out on Their Majesties' house, which was given to me, while in the other- smaller and a walk-through, where the doors never locked and through which passed all the residents of the lower floor to wash up in the mornings, and ensign Nikolsky ran back and forth to his room all day, was where my father and younger brother Gleb settled.

Early 20th century postcard of the Bolshaya Pyatnitskaya Street in Tobolsk. The Governor's house is on the left; Merchant Kornilov's house is on the right

From the 1917 diary of Nicholas Alexandrovich

15th August. Tuesday. Since they do not let us go outside and we cannot get to church right now, at 11 o'cl. there was *obednitsa*[193] service in the hall.

[193] Liturgy without Communion that can be read by a layman

Prayer service at Governor's mansion

After breakfast spent almost two hours in the garden, Alix too. The weather was warm, and around 5 o'cl. the sun came out; sat on the balcony until 6 ½ o'cl. Continued organizing the photographs from the distant seafaring.

16th August. Wednesday. An excellent warm day. Now I have tea with all the children every morning. Spent an hour's worth of time in the so-called garden and most of the day on the balcony, was warmed by the sun all day. Before tea, puttered around in the little garden, two hours on the swings and with the bonfire.

Nicholas and Alexandra on the bacony of Governor's mansion

17th August. Thursday. Magnificent day; 19° in the shade, 36° on the balcony. Alexei had pains in his arm. Spent an hour in the morning in the garden, and during the day- two hours. Yesterday started to read "L'île Enchantée". In the evening played dominos: Alix, Tatiana, Botkin and I. During tea time there was a big rain storm. Moonlit night.

Anastasia to ?[194]

[**17 August**, 1917]. My dear Friend. I will describe to you who [sic] we travelled. We started in the morning and when we got in to the train I went to sleap [sic], so did all of us. We were very tierd [sic] because we did not sleap [sic] the whole night. The first day was hot and very dusty. At the stations we had to shut out [sic] window curtanse [sic] than [sic] nobody should see us. Once in the evening I was looking out we stopped near a little house, but there was no station so we could look out. A little boy came to my window and asked: "Uncle, please give me, if you have got, a newspaper.". I said: "I am not an uncle but an anty [sic] and I have no newspaper." At the first moment I could not understand why did he call me "Uncle" but then I remembered that my hear [sic] is cut and I and the soldiers laught [sic] very much. On the way many funy

[194] Originally written in English

[sic] things happened, and if I shall have time I shall write to you and our travell [sic] father [sic] on. Good by [sic]. Don't forget me. Many kisses from us all to you my darling. Your A.

From the 1917 diary of Nicholas Alexandrovich

18th August. Friday. The morning was grey and cold, the sun came out around one, and the day became really nice. In the morning, Rita Khitrovo, who came from Petrograd, appeared in the street, and went to see Nastenka Hendr.[ikova].[195] This was sufficient for them to search her home in the evening. Devil knows what this is!

Nastenka Hendrikova in Tobolsk photography studio

[195] Countess Anastasia "Nastenka" Hendrikova, Romanov family friend. Followed them into exile and was consequently killed by the Bolsheviks.

From the 1917 diary of Nicholas Alexandrovich

20th August. Sunday. Ideal weather: during the day the temp. reaches 21° in the shade. At 11 o'cl. *obednitsa* service in the hall. Found work for myself in the garden: cutting down a dry pine tree. After tea, as usual these days, read with the daughters on the balcony under the hot rays of sun. The evening was warm and moonlit.

View from a window of Governor's mansion

24th August. Thursday. Wonderful day. Vl. Nik. Derevenko arrived with his family, this was the event of the day. Bad news from the front was unfortunately confirmed; today we found out that Riga was abandoned and our troops had retreated far into North-east.

Dr Derevenko and his wife on the train to Tobolsk

From the 1917 diary of Michael Alexandrovich

25 August. Friday. Gatchina... These last few days the newspapers wrote a lot about the discovery of a counter-revolutionary conspiracy, the center of which was Margarita Khitrovo, who was also arrested. It turned out that due to the discovery of this conspiracy, our arrest and that of Uncle Paul occurred. But apparently there is no such conspiracy...

From the 1917 diary of Nicholas Alexandrovich

25th August. Friday. Warm weather with a strong eastern wind. Our walks in the little garden are becoming incredibly boring; here the feeling of being locked up is a lot stronger than it was in T.S. Worked in the greenhouses with Kirpichnikov[196]. It rained in the evening.

[196] Yard keeper at the Governor's mansion

26th August. Saturday. After a nice rain during the night the weather once again was beautiful. Read with the daughters before our walk, before breakfast and after tea on the balcony. Worked in the garden. Alexei stayed in bed with a cold and earache; it went away in the afternoon. Not much news from the front, the newspapers only get here every six days.

27th August. Sunday. It got cooler today. At 11 o'cl. *obednitsa* was conducted. We like the priest who does the services for us very much; four nuns sing. Alexei stayed in bed as a precaution.

28th August. Monday. In the morning we found out about the passing of Ek.Il. Tatischeva; her son received an emergency telegram on the eighth day! The weather was cool and grey. Alexei got up and walked around the rooms. The daughters also have colds, but they go out into the garden. Obviously no one sat on the balcony. Read a lot. Both Tatischev and Valya are not well.

Pyatnitskaya (Freedom Street), Governor's mansion (left)

29th August. Today is 10 years since we hit a rock on "The Standart". At 11 o'cl. *obednitsa* was conducted. The weather was cold, with occasional rain. Took a short walk. After dinner read telegrams about Gen. Kornilov pronouncing himself dictator, and in another that he was deposed from his post as Supreme Commander, and was replaced by Gen. Klembovsky.

30th August. Wednesday. Had *obednitsa* at 11 o'cl. Took a walk in the little garden during the day. The weather got warmer, but it rained in the evening. The day passed as usual. After dinner played *kosti.*[197]

1st September. Pankratov[198], the new Provis. Gov. commissar arrived and settled in the suite house[199] with his assistant, some unkempt looking ensign. He has the look of a laborer or an impoverished teacher. He will act as the censor of our mail. The day was cold and rainy.

---

[197] Dice

[198] Head of the guards in Tobolsk

[199] Members of the imperial suite who followed the imperial family to Tobolsk lived in Kornilov house located near the Governor's mansion. It can be seen on the right in the photo above, while the mansion is on the left.

Vasily Pankratov

Anastasia and Maria to V.G. Maltseva

6th September, 1917. Tobolsk. [Anastasia:] Thank you so much my darling Vera Georgievna for the letter and your sister as well, who wrote in the very beginning and there was no chance to respond. Not sending photo cards as they can get lost on the way. And so how are you? We remember very very often our cosy infirmary. Do you still go to the infirmary? We are all healthy, everyone thanks you for the greetings and send [their] regards. We settled cosily, and the view is rather pretty. The weather, luckily, is hot, sunny almost every day. I apologize for the horrible handwriting, just now I returned from the little garden, where we played, and now my hands are shaking. In the garden we have a swing (made it ourselves personally) on which we swing a lot and often. We also have here chickens, ducks and a little pig, which eats a lot of rotten cabbage, but we have good ones too. Jemmy [sic] is well and such a darling. How is Nina and her sister? Give them regards from us. Kiss Katya and tell her that we think about her a lot and often. Big regards to V.E. I am writing to you on the balcony, and the sun is warming [me]. Regards to all who remember [us]. All the best, darling. I kiss you firmly. A. [Maria:] We congratulate you warmly, dear Vera Georgievna with day of [your] angel [200] and birthday. From all our hearts we wish you happiness and health. I was happy to her from you. Thank your sister for the greetings. It is probably nice for you to ride to work together with your sister now. Did you get our letter before our departure? And what are you doing now, and your daughter? Vera E. probably returned from the south already. If you see them, give our regards and thank them for [illeg]. I kiss you and Lili very firmy. All the best. M.

---

[200] Aka Name Day

From the 1917 diary of Nicholas Alexandrovich

7th September. Thursday. The morning was cloudy and windy, later the weather improved. Were outside a lot; filled up the duck pond and sawed some firewood for our baths.

Nicholas and Pierre Gilliard sawing wood in the yard

8th September. Friday. For the first time went to Blagoveschenie church[201], where our priest has been serving for a while now. But my joy was spoiled by the foolish circumstances during our procession over there. Along the path of the town gardens stood the marksmen, and by the church was a huge crowd! This deeply disturbed me. The weather was nice, a little cool.

Blagoveschensky Cathedral where the family went for services

[201] Annunciation Cathedral near the Governor' mansion where the imprisoned Roanov family was allowed to worship

From the 1917 diary of Nicholas Alexandrovich

12th September. Tuesday. Warm grey day. During the day sawed firewood and the daughters played with tennis balls on the wooden sidewalk.

Nicholas and Tatiana sawing wood

Tatiana to Ksenia Alexandrovna[202]

18 September, 1917. Tobolsk. My dear sweet Godmother. Finally got a chance to write and thank you for the card. Last, I wrote to you was from the

[202] Grand Duchess Ksenia and her family were in Crimea at the time

steamer named after Sof.[ia] Dm.[itrievna]. Did you get it?

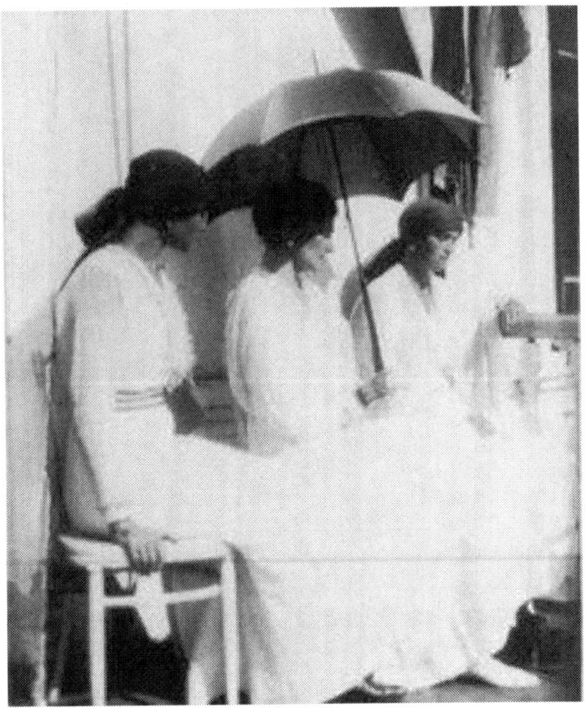

Tatiana, Alexandra and Olga on the balcony of Governor's mansion

We telegraphed N.A.[203] around the 15/VIII [15 August] where we congratulated them with the birth of their son[204]—I do not know whether it reached [them]. I would be terribly pleased if you wrote to me, address it to me directly or to Commissar Pankratov, through

[203] Nikolai Alexandrovich Kulikovsky, Nicholas's brother in law, second husband of his sister Olga

[204] The couple had their first child, Tikhon

whom all correspondence passes; whichever you prefer. Well, then. The weather here is wonderful every day, and today it is about 18 deg. in the shade. So nice, we sit a lot in the garden or in the front yard, where they fenced in part of the street for us, behind which is the town garden.

Olga, Tatiana (with Tolya, child of a washer women), Alexei, Nicholas and Anastasia outside of Governor's mansion

All the roads, that is the streets, are wooden planks and in many places the boards have rotted and [there are] big holes. Luckily no-one fell in. But during rain it is very slippery. – It is awfully pleasant to have a balcony here where we see the sun shining from morning 'til night. It is fun to sit there and watch the street, to see the people walk by. That is our only amusement.

View of the street from a second story window (probably the Grand Duchesses') of Governor's mansion.

We now have a whole farm here. Lots of chickens, turkeys, ducks and five pigs, a cat, [they all] live in the former governor's stables. One accidentally escaped and ran to the street. Looked for him for a long time but could not find, and then in the evening he came back to us himself. Alexei feeds all the animals every day. He and Papa dug a small duck pond, where they swim with pleasure.

Alexei and Nicholas feeding the fowl

From our windows [we have] a beautiful view of the mountains and the upper [part of] town, where there is a large Cathedral. [illeg] ... Arranged to play *gorodki*[205] in front of the house, and we play [a game] something like tennis, but of course without a net, but just for practice. Then we walk back and forth, in order not to forget how to walk. – The length of 120 steps, much shorter than our balcony.

[205] Game similar to bowling or horseshoes

– On Sundays we have *obednitsa* in the hall, [we] went to church twice. You can imagine what joy it was for us after 6 months, as you remember how uncomfortable our camp church was in Ts.[arskoe] S.[elo].

Anastasia, Maria and Olga on front steps of the house

The church here is nice. One big summer [area] in the center, for the parish service, and two winter ones on the sides. In the right aisle they had service for us alone. It is not far from here, we have to walk through town and directly across the road.

Blagoveschenie chapel

We took Mama in a wheelchair, as it is difficult for her to walk. It is sad that she has severe pains in her face all the time, apparently from her teeth, and then from the dampness. But all the rest [of us] are healthy. I hope that all of you are too. How is little Tikhon[206], his parents? Did Aunt Olga get my letter from 6/IX? How are your granddaughter and all the children? And You yourself, how do you feel? What do you do all day—how do spend your time? Did Grandmama recover? Tatischev was very touched that he was remembered.

[206] Tikhon Nikolaevich Kulikovsky, Olga Alexandrovna's new baby

– We sit all together in the evenings, someone reads aloud. We eat breakfast together too but have tea by ourselves. We remember you all very often. Would so much like to see you and talk. Have not seen each other for so long and so much time has passed. – Have you heard about the wedding of little Maria P. and Gulya P. We really did not expect this—and you?

Tatiana outside with the washer woman's child, Tolya

Oh, sorry, I fibbed, the last time I wrote to you was 17 / VIII. How is Sonya's health. Have you heard where

Sasha M. (daughter of Baby L.) is now and what is she doing these days. Do you drive around the neighborhood or to Yalta. I will wait for the letters from you. All the best. May the Lord bless you all. We kiss you all very affectionately, the same as [we] love [you]. [We] pray for you. Your very loving goddaughter Tatiana

The Grand Duchesses' room at Governor's mansion

Maria to V.G. Maltseva

To: Vera Georgievna Maltseva, Sister of Mercy at [Feodorovsky] Infirmary in Tsarskoe Selo. Tobolsk. **20th September**, 1917. I thank you very much, my sweet Vera Georgievna, for the card. I was remembering you on the 28th of August in particular. It was so nice at the infirmary. We remember all of you very very often. Do you ever see the former nurses and Olga Vasilievna? Please pass this letter to Katya. All this time we've had wonderful weather and [it is] even hot in the sun. But today it is snowing and strong wind. Right now, I am sitting in my room. We live in one room all 4, so it is not lonesome. Our windows look over the street and we often look at the passers-by. Well, and what do you do, my dear?

I continue writing on **21st September**. The snow is already sitting on the road. And what kind of weather do you have? Is it still warm or cold already? I remember how we used to go to this infirmary last year. – Did you finish embroidering your appetizing blue pillow case with the grapes? Anastasia kisses and thank you for the card, she will write one of these days. We just took a walk, went to the garden and dug for rutabaga. Here in the garden we only have rutabaga and cabbage. Thank Verochka and Evg. Aleks. very much for the remembering [us], we kiss them affectionately.

Anastasia, Maria, Olga and Alexandra in front of mansion

Do you know anything about the health of Anna Pavlovna? Forgive me for so many questions, but I want to know so much what everyone is doing and how they all are. I wish you all the best, my dear, and embrace you warmly. I hope that you got our letter in time for the holiday. Heartfelt greetings to your sister and all the acquaintances. Do Kolibri and others write to you? How did they settle in at the Infirmary No.36? Probably it is very cozy, were you there? Well time to end. M.

View from a window of Governor's mansion

From the 1917 diary of Nicholas Alexandrovich

24th September. Sunday. After yesterday's incident[207] they did not allow us to go to church, fearing someone's resentment. *Obednitsa* was at home. The day was superb: 11° in the shade with a warm breeze. Walked for a long time, played gorodki with Olga and sawed wood. In the evening read "Zapechatlenniy Angel" aloud.

[207] During a service the priest prayed for the health of the imperial family using their titles

Nicholas sawing firewood with yardkeeper Kirpichnikov

From the 1917 diary of Michael Alexandrovich

24 September. Sunday. Gatchina... At 2 ½ N.P. Makarov (assistant of Golovin) came over to see us. He was telling us in an interesting and detailed way about Nicky and family's journey to Tobolsk...

From the 1917 diary of Nicholas Alexandrovich

25th September. Monday. Lovely quiet weather: 14° in the shade. During our walk, the commandant — the dreadful commissar's assistant, ensign Nikolsky and three marksmen from the committee searched all over our house with the purpose of finding wine. Not finding anything, they stayed for a half hour and left. After tea they started to carry in our luggage which arrived from T. S.

Olga, Nicholas, Anastasia and Tatiana

26th September. Tuesday. Another magnificent cloudless day. In the morning walked a lot and read on the balcony before breakfast. Cut wood during the day and played gorodki. After tea unpacked the newly arrived rugs and decorated our rooms with them. Finished Leskov's novel "Nekuda."

Another view of the mansion and street

29th September. Friday. The other day Botkin received a document from Kerensky, from which we found out that we are allowed to take walks outside of town. To Botkin's question as to when this can start, the dreadful Pankratov replied that this is not even up for discussion right now due to some inexplicable concern for our safety. Everyone was extremely indignant by this answer. The weather got cooler. Finished "Ramuntcho."

Doctor Evgeny Botkin's pass into Governor's mansion

Maria to V.G. Maltseva

Tobolsk. **30th September**, 1917. Darling Vera Georgievna. Thank you for the postcard from 28 August. I apologise that we did not thank you earlier. How are you? The weather here is sunny, very pleasant. Regards to Verochka and your sister. Are you tired from working? We remember the dear infirmary often, it was so nice. Everyone sends you regards. All the best. I kiss you firmly.

From the 1917 diary of Nicholas Alexandrovich

2 October, Monday. Warm day. About 4 o'clock it rained a little. Now all our people who wish to take a walk are forced to pass through the city escorted by the soldiers.

Members of the suite who followed the Romanovs to Tobolsk: Catherine Schneider, Ilya Tatischev, Pierre Gilliard, Nastenka Hendrikova, Valya Dolgorukov. All except Gilliard will be murdered by the Bolsheviks within the next year. They posed for this photo at a professional photography studio and each signed it; it was then given to the Romanov family as a keepsake

Tatiana to Zinaïda Tolstaya

Tobolsk. **2 October,** 1917. My dear and kind Zinaida Sergeyevna, I am so ashamed that I only wrote to you today to thank you wholeheartedly for your nice letter of 30/VIII and I have already received it here. Thank Dalechka very much and I will write to her another time. We often think of you and hope you are well. All of us are here and everything is fine. The house is small but cozy. It has a balcony where we sit often. Almost everyday, the weather is wonderful, very warm but the leaves are falling a lot. We do get a lot of fresh air here. There is also a tiny garden behind the kitchen, with a vegetable patch in the middle. We can walk around the garden in only three minutes (no exaggeration).

They fenced in part of the street in front of the house where we walk, that is back and forth - 120 steps long. The streets here are all covered with wooden planks, and in many places, there are big holes, but they all drive safely. Our windows look out onto the street, so our only entertainment is looking at the passers-by. From our windows we have a splendid view of the mountain, the high city and the cathedral. Too bad we cannot see the river. We went to church three times- it was such comfort and joy! On Saturdays and other times, we have *vsenoshnaya* and *obednitsa.* Certainly, that was nice but still, it cannot replace going to a real church. We have not been to a real one for more than a half a year, since at Tsarskoe Selo we had [only] a camp one [...] Time passes quickly and monotonously. We work, read, play the piano, walk, and have lessons. That is all. How are you, and how do you spend your time? This winter resterez-vous [will you stay] locally or partirez-vous [will you depart] to Tsarskoe? I heard that the husband is fine, [he] lives in S., not far from home. I do not know [...] his address. I would be grateful if you could obtain it for me. If you see Musya, please tell her thanks for the letter and a kiss. Address your letters to me here, or in the name of Commissar Pankratov, through whom all correspondence passes. So, goodbye, my dear and kind Zinaida Sergeievna. I often think of you. Your bags are with us. I embrace you very firmly, and Dalechka. Greetings to your husband and Seryozha. When a finger touches the small leaf, it smells good. I think that its name is geranium. Tatiana

Maria to V.G. Maltseva

Tobolsk. **4th October**, 1917. My darling Vera Georgievna, please give this letter to Katya. How are you? I have not had letters from you in a while. How is Golubev's health now? I feel so sorry for the poor thing. If you see him, give him regards from us and to others we know who remember us. We just returned from outside. We warmed in the sun. Although lessons started, we still sit outside in fresh air a lot. Evg. Aleks. asked to send her our photographs, but I am not sending because almost certainly won't reach [her]. If you write to Kartaeva, then congratulate her for me with 22 Oct. and her girlfriend too. I will be very grateful to you. Since I don't know their address. Time to end. I wish you all the best, darling. I kiss you firmly. M.

From the 1917 diary of Nicholas Alexandrovich

4th October. Wednesday. Today we were reminiscing about the convoy holidays in the old times. It was warmer than it sometimes is in Crimea at the same time of the year. Good for Tobolsk! Spent the day as usual. After *vsenoshnaya,* Alexei got his gifts. Had dinner at 7 ½ o'cl.

Alexei playing in the yard with homemade bow and arrow. This toy will be confiscated from him in Ekaterinburg due to suspicion that arrows were used to get letters to and from the Ipatiev house

5th October. Thursday. Did not get to church for *obednya* on Alexei's name day due to the stubbornness of Mr. Pankratov, and at 11 o'cl. we had a *moleben* service [at the house]. In the morning it was foggy, wh.[ich] dissipated by one o'clock. Spent a long time outside in the fresh air. In the evening Alexei arranged cinematograph for us. The entire family walked before tea. Since yesterday

Kharitonov[208] has been cooking our food, they bring provisions every two days. The daughters are learning to cook from him and are kneading dough in the evenings, and baking the bread in the mornings. Not bad!

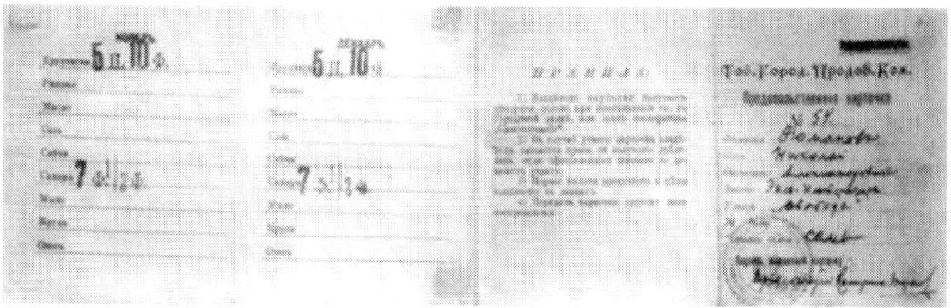

Provisions ration card #54 of "Romanov, Nicholas Alexandrovich"

Poem brought to Tobolsk by Anastasia Hendrikova

THE PRAYER

Grant us patience, oh Lord,
In the time of violent dark days,
To bear the people's persecution
And our executioners' cruelties.

Grant us strength, oh Righteous God,
To forgive evils of our close ones
And to accept the heavy and bloody cross

[208] Ivan Mikhailovich Kharitonov, cook to the imperial family in exile

With Your own meekness.

And in these insurgent days,
When our enemy robs us
To bear humiliation and abasement
Help us, Christ the Saviour!

Master of the world, God of the universe!
Bless us with a prayer
And grant peace to our humble souls,
In this unendurable fatal hour...
And in the passage to the grave,
Breathe into the lips of Your servants,
Formidable strength
To humbly pray for enemies![209]

(Sergei Bekhteyev.. **October** 1917. Town of Eleyi)

[209] After the murders of the imperial family this poem was found at the Ipatiev house, written in Olga Nikolaevna's hand.

Alexandra's corner in the drawing room of the mansion

From the 1917 diary of Nicholas Alexandrovich

10th October. Friday. The weather remained pleasant—around one degree of frost. Klavdia Mikhailovna Bitner, who arrived here two days ago, gave me the letter from Ksenia. Today she started to tutor the children, except Olga, in various subjects.

Klavdia Bitner tutoring Alexei at the Governor's house

Maria and Anastasia to V.G. Maltseva

Tobolsk. **15th October**, 1917. [Maria:] I thank you from my heart, darling Vera Georgievna for the postcards, which arrived, despite the incorrect address, as we live right in the city, in the house of the former governor. I hope that you are now completely recovered. It is so tiresome to be ill and lie in bed. How did you find Roman? He probably grew a lot from last summer. And what is Loshnov doing at D.B.'s? Do you ever see the acquiantances from the infirmary? There is not that much to write about myself, we live as usual. Today aat 8 o'cl. in the morning we went to *obednya*. The church is very close to our house, one needs to only walk through the city garden and a street. We just had tea and now sitting all together. My brother is playing with Kolya, (son of Vlad. Nik.), whom they allow to come over only on holidays. I send regards to your sister and those acquiantances who have not forgotten us. Did Kartashova write? I wish you health and all the best, my dear. I embrace you warmly for remembering [us]. May God keep you. M.

[Anastasia:] Heartfelt thanks, dear Vera Georgievna, for the card. My brother thanks you warmly for the greetings and regards. How are you? I hope your health is better. Sister T. thanks Nina for the letter which was received on 21 September, but she planned on [illeg] therefore she did not thank her. Heartfelt greetings to all who sent regards and thank them for regards. We remember our cosy infirmary often. There is nothing interesting to write specifically, and the rest my sister wrote. Please give this envelope to Katya, I am writing through you, as I think it will get there better this way. All the best, get well. Regards to your sister. I kiss you A.

Alexandra Feodorovna to Anna Vyrubova

[**17 October**]. My darling: We are thinking constantly of you and of all the suffering you have had to endure. God help you in the future. How are your weak heart and your poor legs? We hope to go to Communion as usual if we are to be allowed. Lessons have begun again with Mr Gibbs also. So glad, at last. We are all well. It is beautifully sunny. I sit behind this wall in the yard and work. Greetings to the doctors, the priest, and the nurses in your infirmary. I kiss you and pray God to keep you.

[**21 October**] My darling: I was inexpressibly glad to get the news of you, and I kiss you fondly for your loving thoughts of me. [...] How are Our Friend's[210] dear children, how well does the boy[211] learn, and where do they live? [...] I have heard nothing from Lili D. for some time. We are all well. I have been suffering from neuralgia in the head but now Dr Kostritsky has come to treat me. We have spoken often of you. They say life in the Crimea is dreadful now. Still Olga A. is happy with her little Tikhon whom she is nursing herself. They have no servants so she and N.A. look

[210] Rasputin

[211] Rasputin's son Dmitri

after everything. [...] The needlework you sent me was the only token we have received from any of our friends. Where is poor Catherine [Schneider]? We suffer so for all, and pray for all of you. That is all we can do. The weather is bad these last few days, and I never venture out because my heart is not behaving very well. I get a great deal of consolation [from] reading the Bible. I often read it to the children, and I am sure that you also read it. Write soon again. We all kiss you and bless you. May God sustain and keep you. My heart is full, but words are feeble things. Yours, A. The jacket warms and comforts me. I am surrounded by dear presents, the blue dressing gown, red slippers, silver tray, the stick, etc. The icon I wear. I do not remember the people you are living with now. Did you see the regimental priest from Peterhof? Ask for the prayers of O. Havari for us. God be with you. Love to your parents. Madeleine and Anne are still in St. Petersburg.

Postcard from Tatiana

Tobolsk, **22 October**, 1917. The former Governor's house, now the so-called "Freedom house". Had communion on the 21st, it was as usual every year. Tatiana

Tatiana to Pyotr Petrov

Tobolsk. **23 October** 1917. Dear Pyotr Vasilievich, I am quite embarrassed that I haven't written to you until now. Would you please get my books by A. Tolstoy; they always stood on the 1st shelf of my bookcase, but I don't know what it's like now. I will be very grateful to you if you get them, although I know how hard it is. Send them to Isa if you can manage it, or by mail to the name of Commissar Pankratov, for delivery to me! Now then! We remember you often, I hope that you are completely recovered. Here we have a lot of snow but it isn't very cold. The lessons are going well, so that almost all our time is filled up and the day goes by very quickly- mainly because it is monotonous. Yesterday we partook of the Holy Gifts in church. It was so nice. What are you doing? How is brother doctor and nephew? And where is his former superior, Pavel Pavlovich? I hope that at least for them everything is going well. Did you see Mr. Conrad and Konstantin Alekseyevich? Send them all regards.

Contemporary sketch of the Governor's mansion

24 October. Yesterday I didn't get the chance to finish, so I continue today. The weather was divine all day, bright sun, which makes my mood immediately better, so don't you think that it is always bad. Not at all. As you know, we don't get dejected easily! Were you amazed when you found out about the wedding of your very 1st pupil--?!! We didn't expect that at all. And did Mr. Conrad see the little ones? How do they look now and where are they? Does he continue to give lessons there? Did his family arrive? How did K. A. settle into the new house? Forgive me for so many questions, but I hope that you will answer them all. All the best to you. Everyone sends heartfelt regards. May God protect you. I do not envy your proximity to the repulsive and vile Petrograd. Your student No. 2, Tatiana

Tatiana and Nicholas

Anastasia to V.G. Maltseva

29th October, 1917. Tobolsk. Thank you very much for the letter, my darling Vera Georgievna. We were very happy to learn that you are feeling better. Heartfelt thanks to all for the greetings and give them heartfelt regards from us too. How is Kolibri doing? We we also shocked to find out about Verochka's wedding, we did not get a letter from husband, very hurtful! We have a marvelous sunny weather these days. Snow is still on the ground but very little. When you see Olya from dressings, give her regards. What is Nadya doing? We often talk about and remember the dear infirmary, and the way everything was there. Where is Ekat. Abram. and Elena N., have not heard about them in a while. "Jimmy" is well, goes outside a lot, and everyone plays with him a lot and he entertains many with his appearance. My sister sends a kiss and thanks you for the letter, she will write later. Well, darling, all the best. Send regards to all. I kiss you affectionately. A.

From the 1917 diary of Nicholas Alexandrovich

2nd November. Thursday. During the night it abruptly froze up, in the morning [it was] down to 11°. The day was sunny with a northern wind. Took a walk as usual; during the day hauled firewood. In the evening Olga received some modest gifts.

3rd November. Friday. Dear Olga is 22 years old; pity that the poor thing had to spend her birthday under current circumstances. At 12 o'cl. we had a *moleben.* The weather became mild again. Sawed some wood. Started a new interesting book "The Elusive Pimpernel."

Nicholas and Olga working on firewood

4th November. Saturday. In the morning I was overjoyed by a letter from Ksenia. There was a lot of snow, shoveled the walking path, and during the day hauled firewood to the shed. Already for two days the agents' telegrams have not arrived—must be that dire events are happening in big cities! At 9 o'cl. had a *vsenoshnaya*.

Tatiana to Zinaïda Tolstaya

(Tobolsk) **6th November**, 1917. I am sending you all the four icons from Mama and all of us. They were lying on [top of] the relics of St. Ioann Maximovich of Tobolsk. Unfortunately, we did not go there. Tatiana. [...] I read a lot. I decided to read all the books by our best writers from the beginning to end! I also read books in English and French. I'm working with Alexei on Russian History, which I love...

From the 1917 diary of Nicholas Alexandrovich

10th November. Friday. Another warm day—it went to zero. During the day I sawed wood. Finished the first volume of "1793." In the evening I read Turgenev's "Memoirs of a Hunter" aloud.

11th November. Saturday. Much snow has fallen. No newspapers or telegrams have come from Petrograd for a long time. At such a grave time this is serious. The girls were busy with the swings, jumping from them into a pile of snow. At 9 o'cl. there was *vsenoshnaya.*

From the 1917 diary of Nicholas Alexandrovich

14 November. Tuesday. Birthday of dear Mother and 23rd anniversary of our wedding. At 12 o'cl. *moleben* service; the choristers kept getting confused and making mistakes, must have not practiced. The weather was sunny, warm and with a strong wind. During the afternoon tea I read my old diaries—a pleasant pastime.

Maria and Anastasia to V.G. Maltseva

14th November, 1917. Tobolsk. I thank my darling good Vera Georgievna warmly for letters N◦ 3 and 4. It was very pleasant to learn that you are alive and well. How are you feeling after the illness? I hope you did not get too weak. I am very touched by your nice memories and thank you with all my heart for the wishes. I send regards to Olga. Everyone thanks [you] for the greetings as well, [and] send regards to you, Ak. Iv., V. Alek., [and an] affectionate kiss. Klavdia Mikhailovna is giving us lessons in Literature and History, you probably remember her. We have snow on the ground but it is rather warm, it's even melting these days. Our only acquaintance here is the son of a woman on staff, Tolya, who is 6 years old. He reminds us of Vit'ka Vor. We play with him outside and inside, he entertains us a lot. It is so pleasant to play with little ones, as we love children so much. When we went to... [letter ends].

From the 1917 diary of Nicholas Alexandrovich

17th November. Friday. The same unpleasant weather with stabbing wind. It is nauseating to read the newspaper descriptions of what happened two weeks ago in Petrograd and Moscow! Much worse and more shameful than the events in the Time of Troubles.

18th November. Saturday. Received shocking news that 3 members of the parliament of our 5th army went to the Germans ahead of Dvinsk, and signed some preliminary peace treaty with them!

Tatiana to Lili Dehn

Tobolsk. 1917. **19th November**. My own sweet dear Lili darling, We were so sad that [we] didn't have any news [from you], but in our prayers and thoughts we are constantly with you. I very much hope that you my dear are well and your son too. We are all fine. When it was warm, Mama went outside to the garden a lot, but now [she is] mostly sitting at home. [She] reads a lot and works. We live peacefully. [They] now took away our joy of going to church, and *obednya* and *vsenoshnaya* are always officiated at home. You can probably find out [more] about our lives from Zinochka—I am glad you see [each other], as she is very sweet. We have not walked past the church, It is sad that we couldn't go to the cathedral and venerate the saints' relics. We have breakfast and dinner all together downstairs. Mama and Alexei [eat] upstairs and Papa in his blue study. In the evenings we all sit together in Mama's red sitting room. We work or play some game, while Papa reads to us out loud. The small sitting room is dark, Mama's and Papa's bedroom is brown. Across the hall is Alexei's room, and we 4 have an end room, which is light blue. We have all settled in very nicely and cozily.

The Grand Duchesses' room in Governor's mansion

Tatiana to Zinaïda Tolstaya

19 November, 1917. [...] Everything is the same here. Every day it is almost the same thing. Some rather entertaining incidents happen fairly often. [...]

Tatiana to Ksenia Alexandrovna

19 November, 1917. Open letter [postcard]. Tavrichesky Gub. Crimea. Ai-Todor. To: G.D. Ksenia Alexandrovna. Tobolsk. 19 30/XI, 1917. My dear darling Aunt Ksenia, I am so ashamed that I haven't written to you for so long. How are you all. We are all well. It is all peaceful in our far-away little town. It is nice being so far away from the zh. d. [?] and large cities, with no motor [cars], but only horses. Did A.[unt] Olga get my letter from the 16th and the clothes [we] sent for Tikhon? And your parcel with clothes, wh.[ich] Vera wrote about – [it] never arrived. I will really be waiting for a letter from you. It has been so long since we had something from you. Write directly to us, Kk. A[unt] O[lga]. May Christ be with you all. Did you get the letter from Papa. We kiss you all affectionately. T.

From the 1917 diary of Nicholas Alexandrovich

20 November/3 December. Monday. The frost increased and the day was clear. There was grumbling among the soldiers because they had not received their pay from Petrograd for three months. This was quickly settled by a temporary loan of the necessary sum from the bank. During the day I busied myself with the firewood. At 9 1/2 o'cl, there was *vsenoshnaya.*

Nicholas cutting wood with Valya Dolgorukov

21 November/4 December. Tuesday. This day of the Feast of the Presentation we had to go without church service because Pankratov did not deign to permit it. The weather was warm. Everybody worked in the yard.

Alexandra Feodorovna to Anna Vyrubova

23 November, 1917. My dear Annushka, Yesterday I received your dear letter, dated 6 Nov. and thank you for it with all my heart. It is such joy to hear from you, and God is very merciful to have given us this compensation. Life in town must be more than unpleasant, shut up in stuffy rooms, steep stairs to climb – no lovely walks to take – horrors all around you. Poor child! You know that I am near you heart and soul, sharing all your pain and horror and praying for you with fervent tenderness. Every morning I read in the book you gave me seven years ago – "Day by Day" and like it very much – there are some lovely consoling passages in it. The weather is very changeable, frost, sunshine – then darkness and thaws. Despairingly dull for those that [sic] like good walks and who are deprived of them. Lessons continue as before – mother and daughters work and knit a great deal preparing Xmas presents. How time flies! In two days it will be 9 months I saw red boy for the last time!! Cannot write upon this subject! And my little owl so far away in loneliness and sorrow. But she knows where to seek consolation and strength and God will never forsake her – His love is above all. All are well on the whole, as I do not count chills and colds – knee and arm swell up from time to time, but happily without pain. The heart has latterly [sic] not being [sic] behaving well. Read much, live in the past, which is so full of rich remembrances – trust in a brighter future – He won't forsake those who love and trust in His infinite mercy and when we least expect it He will send help and save His unhappy country. Patience, faith and truth. How did you like the two little coloured cards? Have not heard from Lili over three months. Hard being cut off from all ones [sic] dear ones. I am so glad that your faithful old servant and Nastia are with you – and where are Zina and Mania? So D. Makari has also left us? But he is nearer than he was before. Our thoughts will meet more than ever next month. You remember our last journey together and what followed. After that anniversary it seems to me that God will show mercy. Kiss Praskia and the children from mother. Lisa and the girls have not yet come. All send big Baby very tenderest love, blessings and kisses. God bless you, dearest friend. Keep a brave heart. P.S. Should like to send you some macaroni.

Pass to enter Governor's mansion in the name of Anna Stepanovna Demidova[212]

Alexei to Anna Vyrubova

24/XI. [**24 November**] 1917. Tobolsk. We often remember and miss you, remember the little house. In the afternoon we saw wood for the bath. Snow came a while ago. The day passes unnoticeably, May God keep you. Regards to the girls.

---

[212] Demidova was one of the servants later murdered with the family in Ekaterinburg

Alexci sawing wood with Nicholas

Darling, dear, I hope that you got my postcard. I thank you so so much for the little mushroom. Your perfume reminds us of you so much. I pray to God every day, for us to live together again. May God keep you. Your A.

From the 1917 diary of Nicholas Alexandrovich

26th November. Sunday. Today is Georgievsky holiday[213]. The town arranged a dinner for the Calvary and other entertainments in the People's House. There

[213] Holiday honoring those decorated with the St. George Cross

were a few Georg. Cavaliers but in the ranks of our guards, whom their non-Calvary comrades decided not to relieve, and forced them to serve – even on such a day! Liberty!!! Walked a lot and for a long time, the weather was mild.

Alexei to Pyotr Petrov

Tobolsk, **27 November**. Dear Pyotr Vasilievich. I am very grateful for your letter, everyone read it. I am very sorry that I didn't write to you earlier, but I am really very busy. I have 5 lessons every day, besides homework, and as soon as I am free, I run outside. The day passes by unnoticeably. As you know, I study with Klavdia Mikhailovna, Russian, arithmetic, history and geography. I hug you affectionately. Regards to all. I remember you often. May God keep you. A. How is Pulka!!!

Alexei playing in the yard of the mansion

Tatiana to ?

29 November, 1917. In the evening we sit together, some play bridge, or bezique. We work while Papa reads aloud. Sometimes he plays and someone else reads. Tatiana.

Tatiana to V.I. Chebotareva

29 November, 1917. My sweet Valentina Ivanovna, did you get my letter from 12/X? I am so sad that I have no news from you for so long. How is your health? How are the children? We remembered you, L.F. and her husband. I hope they are both well. It's difficult to think that you are in T.S. during this difficult time. Where is O.P. ? Did she return from Kiev? Does our infirmary [still] exist? If you write, address [your letters] directly to me, as they read all the letters anyway. We are all well, thank God.

From the 1917 diary of Nicholas Alexandrovich

2nd December, Saturday. Both days passed the exact same way. It was rather freezing and sunny. After the afternoon walk we meet at M.Gilliard's daily, and overtly study our roles. At 9 o'cl. had a *vsenoshnaya.*

3rd December. Sunday. Alix and Alexei did not go with us to *obednya* due to the freeze - it was 16°. All morning [we] rehearsed our plays in the hall where, with the help of many screens and all sorts of furniture we set up like a stage. In the evening it was all put away. We took walks while there was daylight. During bezique I now read aloud Turgenev's "On the Eve."

5th December. Tuesday. It seems that real freeze has started –with 15° [below] in the morning, getting down to 20° towards the evening. Gave a lesson to Alexei before tea. At 9 o'cl. there was a *vsenoshnaya.*

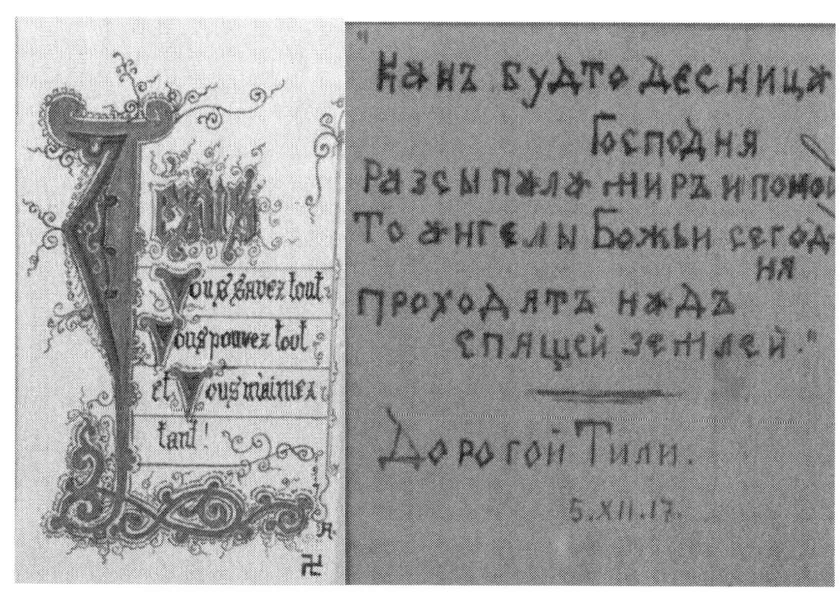

Alexandra's handmade card to Lili Dehn dated **5 December**, 1917

From the 1917 diary of Nicholas Alexandrovich

6th December. Wednesday. Spent my name day quietly and not like in the previous years. At 12 o'cl. a *moleben* service. The marksmen of the 4th regiment in the garden, former guards, all congratulated me, and I them—with the regiment holiday. Received three name day pies and sent one of them to the guards. In the evening Maria, Alexei and M. Gilliard acted in a very friendly little play "Le Fluide de John;" there was a lot of laughter.

7th December. Thursday. The freeze came down to 22° with a strong wind, which cut the face, nevertheless we successfully went outside in the morning and evening. In my study, in the daughters' room and the hall it is very cold—10°, which is why I wear my Plastun cherkesska all day until nighttime. Finished part II of "World History."

Olga pulling Alexei in a sled outside of mansion

9th December. Tuesday. Got a nice letter from Olga [Alexandrovna]. It got colder, it was windy and clear. After my walk I tutored Alexei. Finally, after intense heating it got really warm in the rooms.

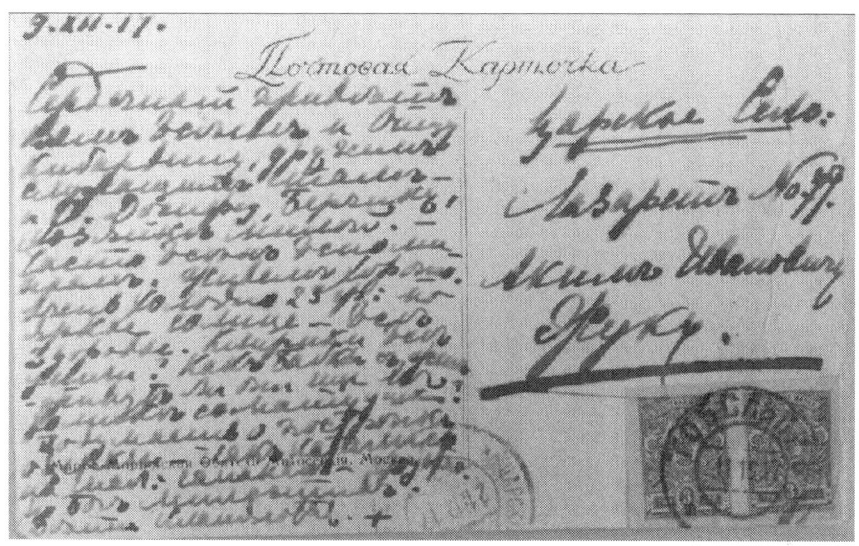

Почтовая Карточка

Царское Село.
Лазаретъ №17.
Акиму Ивановичу
Жуку.

Postcard from Alexandra to a staff member at her infirmary at Tsarskoe Selo, dated **9 December**, 1917

Tatiana to Anna Vyrubova

9 December, 1917. My own little turtledove,

I think of you all the time and pray for you and remember you. It is so hard that we had not seen each other for so long. But God will help us, and we shall surely meet again. I hope however, that this will be in better times than the ones we now live. We remember [our] good guest while wearing her brooches and your little things are always with us. They remind us so much of you. We lead a quiet and peaceful life. The days pass by quickly. In the morning we have lessons.

We take a walk between 11-12 in front of the house in the enclosure that was built for us.

Nicholas and his children in front of Governor's mansion

We have breakfast all together downstairs. Sometimes Mama and Alexei join us, but usually they are upstairs in Papa's blue study.

Nicholas's blue study

During the day we take another walk for about 1 ½ hour, when it's not too cold. We have tea upstairs, after that we read or write. For dinner we all assemble again and after that everyone stays for the evening. Some work, others play cards or something else – sometimes Papa reads to all. And so it is day after day. On Saturdays we have *vsenoshnaya* at home in the hall at 9 o'clock, because before that the Batushka officiates it at the church. There is an amateur choir that sings, before the singing was done by 4 nuns.

Iconostasis at Governor's mansion home chapel

On Sundays, when they permit us to go to the nearby church of Annunciation at 8 in the morning. We walk there through the city park, of course surrounded by men with rifles, who came here with us. A separate *obednya* is officiated for us in the right hand chapel altar, the *obednya* for the public is officiated later. Unfortunately on holidays we are limited to a *moleben* or *obednitsa* at home. For example, on 6 Dec. we had to stay at home. It was sad not to be in church on such a great holiday; well what can one do: one cannot always do as one likes, isn't that the truth? I hope that you can often go to church, provided your health allows. And how is your heart and your leg? Send my love to Marya; ask O.V.[214] for prayers. I kiss her and everyone who remembers us. Do you see Sergei Petrovich? Do you remember how we used to tease you, you poor thing! Regards to Zhuk, Nyura, to the old man and Gorianov if you see him. And where are Tina and her husband – are they in her country? I shall think so much of you all during these days. May God protect you my dear fervently beloved darling. I am glad that Eliebar's parents are so kind. I never saw them, although I know him well. All the letters have to pass through the Commissar. Isa has not arrived yet – has she been to see you? I kiss you as affectionately as I love you. May Christ be with you. Tatiana

[P.S. is written at the top of the first page, upside down in an empty space of the page]: It is sad that we will spend Christmas so far away from each other, but we shall be together in [our] thoughts. Love.

[214] Otetz [Father} Vasiliev

Tatiana to V.I. Chebotareva

Tobolsk. Former Governor's H.[ouse]. **9 December**, 1917. My dear Valentina Ivanovna. Did you get my letter from the 29th? May you be so kind as to give this letter to our Count? You must be very lonesome without L.F. But it is good that they are together. Pity about poor Filatov, that he cannot recover for so long. And he was already sick when we were still there. Could it be that the same wound still bothers him, or something else? And how is our Baron, and Kupych? I hope that O.P. got a good rest at her girlfriend's. Here it is all quiet and peaceful, thank God. There is a feeling here as if we are living on some far away island and that we get the news from another world. There are lots of foolish rumors out there in the newspapers kk. [?] You probably read them, but it is all nonsense. They even sent us a newspaper clipping, where it tells about my escape to America...! I hope you did not believe this? I wonder who is wasting time on these idiotic delusions. Probably many people, the workers who benefit the Motherland - right?

Former Grand Duchess [illegible] Uses Fake Marriage as Means

Reaches New York Next Month to Prominently Aid Russian Relief Work

By Associated Press.

NEW YORK, Nov. 25.—Miss Tatiana Nicolaevna Romanoff, second daughter of Nicholas Romanoff, deposed Emperor of Russia, has escaped from Siberia through a fictitious marriage to a son of a former Chamberlain of the Emperor, and now is on her way to the United States chaperoned by an English woman, according to information made public here tonight by persons connected with the Russian civilian relief.

The former Grand Duchess, who is 20 years old, made her escape from Tobolsk, the present home of the exiled Emperor, to Harbin, in Manchuria, and thence to Japan, where passage was taken on a steamship for the Pacific coast.

Will Soon Reach New York

The New York officers of the Russian Civilian Relief, including Daniel Frohman, Ivan Narodny and Dr. Thomas Darlington, have been informed the young woman will arrive in New York some time in December to play a prominent part in the work of the recently formed organization.

According to an announcement tonight by the News Bureau of the Russian Postoffice Department, Miss Romanoff intends to remain one year in this country, and while in New York her guardian and companion will be Mrs. Margaret Barry Carver, of Denver, who left this city last Friday for the Pacific coast.

Mr. Frohman said tonight that Mrs. Carver is a "wide-awake American woman" who has lived in Petrograd, and from her he had learned that Miss Romanoff soon would arrive in the United States. Mr. Frohman is a temporary member of the Board of Governors of the Russian Civilian Relief.

How Escape Was Made

Ivan Narodny, who is connected with the Russian-American Asiatic Corporation, told tonight how Miss Romanoff succeeded in leaving Russia. He said

A western newspaper clipping telling of Tatiana's rumoured escape abroad

I have not written to Bibi yet, as did not know where – will write now. If you write to your husband, send him regards. I can only imagine his condition now- the wretched ones, I feel such pity for them all, there are no words to express it. Address the letters directly to us, as they pass through the commissar anyway, and this way they arrive faster. I play the piano rather often. Time passes quickly and the days pass by almost unnoticed. The last few days we had frost. It was down to 24, when [it is] windy it really cuts one's face. Today it is more mild. It is sunny every day. In T.S. this does not happen during these months. Well, all the best to you my turtledove, Valentina Ivanovna. May Christ be with you. If anyone decides to write to us – let them write directly. I kiss you affectionately as strongly as I love you. Alusha too and O.P. All the best. Your Tatiana.

Tatiana to E.L. Eristov

Tobolsk. 9/XII [**9 December**], 1917. I am sending you the most heartfelt wishes for the Holy Day. May God grant for it to pass quietly and peacefully. I thank you for the remembrance, was very touched that you remembered. Would you be so kind as to ask your parents to pass this letter on to A.A. We are very grateful that they gave her some affection during this difficult time. All the best. I send you heartfelt regards. Sister Tatiana.

Anastasia to Anna Vyrubova

10 December. Tobolsk. My darling and dear: Thank you tenderly for your little gift. It was so nice to get it, reminding me especially of you. We remember you and speak of you often, and in our prayers we are always together. The little dog you gave [us] is always with us and is very nice. We have arranged our rooms comfortably and all four live together. We often sit at the windows looking at the people passing by, and this gives us distraction... We have acted in little plays for amusement. We walk in the garden behind high planks. God bless you. AN

Maria to Zinaida Tolstaya

Tobolsk. **10 December**. We live quietly, take walks twice a day as usual. The weather is nice, the other day it was very cold. You must still have warm weather? I am so envious that you can look at the wonderful sea! This morning at 8 we went to *obednya* We are always so happy when they let us go to church, of course one cannot compare this church with our *Sobor*[215], but still better than in the rooms. Right now we are all sitting in our rooms. The sisters are also writing, the dogs are running around and begging to sit on our laps. I remember Tsarskoe Selo so often, and our merry concerts at the infirmary; do you remember how much fun it was when the wounded used to dance; we also remember our walks to Pavlovsk and Your small carriage, the morning rides past Your house. It all seems so long ago. Doesn't it? Well, it's time for me to end. I wish You all the best and kiss You and Dalya affectionately. Heartfelt regards to all your [family]. Maria

---

[215] Feodorovsky Cathedral

Nicholas to Anna Vyrubova

10 December. Tobolsk. Thank you so much for your kind wishes on my Name Day. Our thoughts and prayers are always with you, you poor suffering creature. Her Majesty reads to us all your lines. Horrid to think about all you had to go through. We are alright here. It is rather quiet. Pity you are not with us. Endless kisses and blessings from your loving friend, N. Give my best love to your parents.

Tatiana to Anna Vyrubova

Tobolsk. **10 December**, 1917. My darling dear Anya, I was so awfully happy to hear from you. Thank you for the note and the little things. Thank Vikt. Er. for the brooches. I wrote to you yesterday through Eristov. I am glad you met him, he is so very nice. It is strange that we live in a house where you once stayed.[216] Remember that we are sending this parcel secretly, so do not mention it. This is the only chance to do this, probably won't happen again. Yesterday's letter to Katya was sent the same way as the rest, through the commissar. I constantly think of you, my dear. We talk so much about you, but unfortunately only among us

[216] Vyrubova stayed at the Governor's mansion when she was in Tobolsk some years ago

7, Gilliard, Valya, and Mr Gibbs. I always wear the bracelet you gave me on 12th January and never take it off. Do you remember the cozy evenings by the fireplace? How nice it was. Did you ever see A. Linevich and Groten again? Well so long, my own good Anya darling. May God keep you. I kiss you as much as I love you, the girls and O.V. Goodbye... until when? Yours, Tatiana

Grand Duchesses to V.E. Zborovsky

14 December, 1917. Sending you wishes for the holidays and the new year, from all our hearts. May you have lots of happiness and be healthy! Especially during Christmas we will be with you all our dears, in our thoughts. Did you recover completely now? We are all well. The view on this [postcard] is not familiar to us either. Life is the same here. We study a lot, hence the days pass by rather quickly. When we are free, we sit on the window [sill] and watch the passers-by, this is our biggest entertainment [...] May the Lord keep you. I wish you all the best. A.[nastasia]
Big regards and wishes for the holidays. Be well. O.[lga]
Heartfelt greetings. We remember you all often. Tatiana.

So sad to spend the holidays so far from you. Sincerest regards. Maria.

Alexei to Pyotr Petrov

Tobolsk, **19 December**, 1917. Dear Pyotr Vasilevich. Happy upcoming holidays and New Year. I hope that You received my first letter. How is Your health? Right now we have very little snow and therefore it's hard to build a snow mountain. Joy is getting fatter each day because he eats all sorts of rubbish from the trash. Everyone shoos him away with sticks. He has a lot of acquaintances in town and therefore he is always running off.[217] I am writing to You during the French lesson since I have almost no free time, but when I have a break I will write to You more often. Regards to the teachers. May the Lord keep You! Your fifth student. Alexei.

Alexandra Feodorovna to Isa Buxhoeveden

Xmas Eve, 1917. Good morning dear Isa, - I hope you slept well and don’t feel too beaten up and exhausted today. I send you this image with my blessings, from the saint of Tobolsk. His relics lie in the cathedral on

[217] It’s possible that Joy survived the massacre in Ekaterinburg because he was doing the same there – running off

the hill (alas! We have not yet been there). Hang it up, and may he be your Guard and Guide. May you soon get strong, well, and fed again here. We have a service at 12, I wonder whether you may come to it, as the guards will just have changed and it would be nice to begin your entry with prayers. A loving kiss, Darling, fr.[iend]. A.

25 December. A blessed Xmas to you, Isa dearest! And a loving wish and kiss. Above all, I wish for God to give you good health, peace of mind "*dushevny mir*"[218], which is the greatest gift. We can ask for patience, which we all need in this world of suffering (and utter madness), consolation, strength and happiness. "A Joyful Xmas" may sound like mockery, but it means joy over the New-born King, who died to save us all, and does not that renew one's trust and faith in God's infinite mercy? [...] Prayed for you, and shall again at mass – so hard [that] you cannot go. I so hoped by the side door to another church. The Emperor and all the children send many a message and good wishes. They share my regret. God bless you. Won't you look out your window and tell Nastenka when? At one let's say,

[218] Peace of mind – literally "peace in a soul" (Russian)

and then we can peep at the corner window, and perhaps catch a glimpse of you. Just off to church! God bless and protect you. A loving kiss from your affectionate A.

Nastenka Hendrikova in Tobolsk

Tatiana to E.S. Bekhteyeva

26 December, 1917. Thank you so much for the greetings and also the card via A.V. I wish you all the best in the New Year. Tatiana

Tatiana to Zinaïda Tolstaya

26 December, 1917. We had a Christmas party for all who live in the house with us. During the evening of the 24th, at 9 ½ o'cl. we had a *vsenoshnaya*, rather late, but the priest could not get here earlier; and at the table, with all the icons [we] set up a tree and lit it up. It stood there during the entire *vsenoshnaya*. It was very nice and cozy. We did not hang anything on the tree.

From the 1917 diary of Nicholas Alexandrovich

26th December. Tuesday. The same kind of quiet frosty day — 13°. Everyone slept a lot. In the morning stopped by the guard room with the children—the 1st platoon of the 1st regiment was there; yesterday we sent them a tree, a sweet pie and a checkers game. The other day Isa Buxhoeveden arrived, but was not allowed to see us due to Pankratov's caprice.

28th December. Thursday. A lovely sunny warm day, 2° of frost. Stayed outside for a long time in the morning and the evening. Found out with indignation that our good Father Alexei is being investigated and is under house arrest. This happened because during *moleben* on 25 Dec, the deacon mentioned us by title in the presence of a lot of sharp-shooters of the 2nd regiment in church as usual, and they apparently made a fuss, but [it was] most likely not without Pankratov's and his cronies' involvement.

31st December/13th January. Sunday. Not a cold day, with gusty wind. Toward the evening, Alexei got up. He was able to put on his boot. After tea we separated, till the arrival of the New Year. Lord, save Russia.

* * *

YEAR 1918:

Separation and "House of Special Purpose"

Tatiana to Alexandra

To my sweet darling Mama dear with my best wishes for a happy New Year. May God's blessings be upon you and guard you for ever. Yr loving girl Tatiana. Tobolsk 1918. Governor's House

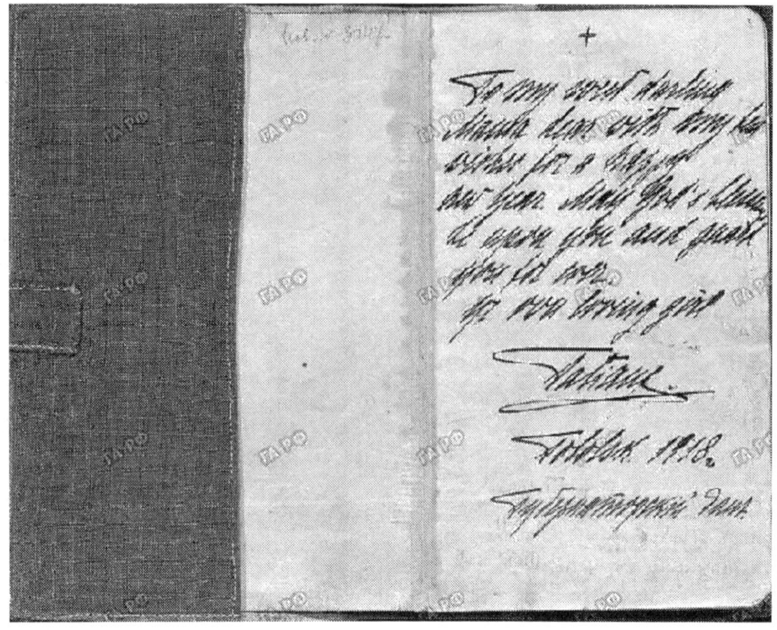

Tatiana's New Year 1918 gift of a diary book to Alexandra

Olga to Lili Dehn

Tobolsk. **1st January**, 1917 [sic]. Saturday. My darling Lili! I was so happy to finally hear from you. To tell the truth, I was afraid that you had forgotten us, but glad that I was mistaken. You probably already heard from one of the sisters how we settled here and that it is really awful. A lot of noise, as we constantly sit all together, and then Kolya Derevenko comes to see my brother for the holidays, so you can imagine the raucous and shouting. All the dogs are with us,

Jimmy[219] lives in our room, but Ortipo is separate, one is enough, and there are four of us too. Rubella is gone, but we still cannot go outside, neither Maria, nor I. Anastasia is healthy for now. Our Christmas tree is still standing in the corner of the hall and smells wonderful, and does not drop needles at all.

Christmas tree in the corner of the hall in Governor's mansion

Yesterday at three in the afternoon we had a service, and today at 8 o'cl. we all went to Blagoveschenskaya church for *obednya.* We go there all the time, as it is the closest church, just walk through the city garden. It is scary to think that we have lived here for almost five months, and don't know even one street, and in

---

[219] Jimmy/Jim was Anastasia's pet Pekinese

general have not seen anything past the fence. We are hoping very much that one day we will be able to get to the cathedral to [see] the relics of saints. We made a hill in the garden, not very high, and sometimes ski down.

Yard and garden of the Governor's mansion

And how are you doing, dear, and [illeg], where is Shurik, he was in Moscow. Did you hear that Gorlin [?] is in Gagry; and have you seen N.N.??? Or any of them? Today there was procession of the cross, saw masses of people returning with fir branches in their hands. In the evenings Papa reads aloud, and we play cards. Well, I will end. Everyone sends regards and kisses. I embrace you affectionately and firmly, my dear; remember and love you. May the Lord keep you + Your Olga.

From the 1918 diary of Nicholas Alexandrovich

6th January. Epiphany. At 8 o'clock went to *obednya,* instead of a *shinel*[220], I wore an overcoat. The daughters all recovered but do not go outside. The weather was holiday-like, sunny, quiet. In the morning sat with the guards for a long time and had a heart-to heart [talk] with them. Unfortunately, could not see the Cross procession to the Irtysh due to the surrounding buildings [blocking it].

Anastasia to Anna Vyrubova

1918 [exact date unknown, but most likely **January**]. Tobolsk. My very own good one, we remember you, good darling all the time. Although we are so far away, we are together in our thoughts... Our life is not bad, thank God. We put on shows with plays and of course act in them ourselves. For entertainment we take walks in our enclosure. We set up a small hill and slide down. All the best, my darling. May God keep

[220] Military coat

you. I kiss you very affectionately. I always remember and love you. A. Big regards to all.

Page from a script of a play handwritten by Olga, titled "Yavlenie" ("The Apparition")

Tatiana to Zinaïda Tolstaya

6 January, 1918. My dear Zinochka, Many thanks to all of you for the postcards. The letters had not yet arrived. I hope that we receive them. How did you spend the New Year? ... In the morning we went to church. Olga and I are still in bed with high fever and skin rash. It was rubella. It was the son of Derevenko who we caught it from. He was sick one day with fever.

He came over during the holidays to play with Alexei. I stayed in bed for three days and only got up today. This morning I went to church. [...] Anastasia was the only one not to fall ill. The weather today is beautiful and despite the 15 degrees of frost, the sun is very warm. We sat outside, and it was really nice. We received your telegram precisely on New Year, and we thank you very much. Isa arrived here. She has been living in the house opposite [to ours] for two weeks. We have seen her only from the window, because they did not allow anyone to come to us. I do not know how long they will remain here [...]. I am pleased that Rita is always with you. Did you receive my letter from 26th December? We had news about Tili, which delighted [us]... And how is Dm.? Did you see Rod [?]? Let him know that I thought about him today for his birthday. I wish you all the best, beloved Zinochka. May God keep you. I embrace you and R. Regards to those who remember me.

Alexei to Pyotr Petrov

Tobolsk, **7 January**, 1918. Dear Pyotr Vasilevich. I am writing You a third letter already. I hope that You are receiving them. Mama and the rest send regards. Tomorrow the lessons start. The sisters and I had rubella, and Anastasia was the only healthy one and walked with Papa. It's strange that we are not getting any news from You. Today was 20 deg. of frost, but until now it was warm. While I am writing to You, Zhilik is reading a newspaper, and Kolya is sketching a portrait of him. Kolya is being rowdy and therefore distracting me from writing to You. Dinner is soon. Nagorny is sending You warm regards. Give regards to Masha and Irina. May the Lord God keep You! Your loving, Alexei

Alexei on the mansion's balcony

Tatiana to V.I. Chebotareva

8 January, 1918. My dear Valentina Ivanovna,

I ask you to please pass this letter to O.P.[221] and her husband. It sounds strange, does it not? Did you go to their wedding? Where was it, which church, etc. and in general please describe how it all went. I will really wait for it. So sad we did not go. Did you get my letter from 9/XII with the enclosed letter for our Prince E.[ristov]? Mama also asks if you got it? Write to her, she will be happy. Enclose it with my [letter] and I will pass it on to her. Address it simply to the "Head of the Guards," and it will be forwarded to me when they see who the addressee is. I remember you often. I finally got a letter from Bibi. There was nothing [from her] for so terribly long. We heard about what Vera Ignatievna has turned into, and how she is walking around. How fast people change – it is even funny! Have you seen her, or was she hiding? How are you and Alusha. Is Grisha with you, and where is L.F. and her husband? Do you remember when I met Grisha on the telephone last year when you were ill – and then finally saw him in real life? It all seems so long ago! We already had the chance to get sick with rubella during three days

[221] Olga Pavlovna Grekova

of the new year, everyone except Anastasia. Awfully foolish – but luckily it went away fast. I already walk outside. Well goodbye, sweet Valentina Ivanovna. May Christ be with you. I kiss you affectionately and remember [you]. Yours, Sister Tatiana.

Tatiana to E. Zborovskaya[222]

11 January, 1918. Sweet Katya,
Thank you for the cards and the wishes. May God grant you all the best in the new year. Did Vitya and others get the cards which were sent to N.V.'s mother's name at the institute? Don't know if she is there, but hope they will forward them [to her] if not. How are you? We constantly remember you all and talk about you a lot. Please send our heartfelt regards to all. "Ortipo" is doing well, but [she] is becoming terribly lazy. [She] is lying down by the fireplace all day or on the sofas. Does not want to walk [outside]. Well, all the best, sweet Katya! Tatiana.

---

[222] Ekaterina Zborovskaya, sister of Viktor Erastovich

One of the Grand Duchesses pulling Alexei's sled in front of Governor's mansion

Tatiana to Rita Khitrovo

11 January, 1918. Rita my sweet, Thank you so much for the sweet letter. I was happy to finally hear from you. Luba writes to Anastasia sometimes, so we do get letters from her. Olya writes, but we only received letter #5, the rest did not get here. Terrible shame. We were so surprised to get a letter from O.P. with the news of her wedding to the Baron.[223] I am happy for both, especially for him. He will be so spoiled now! What are Nina and Kostya doing now? What is he up to? It is so sad and unpleasant to see the soldiers without epaulets now, and our sharpshooters were

[223] Baron D.F. Taube

forced to take them off too. It was so pleasant before, to see the difference between ours and the local garrisons. Ours are clean with burgundy epaulets, crosses, and now they took them off. The stripes too. But happily [they are] still wearing the crosses. Just think – a man shed his blood for the motherland, and got an award, got a rank for good service – and now what? Those who served for many years are now equal to the new ones, who never even fought in a war. So incredibly honest and smart, isn't it? So painful and sad, what they are doing to our poor Motherland, but there is one hope, that God will not leave us and make these madmen see reason. So there. Everything is the same with us. We work in the yard. When they bring wood, we pile it in the shed (built especially for this).

Yard keeper Kirpichnikov with a pile of firewood

We built a small [snow] hill, even with the fence, and it seems that when we climb on top of it, we can be seen, which apparently many [people] do not like, which probably means that soon they will forbid us to slide down on it!!! We have not yet received Zinochka's parcels – hopefully they will arrive. We heard that Pokrovsky (do you remember him?) revealed himself exactly as we all thought of him! What a disgrace! Wherever there is advantage - that's where he goes. – If you see Katya, Nina and her husband, send them a kiss and regards. Have you seen R.[odionov] and how is poor D. feeling? Did he have surgery? Well, all the best. May the Lord keep you. I kiss you affectionately, like I love you. Regards to Zinochka's [family].
Tatiana

Alexandra to Alexander Syrobyarsky

[**11 January**]. [...] The children are sledding their hearts out on a snow mountain and taking the most amazing falls. It's a wonder they haven't broken their necks. They are all covered with bruises, but even so, this is the only distraction they have, either that or sit at the window (which I love to do very much) [...]

From Alexei to Anna Vyrubova

12 January. My darling Anya. We are so glad to have news from you, and to hear that you got all our things. Today it is 29 degrees of frost, strong wind and sunshine. We walked, and I walked on skis in the yard. Yesterday I acted in a French piece with Tatiana and Zhilik. We are now preparing another piece. We have a few good soldiers with whom I play games in their rooms. Kolya Derevenko comes to visit me on holidays. Nagorny the sailor sleeps with me. As servants we have Volkov, Sednev, Trupp and Chemodurov. It is time to go to breakfast. I kiss and embrace you. God bless you. ALEXEI

Grand Duchesses to Tatiana Botkin

12 January, 1918. Tobolsk. To dear Tanya with best wishes for her Angel Day. Olga, Tatiana, Maria, Anastasia

From the 1918 diary of Nicholas Alexandrovich

12th January. Friday. Celebrated Tatiana's name day with a *moleben* in the hall at 12 o'clock. The day was wonderful, 14° of frost, with strong warm sun. Our priest, Father Aleksei was freed from house arrest.

14th January. Sunday. Did not go to church in the morning, *obednitsa* was conducted at home for us. Took a walk prior to that and for a long time in the afternoon. The weather was bright, exactly as it should be in

March. Before dinner presented our play for real. The actors in "Les Deux Timides" were:

Tatiana - Annette.

Anastasia - Cecile.

Valya D. - Garadoux.

M. Gilliard - Fremissin.

Me- Thibaudier.

[We] were aware that it went smoothly and briskly. In the evening, bezique and reading aloud as usual.

Altar in the hall of Governor's mansion

Близокъ Господь сокрушеннымъ сердцемъ, и смиренныхъ духомъ спасетъ. Пс. 33.19.

[illegible] Января 1918 г. + [illegible] (II.)

"Милая, Дорогая, возлюбленная
Сестрица Серафима!
Отъ нѣжно любящаго сердца поз-
дравляю Васъ многолюбивая
страдалица моя съ праздникомъ
Вашимъ. Да ниспошлетъ Вамъ
Господь Богъ всякихъ благъ —
добраго здоровья, крѣпость ду-
ха, кротость, терпѣніе, силы пере-
нести всѣ обиды и гоненія, ду-
шевную радость. Да освѣтитъ
лучъ солнца ярко и ясно путь Ва-
шъ жизненный. Сами погрѣйте
всѣхъ любовію Вашей. Да свѣтитъ
свѣтъ Вашъ въ этихъ темныхъ,
неясныхъ дняхъ. — [illegible], роди-
мая, скорбящая сестра! Господь
услышитъ твои молитвы. Все въ
свое время. Молимся и мы за Васъ
Богоизбранную сестру, [illegible]
Васъ. Уголокъ Вашъ убогій да-
лекъ отъ насъ — всѣ любящіе

Alexandra's handmade card to "Sister Serafima" (Anna Vyrubova)

Alexandra to Anna Vyrubova

18 [?] **January.** [...] Sometimes I see Isa in the street [from the window]. Sister of Mercy Tatiana Andreyevna is now in Petersburg taking care of her sister. Later she will return to Moscow. She seems rather nervous. Give our greetings to our confessor, Father Afanasy [Belyaev], Father Alexander, and my poor old Zio. I don't know anything about my second manservant Kondratiev. What has become of our chauffeurs and the coachman Konkov? Is the old General Shvedov still alive? Holy Virgin, keep my daughter[224] from all danger, bless and console her!

Alexandra to Rita Khitrovo

21st Jan. 1918 T[obolsk]. 卍[225] My darling big, although also little,[226] Rita! Thank You from the bottom of my soul for your dear letter. We are so touched that You all remember us and sent [us] the perfume, etc. The first package got here just fine. Please thank M-me Kadbish for the icons and the rosary, which were sent [to us] now and [back] in the autumn. It makes one so happy when one feels that one is not forgotten by others. Darling, really, do not lose courage - the worse things get, the closer God is, with His earnest assistance. Believe in Him fervently and unshakably. He will save our dear much-suffering motherland. He is patient and forgiving, [He] will not stay eternally angry, but [we] must pray more, be resigned, obedient - and wait patiently. God has storms and [also] sunny weather; the clouds will pass -

[224] Alexandra often referred to Vyrubova as her daughter

[225] The backwards swastika is an ancient symbol for luck and eternal life, which Alexandra often used

[226] Reference to Rita Khitrovo's height - she was unusually tall

and the beautiful "Sunny" will come out. - So much sun we see here, and it warms us so. - Take a look at nature, understand it with your very soul, and She [nature] will tell [you] so much, and [it will] comfort [you]. Such horrors, what's happening all over, my soul is mourning for all these innocent victims, but He knows best, why this is necessary. His ways are unknown to us - we only know that all paths lead to Him. – Life is a difficult school, thorny, but for that we will get peace and calm and pleasure there - one's soul longs for that place. And the Lord will hear the prayers of those who already reached that other place. For others [we] mourn - then fervently pray and give them over into His hands, and He will keep them safe. He gives strength and comfort and peace of mind. You know, all this will be over, and when we feel that all this is ending, then He will show us his endless love and mercy. No epaulets[227] - horrible. [I] understand that everyone wears civilian [clothes]. Al. Vlad.[228] is studying the Engl. lang. assiduously, he moved in with an Engl. family, in 10 days he learned 300 words, [he] is cramming day and night. After surgery he felt very

[227] Nicholas was forbidden from wearing his epaulets in public

[228] Syroboyarsky

badly, but the Lord saved [him]. [I] keep waiting for N.Ya.[229] at least to see [him] from afar. [I] would like to tell You a lot more but cannot. - Sending that by a different route, we think it will get [to you] soon. - So Olga P. and Baron! I am so happy for him. - Everyone has gotten over the rubella. Heart rarely bothers [me], since I live very quietly. - Lord keep you. + [I] kiss you affectionately. Regards from the Little One[230] and Father[231]. Chief. Thanks for the prayers and for the photo of N. D. - Hard to write, hands are so cold. [On the back page]: To Rita.

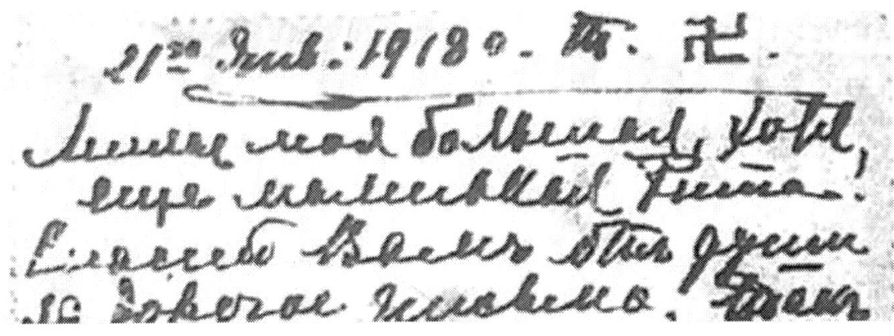

Part of Alexandra's letter to Khitrovo dated **21 January**, 1918

[229]Sedov

[230] Alexei

[231] Nicholas

Alexei to Anna Vyrubova

Tobolsk. **22 January**, 1918. My dear darling Anya, I am happy to have news from you again and that you got our things. Today is 29 degrees of frost, and strong wind and sunny. Took a walk – walked on skis around the yard.

Alexei's letter to Anna Vyrubova, dated 22 January, 1918

Yesterday I acted with Tatiana and Zhilik in a French play. Everyone is preparing some other comedies. We have a few good soldiers, I play checkers with them in the guardroom. Kolya D. comes over to see me on holidays. Nagorny sleeps with me. Sednev, Volkov, Trupp and Chemodurov are with us. Time to go to breakfast. I kiss and squeeze you. May the Lord keep you. A +

Tatiana to Anna Vyrubova

Tobolsk, 22/I [**22 January**] 1918. My very own dear darling, we are always so happy for the news from you. I hope that the letter via E.[ristov] reached you. I think about you a lot and always pray for the Lord to keep and help you. Glad that you met [illeg], he is so sweet. [What an] awful coincidence of the family name [...] Zina is fine, nice letters. A lot of sad things. May Christ be with you, mine own. During cold days, Papa wears a *cherkesska*. I kiss you as affectionately as I love you, [and] congratulate [you] with day of the angel. T.

Tatiana to Zinaïda Tolstaya

Tobolsk, **23 January**, 1918. My dear Zinochka, Many thanks for your three cards and your greeting. I have not yet thanked you for the wonderful perfume. We are all terribly touched by your attention. The rest of the parcels have not arrived yet, but I hope that they will soon. May you be so kind as to mail Alexei's cards. I think they will be more certain to get there. A cadet sent Papa a sweet card. – we don't know him, but he said that Papa spoke to him at some parade. So touching. I am so glad that all ended well for you, thank God, and hope that it is now peaceful in the city... We are all fine here. We live the same way. You probably know all the details from Mr Gilliard. In order to pass time, we memorize short plays, - it is useful for the languages too; both of them, he and Mr Gibbs, are very good directors, as they used to act before. What are you all up to? How do you spend your time? These days we are hard at work sawing and cutting wood. They brought us a lot all at once. The wood is very good – birch. It is so pleasant to have work. Write some more- I very much like getting your letters. All the best. Heartfelt regards to your husband and Seryozha. We kiss you and Dalechka affectionately. I will write to her next time, so that it's not all at once. May Christ be with you. Tatiana

Tatiana to Pyotr Tolstoy

23 January, 1918. Tobolsk. Heartfelt thanks for the greetings and good wishes. An affectionate greeting from us all.

Tatiana to Rita Khitrovo

23 January, 1918. Tobolsk. My dear Rita, darling. Thank you very much for the greetings. I got Ksenia's sweet letter, [she] congratulated me, such a darling. O.P. wrote me a long letter, about her wedding to the Baron. It is sad that everyone from the infirmary could not be there. He also wrote to me and said that he saw Vera Ignatievna at the infirmary. She is [wearing] epaulets, large boots with spurs, did not even ask the Baron how he was doing. So shameful. I did not expect how fast she would change. Although lately she had been very strange. What are you up to? Do you spend your time nicely? Bibi finally wrote, says that Kirilka got ill with appendicitis – poor thing. The only warm room [here] in the entire house is Papa's and our brother's bathroom, where we sat and had tea today. In the hall it is 5 ¾ [degrees] today – we walk around in our *valenki*[232] and thick knitted sweaters. We still take walks outside twice a day. Well, goodbye Ritka darling. Write to me – I will be very happy. Tell Zinochka to address her letters directly to us – they will get here faster. May Christ be with you my dear. If Sashurka and N. Ya. are there, give them regards. All the best. Tatiana

[232] Type of warm snow boots

Alexandra to Boris Solovyov[233]

24 January. I see by your tradesman's clothing that contact with us is not safe. I am grateful to God for the fulfillment of Father's and My personal wish: you are Matryosha's husband[234]: May God bless your marriage and send you both happiness. I believe that you will protect Matryosha and guard her against evil people in an evil time. Let me know what you think about our situation. Our common wish is to achieve the possibility of living tranquilly, like an ordinary family, outside of politics, struggle, and intrigues. Write frankly, for I will accept your letter with faith in your sincerity. I am especially glad that it is you who has come to us. Get to know F.[ather] Vasiliev[235] without fail – this is a person deeply devoted to us. And how long do you intend to stay here? Warn us beforehand of your departure.

Tatiana to Ksenia Alexandrovna

24 January, 1918. My dear Godmother, I congratulate you with all my heart on your name day. I am so

---

[233] Son in law of Rasputin, who was allegedly planning a rescue of the family

[234] Solovyov married Rasputin's daughter Maria (Matryona)

[235] Their former priest at Tsarskoe Selo

ashamed that I did not do this earlier, so decided to write on the day of [it]. We all remember you today. I hope that you spend this day nicely. Today it got warmer here, but it has been very cold these last few days, and most importantly a very strong wind. It really cuts one's face, but we still take our walks twice a day. – How are you, Auntie, my darling. I wish I could see you and tell you so much. There are so many terribly funny stories, but too awkward to write, and not so easy. Do you see Sonia. Or are they not allowing her to see you again? They even kicked Isa out from the Kornilov house, so we only see her from the window now. Another one of those smart contemporary things. I will be so happy if you write. Does your Commissar read all the letters like ours? Is Nastya with you. Give her a kiss, and to Nana. Well, goodbye, Auntie, darling. May Christ be with you. I kiss you, Grandmama, and Aunt Olga affectionately. Regards to the rest, and Yashik. All the best. Your Goddaughter, Tatiana.

Tatiana to Dalya Tolstaya

25 January, 1918. It is cold here; the last few days [there is] strong wind, but it does not interfere with our walks. It is cold in the rooms too, some are only 6 degrees. We sit in our thick knitted sweaters and even wore *valenki*[236] at breakfast, but at least it is warm in the hallways. Your sacks are very useful to us – we only use them now. Well, goodbye dear Dalechka. I will wait for your letters. It is a major event here when we get them, and we are so terribly happy. Everyone takes turns reading them. I was getting a lot [of mail] these past few days due to [my] name day. I kiss you and your Mama affectionately, and think about you a lot. May Christ be with you. Tatiana.

Tatiana to Pyotr Petrov

26 January, 1918. Hello, sweet Pyotr Vasilievich, Thank you very much for your two letters. I was very touched that you wrote so much. We are in good health, thank God, live as quietly as before, and strangely enough so far none of us has fought with anyone else. In the morning we have lessons for two hours, from 9 to 11, walk for an hour, and study for another hour. After lunch we walk again—usually until 4, and if the weather is nice, then longer. Before tea, we work or occupy ourselves for a while with something. After tea and before supper there are often rehearsals for some play. We have already put on

---

[236] Warm tall snow boots

three. All the same, we are still practicing another little diversion, and it's good for conversation. A small [snow and ice] hill has been built in our yard. When we get bored with walking back and forth, we slide down it, and often we take very funny falls. Once Zhilik ended up sitting on my head. I begged him to get up, but he couldn't because he sprained his ankle and it hurt. Somehow, I crawled out. It was all terribly silly and funny, but he had to stay in bed for a few days because of his ankle. Another time I was sliding down the hill backwards and banged the back of my head really hard on the ice. I thought nothing of it, and it turned out that my head did not crack, and it did not even hurt. I have a hard head, don't I? Eh? We are also having very cold weather with a particularly strong wind-- it cut at my face terribly. It was very cold in the rooms. In the hall it was 5 ¾ degrees ... We are not far from Mr. Conrad's. Please console him at least a little bit. Does he get letters from his wife? How can it be that you still haven't gone to a show at the Chinese theater? Oh! What great things you are missing! Did Yury Petrovich get my postcard? All the best. We send greetings to his sister, too. Be well. We send everyone heartfelt regards. Tatiana

Tatiana to V.I. Chebotareva

31 January, 1918. Sweet Valentina Ivanovna,

Thank you so much for your two letters. I am glad that your things arrived successfully and that your little daughter and you all are happy. I remember you often, and feel pity for those who live in town, as they are so close to [Tsarskeo Selo]. It is sad that O.P. was not able to settle together with her husband as a family. Where is Grisha now, and L.F.'s husband? How do you spend your days? Where is Olya Ger. now, who always lived in Pavlovsk. We are fine here. Everything is the same. – The weather is nice enough, sometimes it is cold. Unfortunately, we don't get to go to church. Sometimes have *vsenoshnaya* and *obednitsa* at home. Of course, that cannot substitute church, wh. we miss a lot, as we wish to pray in church more than ever. I feel sad for those who do not understand this. – Address all the letters directly to my name. It is more reliable and gets here faster. I wish you all the best, sweet Valentina Ivanovna. May Christ be with you. I kiss you the way that I love you. It would be best to give all the things for safekeeping to Bar.[on] Vr. How is the Count? What did they do with our old infirmary. – I remember those 2 ½ years we spent there so often. Tatiana.

Tatiana to Anna Vyrubova

5/18 **February**, 1918. Darling my dear, I feel so awfully sorry for you, I pray to God to help you and your poor mother to get through this difficult ordeal. So sad that [your] brother and sister are not with you. I remember you often and kiss you affectionately, like I love you. May Christ be with you. T

Tatiana to Zinaida Tolstaya

Tobolsk, **16 February**, 1918. My dear Zinochka,
It's been so long time since we've written to each other. How are you? Have you received my postcards from the 23rd January? To our great disappointment, the packages have not arrived yet! Probably, someone has taken them. The first [one] arrived. Is Rita always with you? With us nothing has changed and there is nothing new. Your sisters sent postcards. Have you seen N.I.? Did M.D. make it? We often think of you. We pity the unfortunate dwellers of Petrograd. It must be terrible there now. I hope that whichever city you are in, it is peaceful and calm. However, unfortunately it is difficult to hope at this moment. Where is Musya and his family? What are they lacking? It's been so long

since we had news of Katya K.[237]. We stay too far from them. Has N. N. returned? I heard they are in Kiev. I do not know if this is true. Here, the weather has been beautiful, very spring-like. We thought it would never change but today there was lots of snow, then the sun reappeared and the wind blew hard. I hope this letter will reach you. I shall be very glad if you write to me. I wish you much happiness. Greetings to your husband, Seryozha, N.I. and N.D. May God keep you. Tatiana

From the 1918 diary of Nicholas Alexandrovich

19th Feb. Monday. Reading "Anna Karenina" with great interest. Today got a letter from Ksenia. [It] snowed most of the day. Chopped wood in the shed - it's drier there.

Anastasia to ?

20 February. Tobolsk. It is so sad to hear that Nikolai Nikolaevich Vasiliev died. We all find it hard [to believe] that he is not alive. Friends write to us, but many letters don't reach us [...]. We remember the old days, visiting our infirmary. I guess no one goes to the graves of our wounded ones now – nearly everyone was taken away from Tsarskoe. Do you remember

---

[237] Ekaterina Kulneva

Lukyanov – he was pitiful and sweet, always playing with our bracelets like a baby. His visiting card is in my album, but unfortunately the album was left behind at Tsarskoe. Just now I am writing in our bedroom. On the writing desk are pictures of our beloved infirmary [...]. All in all, the times we went to visit the infirmary were awfully good. We often reminisce about our visits to the infirmary, the evening chats on the telephone, and everything, everything...

Maria to ?

22 February/7 March. Tobolsk. In the evenings we get together to work or play cards - bridge or some other games, though I am particularly interested in [card games]. Papa reads out loud. Pretty often, when all 4 of us get together in a proper mood we sing various nice songs. This always ends up with us loudly imitating *zurna*[238] sounds. Some of us knock against the door or any other object that catches our eye in order to produce more noise [...] and create raucous that can be heard almost all over the house.

[238] A musical instrument

Tatiana to Ksenia Alexandrovna

26 February, 1918. My dear darling Aunt Ksenia. I have not thanked you for the card, as Papa and Mama wrote to you, so I decided it wasn't necessary to write on the same day. – We are all terribly happy for your letters. Someone told us that Felix was killed in Kiev, and the next day they told us that it was not him but someone else. So who was it, in truth? How is poor little Nadya now? Poor thing, how many horrors she had to live through. Thank God her husband is with her. And Elena's husband, where is he? Where do they live, in D. or even in Ch. We also heard that Nadya's *beau-pere*[239] had a stroke, is this true or not. There are so many incredible rumors these days, one does not know what to believe. Today the weather is appalling outside, a snowstorm – extremely uncomfortable. But we will still walk outside. We will saw and cut the wood for our stoves. We do it rather well, so we could even be custodians. It's a very pleasant hobby, then time passes, otherwise we just pace around the yard from one corner to another. We shovel the walkway (the only one) and the sidewalk from snow, since they ruined our snow hill so we can't slide down it, they

[239] Stepfather (French)

dug it in half. – Evidently it bothered someone that it was there; although that was not very smart – Well, never mind. At least one less foolish thing, it won't hurt. – Probably your life is hard now due to "money", right? At least it is easier for us to get provisions, but we had to say goodbye to some of [our] people after all, as our state has been reduced, but that is not a problem. – Well, in general these are all trifles, but one feels sorry for the poor people, whom we were able to help before, and many others, and now this is impossible. T.A. wrote to us today from P. [...] We remember you all often, God only knows how long we have not seen you. – So terrible. Do you see Sonya and Vera, or are you still not permitted. How is Grandmama feeling? Isa settled here, and is giving English lessons in town. The Englishwoman came with her, and they both give lessons. – Many [people] here are glad to learn languages. And at least she is able to keep busy and [it is] probably a pleasant feeling to be able to earn her bread. – And what are your eldest sons doing. The second one did not even finish his studies after all. How is little Tikhon? A.[unt] O.[lga] always writes such nice letters about the little one. It is so sad that we cannot see him now. Children are especially wonderful at this age. Occasionally we get letters from old A.[unt] O.[lga][240] and T.K. They live together at "Uncle's", and the rest are in their b.[?] house. They gave them a few rooms, but I think only until May. I have no idea what they will do after that. You probably heard that A.[unt] Olga's old brother died from bronchitis. She wrote to us [about that]. Well, goodbye mine own darling. We have faith in God and are staying cheerful. May God keep you. We kiss you my darling, Grandmama and A. Olga affectionately. – Regards to all. I kiss Nastya and Nono. Your loving goddaughter, Tatiana.

Tatiana to Rita Khitrovo

27 February, 1918. Rita, my dear, Thank you so much for the sweet long letter No.1 from 8th January. I only just got it today, it took horribly long to get here, but still so happy to get it. – I am writing No. 3 on the letter, as it is the third since the new year. Did you get them? Have not received letters from Olya for a while, don't know how she is doing, and we heard from someone at Tsarskoe Selo that she married someone named Malinovky. Have you heard? If you write to Kostya and Nina, send them our heartfelt regards. – Olga asked me to tell you that she wrote you 4 times in

[240] Of Greece

the new year. We read in the newspapers that Gubarev was killed in Simferopol and that he was buried in Petrograd. – Terribly sad, but what happened there? We have not had any news from Veta, I do not know where she is. – Our hair is big – like in my photos after the typhus, with a ribbon in it, do you remember? It is growing a lot faster than back then, I think first of all because we shaved it twice, and then we almost never wore wigs, it was much more pleasant this time. Back then it was embarrassing because it was just me, and now it's all 4 of us together. Oh, how I would love to see the sea, even with one eye! – We had almost spring-like weather here for a few days – it was so wonderful, but these last two days it is windy and cold. We remember you all often. Send heartfelt regards to N.D. from all of us. I hope he is feeling better. Write again, Rita darling. All the very very best. We have not had any letters from Lili either. – May the Lord keep you. I kiss you, Zinochka and Dalechka affectionately. Regards to P.S. and Seryozha. The other day it was a year since we listened to music in the evening together, do you remember, near the fireplace? [...] It was so nice [...] I kiss you affectionately.

Loving Tatiana.

Tatiana to Zinaida Tolstaya

1 March, 1918. Tobolsk. My dear Zinochka,

Thank you very much for your letter for both of us, the beginning of January. I do not know why it took so long. Be so kind and ask R. She sent this letter to Katya Kulneva and this postcard, do you want the good poster. I think that in this way it will reach more certainly. It was a cadet who sent Papa a postcard. We do not know, but he said that Papa spoke to him during a military parade. It's so touching. Lili finally wrote ... She said that he had received our letters sent by you and asks him to write through you. Will you be so kind as to send them to him? I hope everything is quiet again in your city. How are you all? Did you receive my letter of the 25th and R. from the 27th. Ask R. if it is something [from] my Ulyanov and his family? I am not aware of anything. Are they alive? Their property must be occupied by the Romanians because it is in Bessarabia, not far from Kishinev? Rita will explain the correct word but it is bizarre for the uninitiated. Write to me again. I love receiving your letters. Do you know where N.N. is at the moment? I know that his friend was killed in Simferopol and he was there too. Your package did not arrive. I wish you the best. I embrace all three of you firmly. Greetings to

Seryozha and your husband. May God keep you.

Tatiana

From the 1918 diary of Nicholas Alexandrovich

2/15 **March.** Friday. Remembering these days last year in Pskov and on the train! How much longer will our poor motherland be tormented and pulled apart by external and internal enemies? Sometimes it seems that there is no more strength to take this, I don’t even know what to hope or wish for? Nevertheless, there is no one like God! May His holy will be served!

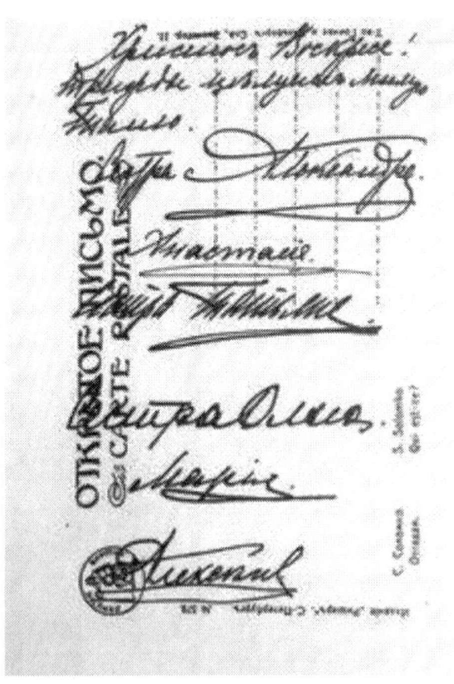

Easter 1918 card to “Tanya’, signed by “Sister Alexandra, Anastasia, Sister Tatiana, Sister Olga, Maria, Alexei”

Anastasia to Ksenia Alexandrovna

Tobolsk **8**/21 **March** 1918. My darling, sweet Aunt Ksenia. Thanks so much for the postcard which just came. For now, we are alive and in good health thank God. We are always so glad when we get news from you. How is Grandmama's health? We often reminisce and talk about you all. These days it's almost always sunny here and it's getting warm – quite pleasant! So, we do our best to get out in the fresh air more. We can't slide down the hill anymore (though it's still standing) as they've wrecked it and put a drainage ditch through it and so we cannot slide down on it.

Anastasia and Olga in the yard

Well, they seem to have calmed down about it now because it was an eyesore for many for some time. It's truly foolish and pathetic. Well, we found new things to do. We saw, chop and split firewood and this is a useful and enjoyable task. We are already quite good at it. By doing this we help many and for us it is a pastime. We clear the paths and the porch – we've become custodians! I have not yet turned into an elephant, though I might yet very soon. I really don't know all of a sudden – maybe it's too little exercise, though I don't know. Please forgive my shocking handwriting – my hand moves something dreadful. We're all fasting this week and sing (hymns) by ourselves at home. Finally, we were able to go to church! And we can have communion there. Well, how are you all, and how are you all getting on? Nothing in particular has happened with us that I need to write about. I must finish now as we are going to our yard to work, etc. We all hug you tightly, and I do too, and so do all the rest of us! Goodbye darling Auntie! God save you! Everyone thanks you very much for your greetings and they send their regards to you too.   Your loving A.

From the 1918 diary of Alexandra Feodorovna

12(25) **March**. Monday. 2nd week of Great Lent. 9-10. Tatiana: Spir.[itual] Readings. 10-11. Maria: The Ray of Spirit. Painted. 12-1. Alexei: Ev.[angelist] Luke 4, Meditat.[ations] on Div.[ine] Liturgy. 1:00 Lunched with Baby. Sat on the balcony - Saw my ex-Crimean Markov pass & Shtein too – 4:30 tea. 5:30-7:30. Looked through money with Tatiana and Zhilik. 8:00. Dined with Alexei. Nicholas read to us. Mme. Syroboiarskaia No: 28.

From the memoirs of S.V. Markov[241]

I saw Their Majesties and Their Highnesses already from a distance, in the windows by the balcony on second floor. The Sovereign stood near the balcony doors, on the nearby window sill sat the heir. Behind him, embracing him by the waist stood Her Majesty. Next to the heir sat Grand Duchess Anastasia Nikolaevna. Next to the Empress stood Grand Duchess Maria Nikolaevna, and behind the Empress and Grand Duchess Maria, apparently standing on something tall, were Grand Duchesses Olga and Tatiana. About twenty paces from the corner of the house, I stopped in order to stall, first taking out from my pocket the

[241] Former officer of Alexandra's Crimean regiment

[cigarette] holder I just obtained, then searching for a cigarette case and matches in my pockets. Their Majesties and Their Highnesses recognized me immediately, and I noticed that they could hardly hold back laughter, this is how comical I looked in my long civilian autumn coat and my rabbit fur hat of a Petersburg merchant.

View from a window of Governor's mansion

When, after much effort to stall time, I stuck my cigarette into the holder, and then raised my head and lit the cigarette, I saw that barely noticeably, Her Majesty nodded her head to me... Everything in me rumbled, and nervous cramps tightened my throat. It cost me great effort not to show my nervousness and restrain sobs which were ready to break out. Having stood at the corner a while longer, I slowly, slowly walked along the façade. Their Majesties and Their Highnesses started to walk from one window to the next. When I reached the edge of the house, I turned back, all the time keeping my eyes on the windows.

This medal of an icon of St Ioann of Tobolsk was conveyed to Cornet S.V. Markov by Alexandra in Tobolsk

Alexandra to Anna Vyrubova

13 March. Peace and yet the Germans continue to advance farther and farther in. When will it all end? When God allows it. How I love my country, with all its faults. It grows dearer and dearer to me, and I thank God daily that He allowed us to remain here and did not send us farther away. Believe in the people, darling. The nation is strong, and young, and as soft as wax. Just now it is in bad hands, and darkness and anarchy reigns. But the King of Glory will come and will save, strengthen, and give wisdom to the people who are now deceived.

Olga to Rita Khitrovo

Tobolsk. **16 March**, 1918. My darling, did you get my letter from the 21st? For some reason I was suddenly compelled to write to you. We heard about you from the letter of Lubusya's mother. How do you like her? We are all fine, healthy. The weather is sunny and frosty; lots of stars in the evenings. We take walks as usual, slide down the hill and romp in the snow a lot. In general, all is the same. I have not heard from Katya in a long time. There are so many disgusting things written in the newspapers, that I am afraid it is not very peaceful. In the evening tonight there will be a *vsenoshnaya*. Pankratov is no longer here with us, for now only the Colonel [is here], it is unknown how it will be, going forward. Everyone is busy learning various comedy plays: English and French. – Did N.N. return? Why have you not seen each other yet? And is the little Chern. here? Big regards if you see them. I wrote for the Holiday. - 3 of Zinochka's packages still did not get here. I'm afraid they are lost, but the 1st with the perfumes, etc. we received. Shura Pet. wrote recently. Kolya left the regiment and moved somewhere. She lives with the children, sews boots. Baron wrote. They live as before, at their respective infirmaries and see each other daily. They seem very happy. Golub with his wife are in Petrograd. Babochkin's sister saw her, and [she said that] Al. Vlad. writes from Vladivostok often. She studies English. He had surgery, now is recovered. Boglanov wrote to Evg. Serg. from Moscow from the infirmary, they are starving terribly. So many revolting things one hears, it is unnerving even, but I still firmly believe that the Lord will help somehow. Right now full demobilization is in process, and they are leaving from here too. I feel pity for the old ones, as they are scttled. Who is S....? and do you know anything about Baron's regiment or any other? Forgive my handwriting and the paper. It is appetizing to write this way-, especially to you. Regards to your landlords from me. I kiss you affectionately my dear. May God keep you. My [family] send regards to you and all, Nik. Dm. and all others who remember. Olga.

Anastasia to ?

25 March. Tobolsk... For the moment, thank God, we are living well. A detachment of Red Army men came from Omsk, up until now they have behaved themselves, and on the whole, all is calm. In the first week of Lent, we fasted and they let us go to church. At all the services through the week we sang by ourselves, as it is difficult to get choristers to come with such frequency for services at home. Lessons for us are as usual, every day, morning and evening. The weather has been marvelous these last days and we often sit on the balcony, glad of the change of scenery, looking at passers-by. Just now, I am sitting and writing by the window. It is already 7:45, but still light outside. The church bells are tolling, which reminds us of the cathedral[242] at Tsarskoe. We've become regular custodians. We cleared snow out of the yard where we go for walks, and now it's not so messy. Then we sometimes chop and saw wood –all is well with us...

Alexei to Kolya Derevenko

[Written on a torn off piece of checkered paper, 5.5cm x 1cm] To Kolya. Urgent. Tobolsk, **March** 1918. Dear Yalok, bring your bullet which you found in T.S. I will also bring two of mine. Bye. Yeskela. P.S. tomorrow.

---

[242] Feodorovsky Cathedral

Alexei, Kolya Derevenko and Pierre Gilliard at the entrance of Governor's mansion

From the 1918 diary of Nicholas Alexandrovich

29 March. Thursday. During the morning walk saw the "special commissar" Demianov, who with his assistant Degtyarev, escorted by the commandant and marksmen, made rounds of the guard house and the garden. Because of him, i.e. this Demianov, and the marksmen's unwillingness to miss him, was why the all the fuss started three days ago.

30 March. Friday. Another day, another surprise! Today Kobylinsky brought the instructions paper he received from Central Executive Committee in Moscow yesterday, which stated that everyone residing in that house [Kornilov] will be moved to our place, and consider us all arrested again, like in T.S. Immediately the moving of house maids started from one room downstairs to another, in order to make room for new arrivals. Alexei has a pain in the groin from coughing, and he stayed in bed all day.

31 March. Saturday. He did not sleep at all during the night and suffered much during the day, poor thing. The weather was, as if on purpose, marvelous and warm, snow is melting quickly. Took a long walk. Clothes and furniture from Kornilov house was dragged over before breakfast, the residents settled into the new place. At 8.45 we had a *vsenoshnaya.*

1 April. Sunday. Today the team committee decided that according to instructions in that paper from Moscow, the people who are residing in our house are no longer allowed to go outside either, that is into town. Therefore, the entire day there was talk about how to fit them into this already crowded house, as several people were supposed to move in. All this is being done in such a hurry due to the arrival shortly of the new detachment with a commissar who is bringing instructions. Therefore, our sharpshooters, in order to avoid any possible conflict, wish for them to find us following a strict order! At 11 ½ o'clock *obednitsa* was conducted. Alexei was in bed all day; the pains continued, but with short breaks. The weather was grey, windy.

2 April. Monday. In the morning a committee of two officers and two sharpshooters made rounds of some of the rooms of our house. The result of this "search" was confiscation of sabers from Valya and M-r Gilliard, and from me – a dagger! Again, Kobylinsky explained this matter only by the necessity to pacify the sharpshooters! Alexei felt better, and from 7 o'cl he fell deeply asleep. The weather stayed grey, mild.

3 April. Tuesday. He slept with short breaks for twelve hours, had almost no pains. The weather became unpleasant, wet snow was falling, and a cold wind blew. The day passed as usual.

Alexei to Kolya Derevenko

Tobolsk. **April** 1918. My dear Kolya, thanks for the letters and drawings. I feel better now. In the garden the mud is terrible. Everywhere planks were laid. I am sending you a *prosfora.*[243] The Blue one says that he yelled at Feffer, serves her right, ha-ha-ha!!!!!! The Blue one is your Papa, I called him that in Crimea. Regards to all. Kisses. Your Ieskela.

Tatiana to Zinaida Tolstaya

Tobolsk. **3 April**, 1918. Christ Is Risen! We all send you and the others our best wishes for Holy Easter. We

[243] Bread used in Holy Communion

hope you are all healthy and everything is going well T.

From the 1918 diary of Nicholas Alexandrovich

4 April. Wednesday. The weather was grey, mild, around 4 o'cl the sun came out. In the morning I walked for an hour, and in the afternoon, I took a walk and sawed wood for two hours. Alexei feels better, but he is tired of lying in the same position; fever, like yesterday is not high – 38.4°. Vl. Nikol. Derevenko feels that this type of temp is necessary, as it aids in the resorption of thc inflammation.

Olga to Rita Khitrovo

4/14 **April**, 1918. My beloved darling. I just got your letter from 14 December with the poetry. Although it is very old, I was still really happy and thank you for it. I don't know if you get any of my letters? This is the 6th one since the New year [sic]. I gave Papa the letters from the coeds and he thanks [them]. Thank God that all is well with you now. It was scary, learning from the newspapers what was going on where you are and not have any news from you for such a long time. All is well with us for now, more or less. The red army men are here too, recently a detachment arrived, but for now they are behaving decently. Everyone fasted and attended divine services during the first week, and were also in Church three times. And now *vsenoshnayas* and *obednitsas* are at home again. Oh, you know, they moved Nastenka, Trina, Valya and Tat.[ischev], and also all our people to our house, and locked everyone up tightly. That's right. So our house is now crowded with screens, people, etc. These last few days were cooler and overcast, but still the sun comes out just before sunset, like right now for instance, and it warms so nicely. Recently it was 21 deg. on the balcony, nice? The snow is melting and the mud in the streets, and especially in our little garden, is incredible. Also a lot of water. We live as always in general – take walks, sit in the sun on the porch, saw, chop firewood and etc. When it is sunny, then all feels nice even when there is nothing to do, while vice versa is boring. – No news from Katya since Christmas. Olya wrote in January, Bibi too. I know that they write often, but for some reason [letters] don't reach [us]. Baron with Olga Porf. are in T.S., each in his own infirmary. The poor Countess has a new sorrow – her Father has died. Recently we got a very sweet letter from [illeg]. – Well, I think this is all I know. Oh yes one more thing, Ivan Gor. Trof.'s son was born in Yeltz.

He wrote to Evg.Serg. - We can see Isa from the window. Babochka's family and he himself dispersed to different places. His godmother stayed in Petrograd though. Everyone sends regards. I embrace you warmly. May God keep you. Your Olga. Send lots of good wishes to little Cher. and your landlords.

5th April, 1918. As we were about to submit the envelope, we received your letter from 3/16 March, thank you dear. I can only imagine what you lived through, my poor ones. And how is it now? I don't know if you heard that our poor Gubar., and also Sasha Dum. and little Kablukov were killed. Horrible stuff. Everyone from Ai-Todor moved to Dulber, [they] are well. The letters now take a long time. For now P. Kob. receives letters for us, but soon some sort of a commissar will arrive and then we don't know how it will be. Whatever God sends – since all comes from Him, and no matter how hard it is, then it is because it's necessary for some reason. – Now it is unclear, but later we will understand. I wait impatiently for another letter. Oh yes, about the violets, and little rock, everyone is very grateful. We put it into the Bible. I kiss my darling firmly one more time. Your Olga.

From the 1918 diary of Nicholas Alexandrovich

5 April. Thursday. An excellent day, my window remained open for half a day. Alexei slept with breaks, pains bothered him occasionally, when he changed positions in bed or sat up. But in general, he was merry and talkative. Temp. – 38.8.

6 April. Friday. Today Alexei suffered more and did not sleep much. The day was excellent; around 5 o'cl a nice spring rain passed. I finished history of England [by] Green Ann [sic] started the novels by Vsev. Soloviov.

7 April. Saturday. Alexei slept well, the pains came a lot more seldom. The morning was warm and sunny, and from 2 o'cl wet snow started, and towards the evening it started to drizzle. At 9 o'cl there was a vsenoshnaya, the bass sang wonderfully.

8 April. Sunday. Twenty fourth anniversary of our engagement! The day stayed sunny, with a cold wind, all snow melted. At 11 ½ there was an *obednitsa*. After that Kobylinsky showed me the telegram from Moscow, which confirmed the decision of the detachment committee to take off mine and Alexei's epaulets! Therefore, I decided not to wear the for the walks, and only wear them at home. I will never forget this kind of beastliness! Worked in the garden for two hours. In the evening we read aloud "Volkhvy" – also by Vsevolod Soloviov.

9 April. Monday. Found out about the arrival of the extraordinary authorized [commissar] Yakovlev[244] from Moscow; he settled in Kornilov house. The children imagined that he will come today to do a search, and burned all letters, and Maria and Anastasia even [burned] their diaries. The weather was revolting, cold with wet snow. Alexei felt better and even slept for two-three hours during the day.

10 April. Tuesday. At 10 ½ o'cl in the morning Kobylinsky showed up with Yakovlev and his suite. I received him in the hall with the daughters. We expected him at 11 o'cl, therefore Alix was not yet ready. He came in, clean shaven face, smiling and embarrassed, asked if I am happy with the guards and the building. Then, almost running he stopped by to see Alexei, without stopping, looked around the rest of the rooms, and, having apologized for bothering us, went downstairs. In the same hurried manner, he also stopped by the others' [rooms] on the rest of the floors.

---

244 Vasily Yakovlev, Commissar "Extraordinaire" who transferred Nicholas, Alexandra, and Maria from Tobolsk to Ekaterinburg

In a half hour he appeared again, in order to present himself to Alix, again hurried to Alexei and went downstairs. This was the extend of inspecting the house for now. We took a walk as usual; the weather was interchangeable, first sunny, then snowing.

11 April. Wednesday. The day was nice and relatively warm. Sat on my favourite greenhouse roof a lot, there the sun warms one nicely. Worked by the hill and on the clearing of the deep ditch along the inner fencing.

Nicholas and his children on the roof of the greenhouse

12 April. Thursday. After breakfast Yakovlev came over with Kobylinsky and announced that he received an order to take me away, without saying where? Alix decided to go with me and take Maria; it was useless to protest. To leave the other children with Alexei – ill under current circumstances – it was more than difficult! Immediately we started to pack the most necessary things. Then Yakovlev said that he will return for O., T., An. And A., and that most likely we will see them in three weeks or so. We spent a sad evening, of course no one slept that night.

From the 1918 diary of Alexandra Feodorovna

Tobolsk. **12**/25 **April**. Thursday. Baby had a better night 36°. 9:00-10:00 Anastasia: Isaiah 38-42. Sat with Baby. Played cards & worked.12:15-1:00 Maria: J. Sirach 18-26. After luncheon the Com. Yakovlev came as I wanted to arrange about the walk to Church for Passion Week. Instead of that he announced by the order of his government (Bolsheviks) that he has to take us all away (to where?) Seeing as Baby is too ill wished to take Nicholas alone (if not willing then obliged to use force) I had to decide to stay with ill Baby or accompany him. Settled to accompany him as can be of more need & too risky not knowing where & for what. (we imagine Moscow) Horrible suffering. Marie comes with us, Olga will look after Baby,

Tatiana the household & Anastasia will cheer all up. Take Valia, Niuta, Yevgeny Sergeevich offered to go. Chemodurov & Sednyov [sic]. 10:30. Took meals with Baby, put few things together, quite small luggage. Took leave of all our people. After evening tea with all. Sat all night with the Children. Baby slept & at 3 went to him til we left. Started at 4:30 in the morning. Horrid to leave precious children. 3 of our rifles went with us.

From the testimony of E.S. Kobylinsky

At 2 o'clock we entered the hall with Yakovlev. In the center of the hall, next to each other stood the Sovereign and Empress. Having stopped at some distance and bowed to them, Yakovlev said: "I have to tell you (he was speaking to the Sovereign in particular), that I am the extraordinary authorized person from the Moscow Executive Committee, and my authorization consists of the fact that I must take away the entire family from here, but since Alexei Nikolaevich is ill, I received secondary order to leave with you only". Sovereign replied: "I am not going anywhere". Then Yakovlev continued: "I ask you not to do this. I have to execute this order. If you refuse to go, I will have to use force, or refuse the assignment entrusted to me. Then they may send someone else instead of me, a less humane person. You can be at peace. I am responsible for your life with my own. If you do not wish to go alone, you may bring whoever you want. Be ready. We will be departing tomorrow [morning] at 4 o'clock". With this, Yakovlev once again bowed to the Sovereign and the Empress and left. At the same time, having said nothing to Yakovlev, the Sovereign turned abruptly, and both of them with the Empress they left the hall. Yakovlev headed downstairs. I followed him. But when I was leaving with Yakovlev, the Sovereign made a gesture for me to stay. I went downstairs with Yakovlev, but when he left, I came back upstairs. I entered the hall where the Sovereign and Empress, Tatischev and Dolgorukov stood near a round table in the corner of the hall. The Sovereign asked me, where are they planning to take me? I reported to the Sovereign that it is unknown even to me, but based on a few clues from Yakovlev, it is possible to figure out that they want to bring the Sovereign to Moscow. This is why I thought so then: when Yakovlev came to me on the morning of 12 April and initially told me that he will be taking the Sovereign, he said to me that he will return again for the family. I asked him: "When do you think you will return?" To this Yakovlev replied: "Well, let's see? We will get there in about 4-5 days; say, a few days over there, and back; will return in 1 ½ - 2 weeks". This is why I reported to the Sovereign that Yakovlev apparently wants to take him to Moscow. Then the Sovereign said: "They must want me to sign the Brest treaty. But I would rather let them cut off my hand than do this". Very anxiously, the Empress said: "I am going too. Without me they will force him to do something again, as they forced him once before", and with this she brought up something about Rodzyanko. Undoubtedly, the Empress was hinting at the Sovereign's act of abdication from the throne. After this the conversation was over, and I went to the Kornilov house.

From the memoirs of Pierre Gilliard

A bit before 3 o'clock, walking down the hallway I ran into two lackeys who were sobbing. They told me that Yakovlev arrived to announce to the Sovereign that he is being taken away. What is going on? I did not dare go upstairs without being asked and returned to my room. A minute later, Tatiana Nikolaevna knocked on my door. She was in tears and said that Her Majesty is asking me to go to him. I follow her. She [the Empress] confirms that Yakovlev was sent from Moscow in order take the Sovereign away, and that the departure will take place this night: "The Commissar promises that nothing bad will happen to the Sovereign, and that if anyone wishes to accompany him, there will be no objections. I cannot allow the Sovereign to go alone. They want to separate him from me, like last time, and push him into [doing] something bad, causing him to feel anxiety for the lives of his dear ones... The Tsar is necessary to them; they know very well that he alone represents Russia... together we will be able to resist more strongly, and I must be next to him during this trial... But the boy is still so ill... what if there are complications... My God, what awful torture!... For the first time in my life I do not know what to do. Every time I had to make a decision, I always felt that the answer would be given to me from above, and now I feel nothing. But God will not allow this departure, it cannot, it must not happen. I am convinced that this night there will be an ice drift..."

Pierre Gilliard

At this moment Tatiana Nikolaevna intervened into the conversation: “But, Mama, if Papa will be forced to leave after all, one must make some kind of decision! ..” I supported Tatiana Nikolaevna, saying that Alexei Nikolaevich feels better and that we will take good care of him. The Empress, was obviously tortured by doubts; she paced back and forth in the room and continued speaking, but mostly to herself rather than to us. Finally, she came over to me and said: “Yes, it is better this way; I will be going with the Sovereign; I entrust Alexei to you...” The Sovereign returned in a minute; the Empress rushed to him with the words: “It is decided – I am going with you, and Maria will go with us". The Sovereign said: "Fine, if you wish…" I went down to my room, and the entire day passed in preparations. Prince Dolgorukov and Doctor Botkin, as well as Chemodurov, Anna Demidova and Sednev will accompany Their Majesties. It was decided that eight officers and soldiers from our guard will go with us. The family spent the second half of the day by the bed of Alexei Nikolaevich. In the evening, at 10 ½ o'clock we went upstairs to have tea. The Empress sat on the sofa, with her were two daughters. They cried so much that their faces were swollen. We all hid our torment and tried to appear calm. We all had a feeling that if one of us breaks down, the rest will break too. Sovereign and Empress were serious and focused. It was apparent that they were willing to sacrifice everything, including their lives, if the Lord, in His inscrutable ways, would demand this to save the nation. Never before had they shown us more kindness and caring… At eleven and a half o'clock, the servants gather in the large hall. Their Majesties and Maria Nikolaevna are saying goodbye to them. The Sovereign embraces and kisses all the men, the Empress – all women. Almost everyone is crying. Their Majesties leave; we all go downstairs to my room. At three and a half o'clock in the morning equipages are driven in the yard. These are most awful tarantasses[245]. Only one has a top cover. We find some straw in the back yard and line the tarantass floors with it. We put a mattress into the one intended for the Empress. At four o'clock we go upstairs to Their Majesties, who leave the room for a minute to see Alexei Nikolaevich. The Sovereign, Empress and Maria Nikolaevna say goodbye to us. The Empress and Grand Duchesses are crying. The Sovereign seems calm and finds a cheering word for each of us; he embraces and kisses us. While saying goodbye, the Empress asks me not to go back downstairs and stay with Alexei Nikolaevich. I head over to him, he is crying in his bed. A few minutes later we hear clamor of equipages. The Grand Duchesses are returning to their rooms upstairs and pass by their brother's door, sobbing.

From the memoirs of V.V. Yakovlev

[**12 April** O.S.] All the residents of the house were up and about. In all corners of the house one could hear sobbing. The Romanov daughters and their entire "court" staff came out on the porch to see off their

[245] Type of a flat sleigh or wagon

"patrons". Nicholas Romanov bewilderingly paced around in his wobbly gait from one person to another, and with sort of convulsive movements crossed his daughters as goodbye. His haughty wife restrained the sobs of those remaining behind. Her every gesture, every word showed that one should not show any weakness in front of the "red enemy".

Anastasia to Nicholas

Tobolsk. **12th** / 25th **April**, 1918. My dear Papa! May the Lord and all Saints protect You, my dear and beloved Papa. In our thoughts and prayers, we are always with You. I cannot even imagine how we can be without You. I believe and hope that the Lord will help us all. Good night my precious and wonderful Papa. I kiss you a thousand times, strongly, strongly as strong as my love is for you. *May the Lord be with You and bless You, darling*[246]. Your loyal and devoted Shvybz/Anastasia

Olga to Nicholas

Tobolsk, **12th April**, 1918. My Dear Papa! May the Lord protect You, bless You and have pity on you, my

[246] This sentence was written in English

dear, beloved Papa. Do not worry about Alexei. I cannot express to You how painful it is [...]. but the Lord knows the reasons why we are going through all of this. I kiss you and I love you as much as I can, my angel, my Papa. Your Olga

From the testimony of E.S. Kobylinsky

At 4 o'clock in the morning they brought Siberian "crochets" – wicker wagons on long horns, one had a top, the seat was made of straw, which was held together by ropes, attached to the sides of the body of the wagon[247]. The Sovereign, Empress and the rest came outside. The Sovereign embraced and kissed me, the Empress gave me her hand. Yakovlev sat down with the Sovereign, the Empress sat down with Maria, Dolgorukov sat with Botkin, Chemodurov – with Sednev. In front and in back there were several carts with our soldiers and infantry from Yakovlev's detachment, and there were two machine guns on these carts, as well as cavalry guards from Yakovlev's detachment.

[247] Aka "tarantass"

From the 1918 diary of Nicholas Alexandrovich

13 April. Saturday. At 4 o'clock said goodbye to our dear children and climbed into tarantasses: I – with Yakovlev, Alix - with Maria, Valya – with Botkin.

Among our people, the following went with us: Nyuta Demidova[248], Chemodurov and Sednev,[249] 9 marksmen and Calvary convoy (Red Army) of 10 men. The weather was cold with unpleasant wind, the road was very bad, and awfully bumpy from the frozen tracks. Crossed Irtysh in rather deep water. Changed horses four times,

[248] Anna Demidova, chamber maid

[249] The imperial family's cook

making 130 versts the first day. Came to Ievlevo village to spend the night. Got settled in a large clean house; slept deeply on our cots.

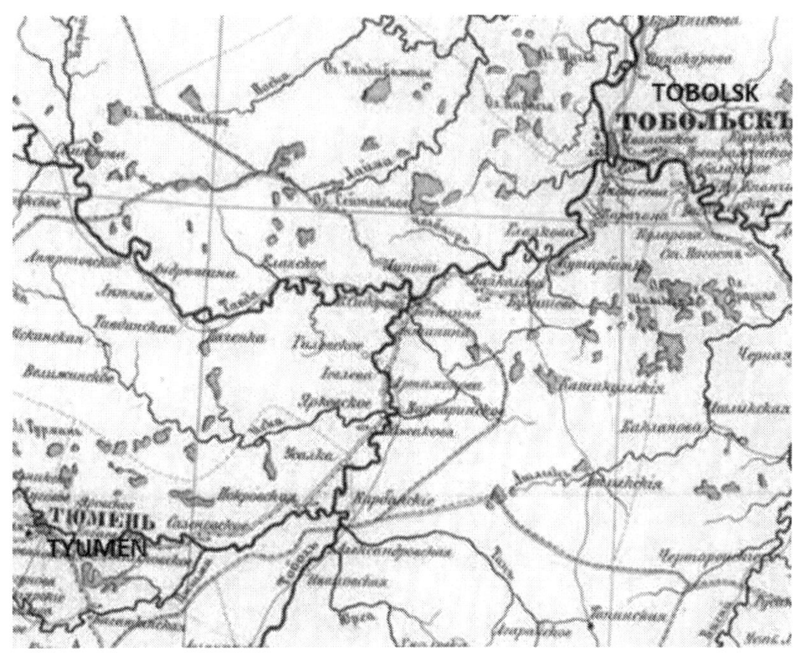

Tatiana to Syroboyarsky

13/26 **April**, 1918. […] They asked me to write to you and thank you very much for the two letters. Today [we] received the letter where you wrote that you got No.15. But ours unfortunately was late, as Sunny with husband and [their] third daughter left town unexpectedly, where you lived through so awfully much on your way from P. It was terribly unexpected for all of us. Everyone was supposed to go, but the little one was sick and therefore they left us with him for now.

From the 1918 diary of Alexandra Feodorovna

13 (26) **April.** Friday. Marie & I in a tarantass. Nicholas with Com. Yakovlev. Cold, grey & windy, crossed the Irtysh. – After changing horses at 8 & at 12 stopped in a village & took tea with our cold provisions. Road perfectly atrocious, frozen ground wind, snow, water up to the horses' stomachs, fearfully shaken, pain all over. After 4th change, a linchpin popped out & we had to climb over into another basket. Changed 5th time horses & and got over into another basket. The others change carriages every time. At 8 got to the town of Ievlevo where we spent the night in house where was the village shop before. We 3 slept in one room we on our beds, Maria on the floor on her mattress, Niuta[250] in her sitting room where we eat of our provisions & our luggage stood. Valia & Yevgeny Sergeevich in our room, our men in another, all on the floor. Got to bed at 10, dead tired & ached all over. – One does not tell us where we are going fr. Tiumen – some imagine Moscow, the little one are [sic] to follow as soon as river free & Baby well.

---

[250] Or "Nyuta" - Anna Demidova

– By turn each carriage lost a wheel or something else smashed. Luggage always late. – heart aches, enlarged, wrote to the children through our first coachman.

From the diary of Pierre Gilliard

14/27 **April**, 1918. The coachman who drove the Empress to the first post station, brought a note from Maria Nikolaevna: the roads are ruined, conditions of the journey are terrible. Will the Empress be in any condition to tolerate the trip? What burning anxiety one feels for them!

From the 1918 diary of Nicholas Alexandrovich

14 April. Saturday. Got up at 4 o'cl, as we were supposed to depart at 5 o'cl., but there was a delay because Yakovlev overslept and besides, he was waiting for a lost package. Walked across Tobol on boards, but at the other bank we had to cross for about 10 *sazhens*[251] in a steamer. We met Yakovlev's assistant – Guzakov, who was in charge of the entire guard on the route to Tyumen. The day became excellent and very warm, the road got softer; but it still shook strongly, and I was concerned for Alix. In the open spaces it was very

[251] A *sazhen* is a unit of measurement of about seven feet

dusty, and in the forests very dirty. In the village of Pokrovskoe there was change of horses, we stood for a long time just across from Grigori's house and saw his entire family, who were looking out of the windows.

Maria made this sketch of Rasputin's house in Pokrovskoe during the change of horses

The last change of horses was in the village of Borki. Here E.S. Botkin got very strong kidney pains, they put him in the house for an hour and a half, and then he resumed forward, unhurriedly. We had tea and snacks with our people and the sharpshooters at the village school building. The last leg was slow and with all the manner of military precautions. Arrived in Tyumen at 9 ¼ in the presence of a beautiful moon, with an entire squadron, which surrounded our wagons at the entrance into the city. It was pleasant to end up in a train, although it was not very clean; we ourselves and our belongings had a desperately dirty appearance. Went to bed at 10 o'clock without undressing, I – above Alix's bunk, Maria and Nyuta in the next compartment.

From the 1918 diary of Alexandra Feodorovna

14 (27) **April**. Saturday. Got up at 4, had tea, packed up, crossed the river at 5 on foot on planks & then on a ferry. Waited ages before driving off, 7:15. (Com. fidgety, runing [sic] about, telegraphing). – Lovely weather, road atrocious. Changes horses, again 6 times, & our horsemen oftener, as both days the same men. About 12, got to Pokrovskoe, changed horses, stood long before our Friend's house, saw his family & friends looking out of the window. At village Borki took tea & our provisions in a nice peasant's house. Leaving the village, suddenly saw Sedov in the street!- Changed our carriage once. Again all sorts of incidents, but less than yesterday. Stopped in a village school, drank tea with our soldiers. Yevgeny Sergeevich lay down as awful kidney pains. When darkness set in one tied up the bells of our troikas, lovely sunset, & moon. Tore along at a wild rate. Approaching Tiumen a squadron on horseback formed a chain around us & accompanied a far [sic] as the station crossed the river on a movable bridge, from 3 versts through the dark town. At midnight got into the train. Write 2 [letters] to the children.

Alexandra to Olga

[...] Your old mother is always with you in her thoughts, my dear Olga. The three of us are constantly talking about you and wonder what all of you are doing. The beginning of the trip was unpleasant and depressing; it was better after we got into the train. It's not clear how things will be there.

From the 1918 diary of Nicholas Alexandrovich

15 April. Sunday. Everyone got substantial sleep. By the names of stations we guessed that we are heading towards Omsk. Started to try guessing, where will they take us after Omsk? To Moscow or Vladivostok? The commissars of course, did not say anything. Maria went to see the sharpshooters often – their compartment was at the end of the car, here there were four, the rest in the next car. Had dinner at the stop, at Vagai station at 11 o'cl., very tasty. At the stations we closed the curtains, as there were a lot of crowds due to the holiday[252]. After some cold snacks with tea, we went to bed early.

Olga to Alexandra

15/27 **April**. Tobolsk. Palm Sunday, 1918. Mama, dear Mama, tenderly beloved! We hug the three of you tightly. We kiss you fervently and we are with you, with all our hearts and souls. May the Lord protect you. Here, for the moment everything is fine, thank God. The Little One's temperature is normal and his spirits are good. We stay together and take turns eating with him. We play cards and read episodes of "*Notres a l'etranger*" [sic], I mean, Zhilik reads to us in French. Today the weather was summer-like, 13 degrees in the shade and in the sun it was horribly warm and we basked on the roof. Ah! the little one has a cold and coughs like Zhilik. He is not in pain but has a stuffed nose, just like when you were here. Mama, little soul, how much we miss you! Around us everything seems empty. When I enter your bedroom, it seems to me that you are still there and that feels so good... Mama, my little soul, you drive yourself to exhaustion. We were terribly happy to have received your little notes. A letter from Madam Zizi arrived for

[252] Palm Sunday

you. She is fine, she writes in a kind manner and wishes us all the best. She says that probably her grandson is dead. We set up the altar this morning, but the service did not start until 1 o'clock. The altar is very nicely arranged by the corner window. Five nuns sang and yesterday there were also singers. The palms were very bulky and soft and I placed one palm by your icon of the Saviour. Every evening I lock your door and Tatiana locks the one to Papa's study. Masha's drawing is in my room, near the icon of Tikhon. Tatiana [Konstantinovna] wrote to us about Vol. They live in two rooms; she, with two children in one, and Diar with Korach in the other room. Oh yes, Al. Vl. wrote to us and we already answered him, everything was done as was needed. Everything is fine. Mama, my little soul, how are you? We would like very much to know what is going on with you. It seems that they allowed Isa to leave.[253] Today there was an enormous religious procession, with banners, icons, many members of the clergy and the faithful. It was very beautiful, under the sky sparkling from the sun

[253] Sophie Buxhoeveden ("Isa") followed the family into exile but, unlike many other imperial retainers was later released by the Bolsheviks and emigrated abroad

and the bells ringing. In the evening, I do not know why, but the local bishop was arrested.

Tobolsk, **16th** /28th **April**, 1918. I continue writing to you this Monday, before the service. We intend to take the Little One to your bedroom to hear the service, and then we will take him to Papa's study. In the evening I prayed with him and blessed him, in your absence. Mama, you are our joy and light. Today was warmer than yesterday and the windows are wide open. Yesterday evening the two of us with Trina and the general, played bridge in Nastenka's room, while Nast.[enka] and Shvybz played *bezique* taking turns with Ilyusha[254]. We had the evening tea in the dining room (before the church installation we took tea in the sitting room).

[254] General Ilya Tatischev

Olga, Tatischev, Gilliard, Nastenka, Tatiana and Trina in Governor's mansion

What a pity that *Koziol*[255] and old Fedya have not left. Tell Mashka that everyone is fine. *Koziol* disguiscd himself as Volkov and, being embarrassed, hid himself in the back of the *camar* [?]. I gave him a hard time. One could say that the little peasant disappeared. Pimy came forward and Shvybz, of course, understood well and was encouraged by them. Yesterday, we ate the "poor" turkey. Mama, you would have said "one should not", dear little soul. *Yolochka*[256] has grown and its foliage is long... For the moment, they detain

[255] "The Goat" again, probably peasant messenger

[256] Little fir tree (Russian)

everyone as before and do not permit even those with families to leave, which is foolish and makes no sense.

From the 1918 diary of Nicholas Alexandrovich

16 April. Monday. In the morning we noticed that we are going back. It turned out that in Omsk, they did not want to let us through! At least we felt freer, even took a walk two times, the first time along the train, and the second – rather far off in the field together with Yakovlev himself. Everyone was in a merry mood.

From the memoir of V.V. Yakovlev

On the morning of the [**17th**]30th[257] [**April**] we arrived in Ekaterinburg without any incident. Despite our early arrival, the Ekaterinburg station was overflowing with people. As it turned out, the residents of Ekaterinburg found out about our pending arrival – we had no idea about this. Especially large was the crowd concentrated at the freight platform. Our train was standing on the fifth track from the platform. When they saw us, they started demanding for me to bring Nicholas out and show him to them. There was a roar in the air, and here and there threatening cries could be heard: "Strangle them all!", "Finally they are in our

---

[257] Yakovlev was using new style dates

hands!" The guards who stood on the platform weakly restrained the pushing crowd, which started chaotically moving towards our train car. I lined up my guard team around the entire train… prepared machine guns. To my great horror I saw that somehow the station commissar ended up at the head of the crowd. He yelled out to me, still from afar: "Comrade Yakovlev, bring the Romanovs out of the train. Let me spit in his face, at least!". The situation was becoming extremely dangerous. The crowd was pushing against us and kept getting closer to the train. Its mood was becoming more threatening. To wait for someone from the Soviet was useless – no one among the local leaders came to our aid, although they were already warned not only of our arrival, but also of what was going on at the train station! It was necessary to take some decisive measures. I sent comrade Kasyan to the station head, with a demand to immediately put a freight train between the platform and our train, and then send our train towards Ekaterinburg II [station] as soon as possible. The shouts were getting more insistent. Persuasions did not work. The crowd kept demanding to see the Romanovs more and more insistently. In order to at least temporarily restrain them until Kasyan returns, I shouted loudly to my lined-up guards: “Prepare the machine guns”. The pushing crowd fled, but threatening shouts towards me could be heard. The same fat commissar with a big stomach yelled in a frenzied voice: “We are not afraid of your machine guns. We have prepared cannons against you. See them sitting on the platform”. I looked in the direction he was pointing. Indeed, three-inch muzzles were moving there, and someone was swarming nearby. While we were exchanging these niceties, trying to somehow stall for time, Kasyan returned, he was able to obtain from the station head an execution order for our demand, despite the chaos happening at the station. Right after Kasyan’s arrival we saw that a freight train was moving towards us. In a few minutes we were behind a wall of train cars, isolated from the crowd. Shouts and curses could be heard towards the machinist, and while the rushing people were trying to get to our side through the buffers of the freight train, we, having an attached locomotive, took off and disappeared among endless tracks of the Ekaterinburg train station, and in 15 minutes were already in complete safety of II Ekaterinburg.

From the 1918 diary of Alexandra Feodorovna

17/30 **April**. Tuesday. Yekaterinburg. Stood ages & moved up & down with the train whilst our two com. Yakovlev & Guzakov spoke with the Sovdep of here. At 3 were told to get out of the train Yakovlev had to give us over to the Ural Region Soviet.

Artist's rendition of the transfer of the Romanovs at Ekaterinburg train station; the station as it looks today

Their chief took us three in open motor, a truck with soldiers armed to their teeth followed us. Drove through bystreets till reached a small house, around whi.[ch] high wooden pailings [sic] have been placed. Our soldiers not allowed to accompany us. Here a new guard & officer & other civilians, looked through all our baggage. Valia not yet let in. got our lunch at 4:30. (rations) fr. an hotel, borcht & a dish, we 3, Niuta in the dining room, then sitting room in wh. sleep [sic] Yevgeny Sergeevich & our two men. (Canalisation does not work.)- Had tea at 9:30. Then one brought beds for the others & found us a basin. Went to bed at 11. Weather was glorious, so warm & sunny. Nicholas read the Bible to us.

From the 1918 diary of Nicholas Alexandrovich

17 April. Tuesday. Another marvelous warm day. At 8.40 we arrived in Ekaterinburg. For about three hours [we] stood at one station. There was major altercation between the local and our commissars. In the end the former won, and the train moved to another – freight station. After an hour and a half of standing still, we came out of the train. Yakovlev transferred us to the local regional commissar, with whom the three of us got into a motor and drove down deserted streets to the house that was readied for us – Ipatiev's. Little by little our belongings also arrived, but Valya was not allowed in.

Wide view of Ekaterinburg and the Ipatiev house (left of center)

The house is nice, clean. They assigned us four large rooms: corner bedroom, lavatory, close by a dining room with windows looking over the garden and view of the lower part of vegetable garden, and finally an open hall with an arch instead of doors. We could not unpack our things for a long time, as the commissar, the commandant and the officer of the guard still had not been able to inspect our luggage chests. The inspection later was similar to customs, very strict, down to the last bottle from Alix's travel first aid kit. This made me explode, and I sharply expressed my opinion to the commissar. By 9 o'cl. we finally settled in. Had dinner at 4 ½ from a hotel, and after clean up, had tea for dessert.

Ipatiev house and surroundings circa 1918

We settled this way: Alix, Maria and I in the bedroom all three, the lavatory is shared, in the dining room – N. Demidova, in the hall – Botkin, Chemodurov and Sednev. Near the entrance is the room of the officer of the guard. The guards were staying in two rooms near the dining room. In order to get to the bathroom and W.C., one had to pass by a guard by the door of the guardroom. Around the house a tall picket fence was erected two *sazhens* away from the windows; there, a chain of guards was standing, in the garden as well.

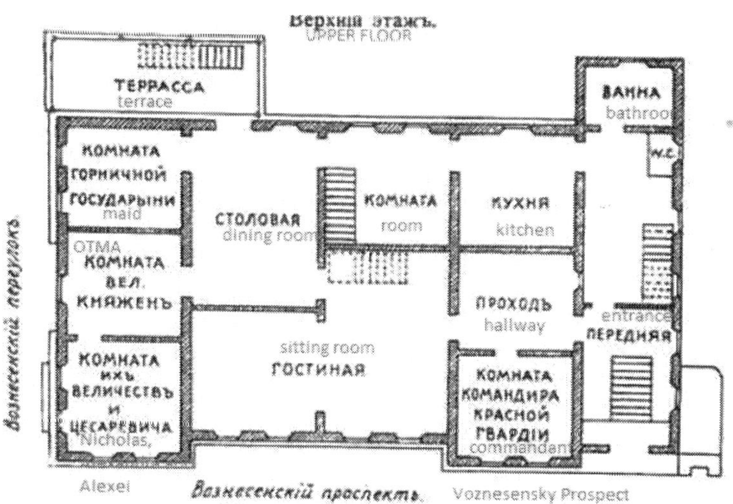

Plan of the upper floor of the Ipatiev house

18 April. Wednesday. Slept marvelously. Had tea at 9 o'cl. Alix remained in bed in order to rest from everything she went through. In light of 1 May, we heard music of some sort of a procession. We were not allowed to go out into the garden today! One wanted to wash in the excellent bathtub, but the plumbing was not functioning, and they could not bring water in a barrel. This is tiresome, as my feeling of cleanliness was suffering. The weather remained wonderful, the sun shone brightly, it was 15° in the shade, I breathed in the fresh air through a window flap.

From the 1918 diary of Alexandra Feodorovna

Yekaterinburg. **18 April**/ 1 May. Ipatiev house. Wednesday. Sunny morning again. 25° in the sun. Remained in bed because of enlarged heart, tired & head ache. 1:15. The others got soup & eggs brought. I had some good bread. Marie read to me *Spir. Readings*.

3:30. Tea, bread & Maltz extract.[258] Marie read to me, Nicholas sat as his writing table also in our bedroom. Reading & writing. 8:45. tea. Wrote to the children. Our Commandant is Avdeev[259] (acc.[ompanied] us fr. Tobolsk it seems) his aid [sic] Ukraintsev (former soldier was a beater when Misha went shooting near Borzhom.[260]) (as a little boy Olga played with him at Gagri 15 years ago), - he works in a fabric [factory], receives 300 a month, has a large family. ♥ 3

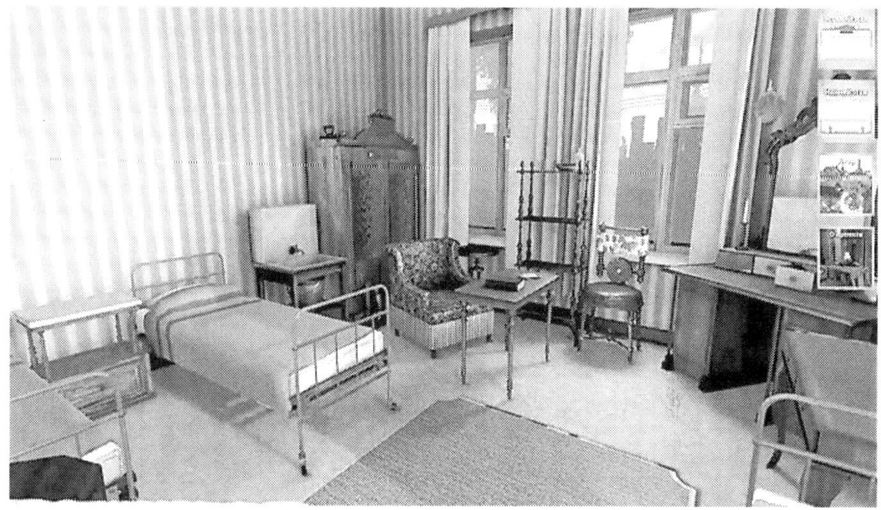

Digital recreation of Nicholas and Alexandra's room at the Ipatiev house

[258] She probably meant "malt extract" which is something like marmite spread
[259] Alexander Avdeev (Avdeyev) was the first commandant at the Ipatiev house
[260] Town in Georgia

Maria, Alexandra and Nicholas to Anastasia

[Maria]: Ekaterinburg, **18 April**/1May. Christ Is Risen! I send you my greetings for the feast of light, my sweet Anastasia. We arrived here by car after the train. We had breakfast at 4.30 in the dining room. Only unpacked our things in the evening, because the luggage was searched, even the "medicines" and the "candy"[261]. After two days in the cart, with bumps, our belongings were in a terrible state. Extraordinary thing – the frames and perfume bottles were not broken, only the top of the Malzeket[262] spilled out, which stained the books, but Nyuta and Sednev put everything back in order. Even inside the bags, there was dust and dirt and all the wrapping paper was untidy and torn. We had tea together at 9.30 in the evening. After that we rested a little; we set cots up ourselves and went to bed at 11 o'clock. Papa read to us, the Gospel of the week. Mama teased Mashka, imitating, with success, Pankra[tov]'s enthusiasm, but despite all of that, everything again is "a little depressing".

---

[261] Code word for jewelry

[262] Possibly perfume

[Alexandra]: I bless you and kiss you affectionately, my little soul.

Contemporary sketch of Ipatiev house

[Maria]: We have not unpacked everything, because we were told that we would be moved to another place. I am not going to write to anyone else, so please give my Easter wishes to all and tell them that I send them regards with all my heart. Tell Madelen and the others how we live.

[Nicholas]: I am bored without you, my dear Shvybz. I miss the funny faces you make at meals. How were the religious celebrations during the Holy Week? Did you set up a good icon altar? See you soon. I kiss you thrice. Your Papa

[Maria]: My best wishes to my dear Shvybz. May God protect you. Your M.

[To the left of Maria's signature, Alexandra wrote]: Your old Mama.

Alexei to Kolya Derevenko

Tobolsk. **April** 1918. To Kolya. Dear Kolya, what word ends with three e's. Write it down and give to Zhilik. [On lower right of reverse side of folded piece of paper]: To pass on to Nikolai Vladimirovich Derevenko.

From Olga to Alexandra

Tobolsk, Thursday, **19th April** / 2nd May, 1918. I have not written for two whole days. I thought I would never be able to send this one. Today we took communion. We thought about you all the time, dear ones. We miss you very much! Yesterday, we dressed the Little One and took him for a walk for two hours, in a wheelchair. He was very happy and it was not expected that he would be so sweet. Today it is colder and he rests in the house on a cot. It is better this way, as he was feeling tired. He slept in Papa's room and during the service, in your bedroom. Tutels packed all your belongings, Mama, my little soul, now it feels so empty here. Yesterday we received a letter and a small package from Zina. As always, she writes very nicely. In the package there was a candle from the tomb of Christ, a cake, two colored eggs and marmalade. For you, a napkin and a bookmark from her daughter. We received 3 letters from Rita. There is one also for you. They sent us all their best wishes. Kupov wrote. He saw Mitya and Boris in Petrograd [and they] also send their greetings. Djour wrote - he left with his division, because after the peace treaty he could not stay here, but he does not say where they went. Lubasha's mother also wrote. Nik. Dm. works as an assistant to her husband. He lost weight - on a diet. He did not have the surgery yet. He sees Rita very often, etc. He is very kind. Today I will write to my godmother.

Alexandra to Dr V.N. Derevenko

[On the right-hand side]: To V.N. Derevenko, Tobolsk. **19 Apr.**/2 May. 1918. Ekaterinburg. Christ Is Risen! Our heartfelt wishes to You and Your family for the Holy day. We hope that Kolobov visited You. Already for 4 days we know nothing about them [the children] – very hard. Is [Alexei] allowed on his feet yet? How is [his] strength, appetite, well-being. Does he lay out on the balcony? Want to know everything. We do not know where we will be moving, but probably close. The weather is splendid. I am very tired, heart is enlarged. We are alright, missing [everyone]. May the Lord keep [you] +

Maria to Anastasia

Ekaterinburg, **19th April**/2nd May, 1918. [To] An.N. Christ Is Risen, my little and dear soul. I kiss you three times. I hope you receive all my little eggs and icons. We think about you all the time and dream about the happy day when we will see each other again. Have you received all our letters? It is already one week and we have not seen each other and we have written every day. It is silly, what is there to write about, but we cannot write everything. There were some amusing incidents. Every night I wish you good night's sleep. And you? In the entire house there is no water and we wait a long time for the *samovar*[263] to be brought, which is slow to heat. Mama has her meals on the cot and I have mine with Papa, Nyuta, Evg. Serg., Sednev and Chemod[urov] in the dining room and Nyuta sleeps there. She sends regards to all of you. Do little Tresses[264] and the "good Russians" still take walks together?

Dining room at the Ipatiev house

[263] Heated metal container traditionally used to heat and boil water in Russia
[264] Messenger

Christ Is Risen! **19 April**/2 May, 1918. Ekaterinburg. I kiss you fervently thrice, darling, and remember you. Today [Mama's] health is better I think, the others took a walk for an hour in the tiny garden, were very happy. [They] brought water in a barrel, so Papa can take a bath before dinner. I swung on the American swing with Nyuta, walked back and forth with Papa. – Mama is lying down on a cot today, a bit better, but head and heart ache. They asked us to make a list of everyone who will arrive with you – I hope we did not forget anyone - I don't know whom Isa will bring [?]. We must explain the reason [to have] each person with us. How very complicated everything is, 8 months of living a peaceful life and now everything is starting again. I feel such pity for you, that you have to pack and resolve [everything]. I hope that Stepan is helping. [I wish] only to have some news from you. May the Lord keep you + Maria

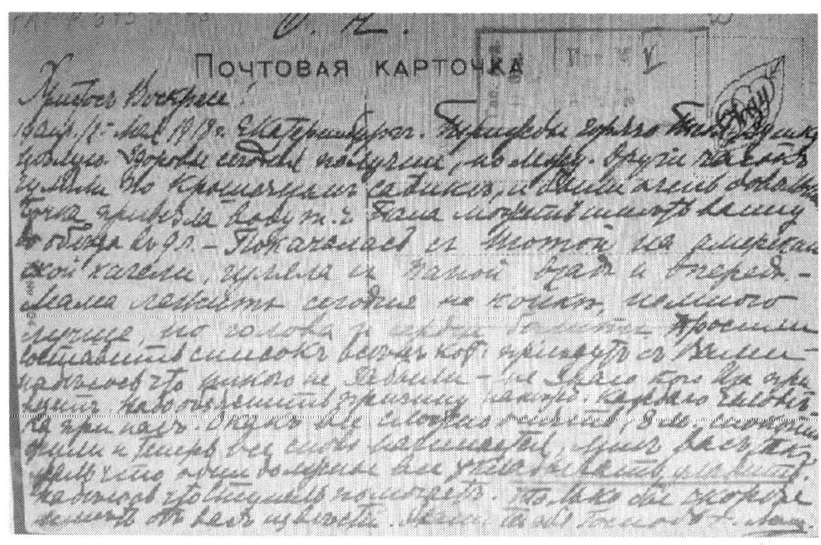
Почтовая карточка

Maria's postcard from Ekaterinrg, translated above

From the 1918 diary of Nicholas Alexandrovich

19 April. Great Thursday.[265] The day remained excellent, windy, dust flew around the entire city, the sun burned through the windows. In the morning I read to Alix the book "La Sagesse et la Destinee" [by] Maeterlinck. Later continued reading the Bible. Breakfast was brought late - at 2 o'clock. Then all of us, except Alix, took advantage of permission to go out into the little garden for an hour. The weather got cooler, there were even a few raindrops. It was nice to breathe the fresh air. Hearing the bells tolling made one sad to think that it is Passion [week] and we do

[265] Maundy Thursday

not have the chance to be at these wonderful services, and besides we cannot even fast. Before tea I had the joy of taking a thorough bath. Had supper at 9 o'cl. In the evening, all of us residents of the four rooms gathered in the hall, where Botkin and I took turns reading the 12 Gospels, after which we went to bed.

Olga to Alexandra

20 April/3 May, 1918. [Tobolsk]. Today is Good Friday. The weather changed. After a sunny morning strong wind started, and then clouds appeared and it started to rain. It is only 4 degrees and we also had hail. We cut wood with Shvybz - not so bad. I cannot remember if I wrote to you on 1st May "New Style".

There was a manifestation or demonstration, I do not know what it is called, and everybody paraded with red flags, guns, etc.

May Day street march in front of Kornilov House, probably photographed from a window of Governor's mansion

Alex. Petr. sold the pigs for 900 rubles, and we kept one - the female who I think found a way to fight with Ortipo. Jim has a cough and stays indoors. Yesterday the Little One had pain in the legs all day and was gloomy and nothing would distract him. During the service he followed the reading of the Twelve Gospels and was very happy. Today he is in good spirits and there is no pain. He continues to cough but his stuffed nose is much better. Alexei was nauseous and was not feeling very well, and that is the reason why he did not leave. He is sad. Do you understand?[266] St.[epan] sends thanks to Mashka. He had accumulated a lot of little things that I would love to tell you, my little soul. We found a small *Saint-Suaire*[267] and put it on the game table, on top of the white cloth. Underneath it is the carpet of the brother and around the pink flowers, with which Shvybz played the comedy. We put the Little One's roses on the ... I forget what you call the thing that the priest holds at the same time as the cross during the midnight mass; I mean, it is with the candles and the priest asked us to hang it there. He was very pleased when he saw the *Saint-Suaire*, etc. Mama, little soul, I want to know only where you are and what is happening. O.

From the 1918 diary of Alexandra Feodorovna

21 April/4 May. Great and Holy Saturday. 2°. Slightly snowing. Wrote to the children 8th time. Nicholas read to us Gospel & book. 1:40. Brought their luncheon. Nicholas had a bath. 2:00. Sednyov cooked vermicelli again for me. 3:00. Had a bath. Niuta too. Lay down

[266] Apparently a code they agreed upon

[267] Shroud

again. Wrote to the children, the others went out for 20 min. 5:30. Tea. Nicholas read to us. Arrayed our images on table. 8:20. Priest & Deacon came & served matins – soldiers of the guard came too. – 9:00. Dined. 10:00. Went to bed. - Marie read to me.

Olga to Ekaterinburg

Saturday, 6 o'clock, [**21 April**] 4 May. We learned from a telegram from Matv.[eyev] that everything is fine. Oh my God, how are you? It is horrible not to be together and to know nothing about you, because what we are told generally is not always the truth. [...] May God protect you. O.

Olga, Tatiana and Alexei in Tobolsk

[**22 April**] 5 May [continued]. ХРИСТОС ВОСКРЕСЕ![268] Dear beloved ones. We would love so much to know how you celebrated your Easter. Dear Mama, when will we finally be together? May God look after you. The midnight mass and the service afterwards were well done. It was beautiful and intimate. We put on all the side lights, except for the chandelier and there was enough light. The Little One slept during the service and did not participate in the Easter supper and did not even notice that we moved him to his bedroom. Today at 10:30 we offered Easter greetings to everyone and gave eggs. Everyone thanked us, in fact the nuns sang well as a whole, but the Easter hymns were dreadful, in the style of popular dances and at top speed. The candles were beautiful, with golden stripes and it was for you that we lit them, in turns during the Easter mass, as well as Zina's candle. There are a lot of eggs, *kuliches*[269] and *paskhas*[270], etc. Mama, my little soul, how are things with you? I feel sad—when I think about you—why do we have everything and you, what do you have? Dear and beloved Mama, how I would love to see you and kiss you!! At this moment Klavd[ia]

---

[268] Christ Is Risen! (Russian)
[269] Easter bread
[270] Easter cake

Mikh.[ailovna],[271] Nastenka and the general are with the Little One. Rostovtsov sends his greeting by telegram as well as Kupytch, who writes about Voronezh and remembers the year 1915. We hear the sound of bells all the time. The weather is bad.[272]

Alexei with Klavdia Bitner

[271] Klavdia Mikhailovna Bitner

[272] Letter ends here abruptly, so it is probable that a page is missing

From the 1918 diary of Alexandra Feodorovna

Yekaterinburg. **22 April**/5 May. Pascha. Sunday. -3°. Marie read to me Spir. Readings, & Nicholas the Gospel & French book. 1:00. Sednyov prepared us luncheon warmed up yesterday's food, I was up too & then lay down again. Wrote to the children. The others walked a little. Had coco. Nicholas read "Small in the Great" to us. 5:00. Tea - sun came out. Nicholas read the evening's Gospel to us. 8:00. Supper, I had it with them. We sat in Yevgeny Sergeevich's room for an hour. -4°. Talked with Ukraintsev. Early to bed again.

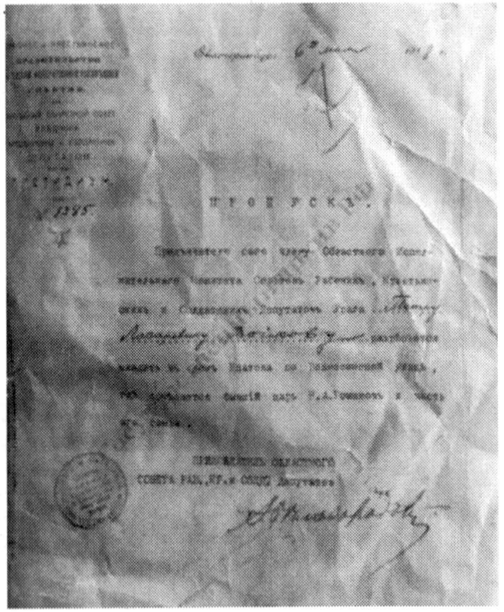

A pass to enter the Ipatiev house for Pyotr Lazarevich Voikov[273], dated **23 April**/6 May, 1918 (New Style)

[273] People's Commissar of Ural Soviet

Anastasia to Maria

24 April/ 7 May. Tobolsk. Indeed He Is Risen! My dear sweet Mashka. We were so terribly happy to get the news [from you] and shared our impressions. I apologize for writing crookedly on the paper, but this is just my foolishness. What we rec.[eived] from An.Pav. was very sweet; [sends] regards, etc., to you. How are you all? Sashka and so on? You see, of course that there is always a massive number of rumors; well and you sometimes understand how hard it is and one doesn't know whom to believe and sometimes it's all so disgusting! As they only tell us half of it, but not the rest, and that's why we think he is lying. Ks. Mikh. [sic] Bitner comes and spends time with the Little One. Alexei is so sweet; he eats and tries so [hard] (remember how it was at the little bench when you were here?) We take turns having breakfast with Alex.[ei] and making him eat, although there are days when he eats without needing to be told. Dear ones, in our thoughts we are with you all the time. It is terribly sad and empty; I really don't know what possesses me.

Anastasia in the Grand Duchesses' room in Tobolsk

The baptismal cross is with us, of course, and we got your news. So. The Lord will help and does help. We set up the iconostasis awfully nicely for Easter, all in spruce, which is the way they do it here, and the flowers. We took pictures. I hope they come out. I continue to draw, not too badly they say; it's very pleasant. We swung on the swing; boy did I laugh when I fell off so splendidly! Yes, quite! I told the sisters so many times last night, that they are sick of hearing about it, but I could tell again and again, although there is no one left to tell. In general, there is a whole trainload of things to tell you all. My Jim caught a cold, and coughs, so he sits at home and sends regards. There was such incredible weather! One could shout from the pleasantness of it. Strangely enough, I tanned more deeply than anyone else, a regular Arab woman! But these days I am boring and not pretty. It's cold, and this morning we froze, although we were inside, of course, and didn't go out. I very much apologize: I forgot to extend good wishes to all you dear ones for the holiday; I kiss you all not thrice but lots of times. My dear, all of us thank you for the letters. There were demonstrations here too, but they were not much of anything. We sit here together as always, but you are missed. Tell precious Papa that we are very grateful for the figs; we are savouring them. I apologize of course that this is such a jumbled letter; you understand that my thoughts are racing and I can't write anything and so I put down whatever comes to mind. Soon we will go for a walk; summer hasn't come yet and nothing is blooming, but things are starting to come up. You know, I want to see you so much, it's sad. I go for walks and then I'm back. It's boring whether you go out or not. I swung. The sun came out but it's cold and my hand can barely write. Your regards were transmitted to us word for word, and we send you big thanks and the same. In the evenings we sit around; yesterday we read fortunes using the book. You know which one. Sometimes we work. We do everything they ask. A kiss to you, and to your dear ones, and much else I won't elaborate on, for you will understand. Thought about it already some time ago. Russa [?], although sweet, is strange and makes one angry, for she doesn't understand and simply can't bear it. Once I was almost rude, a real cretin. Well, it looks like I have written enough foolishness. Right now, I will write some more, and then I will read it later, during free time, that is. For now, good-bye. I wish you the best, happiness, and all good things. We constantly pray for you and think, Help us Lord. Christ be with you, precious ones. I embrace all of you tightly and kiss you. A.

Olga to Maria

[Telegram **24 April**/7 May, 1918]. To the Chairman of Ekaterinburg Regional Executive Committee for Maria Nikolaevna Romanova. 19 o'cl. 31 min. from Tobolsk. All grateful Easter cards little one slowly recovering feels well kiss affectionately Olga

Olga, Tatiana and Anastasia to Alexandra

25 April/8 May. [Olga]: Mama, my dear little dove. Yesterday we sent you long letters and a telegram and we hope you will receive them. Here, thank God, everything is going well at the moment. The little one is better but evidently, he has not yet gotten up because this illness lingers for a long time. He takes a bath every other day. He is in high spirits and does not complain of pain. His cough has almost ceased. His appetite, as always, is not great. But you Mama, little soul, how are you? Is your heart better? We would really like to know more about how you are. The letters dated the 18th only arrived yesterday, but they brought us immense joy. We told and repeated to everybody what you wrote. Tutels, the servants, ladies, etc., send regards to you, kiss your hands and send words of encouragement. Isa herself wrote kindly. The weather does not seem to be getting better. Today the sun is shining, however there is also wind and clouds periodically. There is no more ice in the Irtysh River and the first boat arrived yesterday with "Sashka and her family".[274] On the 23rd there was a mass and the old Mother Superior sang with the choir. Our game of *gorodki* became very popular and it is played now a great deal. The sow had six piglets. They look like big rats. They are not very appealing. I hear my brother who is splashing in the bath. Shvybz is reading near the window. Jim is on my knees and the cat is snoring

[274] A code

on the floor. Tolya sent us colored eggs and greetings. Klim saw them. Oh yes, yesterday I wrote to Aleks. Al. Since the arrival of the letters, I received nothing from his mother and we cannot expect anything from anywhere, because communications are disrupted. We learned of the death of Prince Finikin in Dulber, the poor man! News from elsewhere is no longer received. Rumours circulate that the Germans occupied Crimea – what horror!! Mama, little soul. Everything is well in the room, for the moment. There are plenty of various green plants, the altar doors are opened all the time and the balsamic fir trees smell very nicely. We will finally learn how to close the doors. We always fear that Joy, Ortipo and Jim may get into "hot water". Shvybz tells me whenever there is anything interesting [happening] in the street. At this moment *Koziol* appears from some place. The amazon, you know the one who goes riding, passes by very often. We read today in the little telegram, as Protz calls it, an article about your transfer from Tobolsk to Ekaterinburg. Olya[275] has become very nice. Mama, little soul, all

[275] May be a code

these funny things are for Mashka. Nik. Dem. seems attracted to O.

[Tatiana]: Mama, my dear, my beloved little soul. Thanking you immensely for the little icons and egg. I miss you terribly, my beloved ones. The rooms are so sad and empty. We spend the evenings with Nastenka downstairs, and then we all take tea. We go to bed early. I help Zhilik when he is in need. Zhilik and Cig.[276] take turns having tea with us. With the latter everything is very peaceful but with the other it is truly eventful and we tease one another and argue. I finally received a letter from Boris R. who sends best wishes and his greetings for the holy days. He is in Moscow with his sister and foolishly he forgot to give his address. Yesterday we sent letters and a telegram to all three of you. The weather is still cold here and our brother went out only once. We have no news from *Znamenskaya* nor from the peasant. We cannot write to Zinochka because we are isolated from the south and Kiev. We heard that Irina T.'s brother married one of Victor Kotch's daughters and the other daughter married the younger brother of "God's Servant

[276] Charles Gibbs, their English tutor

Sergei"[277]. You saw him when he was wounded at the beginning of the war. For the moment we have not had letters from Serafima[278], but we learned that she received ours and thanks us. Mama, my dear little soul, we are very lonesome without you and we torment ourselves with the thoughts that we do not know how you are doing. I pray a lot for you so that God will come to help you all, our dear angels. Do you have books to read or should we send some to you? I read the book sent by Zina. It is very interesting and educational. It is a gift and we will take it with us. I hope that the sugar was useful. How do you receive fresh supplies? Can we bring something that you need or are you able to buy yourselves? We think about you all the time and talk about you. In fact, we cannot even imagine how you live nor what you do. For you it is easy because you know how we live. I hope Mama, little soul, that you have no difficulty deciphering my charming handwriting which you love so much!! What will we do with the bags of cid[?]? Now goodbye, may Christ protect you from all evil+++++. I kiss you my

---

[277] Georgi Voyevodsky

[278] Anna Vyrubova later took the name "Sister Serafima" when she became a nun

beloved dear ones as much as I love you. I miss you. Your daughter who loves you very much, Tatiana.

[Olga]: Hello!! I believe that the news, to tell the truth, is not very interesting but there is nothing better. Iv.[an] Iv.[anovich][279] left today. I could not see him, not once, even from a distance. Beloved and dear Mama, may the Lord with His goodness protect you, give you strength and bless the three of you. I kiss you and love you so much, as much as I can, dear Mama, Papa and Mashka. Your Olga. Greetings to the others from us.

[Anastasia]: Beloved and dear Mama. Thanks enormously for the letters. You have no idea how much joy this letter brought us. I hope that your heart is not bad and you have no more headaches. What happened with Garad is very sad and hurtful but it seems to me that he was quite an idiot. We had tea today, as usual with Zhilik, who tormented and crushed us terribly. We spend the evenings working with Nast.[enka], who kisses your hands, and sometimes play bezique. We have the evening tea early and in the dining room. It is very good to have a

---

[279] Footman

church here. It is very sad without you, my dear ones. All the time we feel that something is missing. The boats have now started to sail and we often hear their sirens. That noise is so familiar, do you remember? There are a lot of things that we would love to know about you, our infinitely dear ones. How do you feel and what is going on now? We need to go downstairs for dinner and Olga will stay with the little one. Bronislav and his wife send you greetings. He has recovered, thank God, and goes for walks. Kay wrote, she sent us her good wishes and kisses. Her grandmother is dying, her mother had gone to be with her but now she has returned. Goodbye for now, my immensely dear Mama. You are constantly in our thoughts, our precious ones, and we pray for you. May the Lord and Ioann of Tobolsk protect you all. Good night, I kiss you three very affectionately my dear ones, how I love you ++++. May the Lord come to your aid. Your faithful A. My good thoughts to everyone.

From the 1918 diary of Alexandra Feodorovna

Yekaterinburg. **25 April**/8 May. Wednesday. 5°. Sunshine and strong wind. Nicholas as daily read the Gospel to us & then “Great in the Small”. 1:15. Had Sednyov: [sic] excellent vermic. & bread & butter. 1:30.

Lunch was brought to the others. Snowed a little. Wrote to the children. Lay with shut eyes as head continues to ache. 4:00-5:00. The others walked in the sunshine. Marie read to me after tea. 8:15. Supped – got first wire from children. Played bezique. Cannot get them to tell us anything about Valia.

Maria and Alexandra to Tobolsk

[**Maria**]: Ekaterinburg, **26th April**/9th May, 1918. Thank you, our little souls, for the telegram which we received yesterday before dinner; we are very happy, because this is the first news we received from you since we [have been] here.[280] We are happy to learn that you received our letters. Do you remember, Shvybz, our special corner near *Feodorovsky Sobor*, of T.G. [?] and of his students "Bokche" and of others; the story of the parrot that Al.[exei] told us and [which] always pleased Nyuta? We began to look like Vl.Al., do you understand? Do not forget that one of you asks for the address of P.Iv. and Styopa. Our life continues without changes. Yesterday we walked for such a long time in the little garden, because the weather was better and the sun warmed us – this reminded us of last summer at Tsarkoe Selo. We thought a lot about

[280] They received previous letters written from Tobolsk late, or not at all

you, when we were listening to a polka, at the station waiting room. Afterwards, someone sang a duet. Does Maksimochin still sing so loudly that the entire Tobolsk can hear? It is a shame that we do not know the words to “I do not mind”. You could probably ask for the words and of other songs.

Time goes so fast, that I have not had the time to read, not even once, the words of the songs that we have written down. Write to M. Zizi and Maria Nik. and tell them that we kiss [them] and think about them. I hope that Ch. wrote to all the sisters. Have you had news from Zinochka? While I write, Papa organizes his cigarettes that were packed loosely together during the

voyage but were not totally damaged. Papa kisses you all. A big "good morning" to A.A.[281]. You will see him tomorrow for sure. We have retained good memories of him. What do Baby and the others do? [...] We think about everybody with affection. We talk a lot about you and think about you all the time, dear ones. We wait for a letter from you. I kiss you affectionately, my precious ones. May the Lord protect you+++
Your Masha. It seems to me that you are being formal in using "Vous" in your letter. What became of Jimmy, Joy and Ortipo[282]?

[281] Alexei Volkov

[282] Three dogs they brought with them

[**Alexandra**]: We were very happy to receive Olga's telegram. Finally we know something about you and now we wait for a letter. My dear little souls, tomorrow it will be two weeks since we said goodbye. We are sad without you and miss you. Did you ask for a bag for the "medicines"? Do not forget to thank Marusya specifically and the others who conscientiously worked for nine months in the house. I believe that there are no people like them. Papa would have wanted Titar to come, to give old Chemodurov free time to rest, but he was not allowed to come with us after Petrograd or Tsarkoe Selo. On the other hand, anyone has the right to leave us. We do not know with whom, or how you are going to arrive, and that worries us a lot. But the Lord is merciful and will protect you. I hope that Tatiana and Zhilik have finished everything. Yashka probably does not understand anything. My dear ones, it is difficult to write and therefore my heart overflows. I hold you all tightly in my arms and bless you. My [good] wishes with affection to all.

Mama

From the 1918 diary of Alexandra Feodorovna

Yekaterinburg. **26 April**/9 May. Bright Week. 2°, Thursday... Every morning have to get out of bed for the guards & Com. who came to see if we are there...

27 April/10 May. 2°. Friday. 8:15. Told us to get up as Com. wished to see us before changing in ¼ of an hour & to look at the rooms. 0°. Yesterday they changed 3 times. - ... Again people came to ask now how much money we all have (we both have) & all had to write down the sum & give it up to the Sovdep to take care of... 8:15. Dined with the others. Played cards in Yevgeny Sergeevich's room. Talked with the Chief of the Guards. –

Maria and Alexandra to Tobolsk

[Maria]: Ekaterinburg, **27th April** / 10th May, 1918. Yesterday, we did not have time to send the letter because the guards were changed three times. I hope that today the letter is sent. All new guards come inside and check everything. Each time, Mama is obliged to get up from bed and meet the guards in her dressing gown. Yesterday an extraordinary event happened: Nyuta and I washed Mama's hair. Everything went well and her hair was not tangled, but I don't know what is going to happen today and everything is, for sure, going to come undone. The water here is very good, almost as good as in Tsarskoe Selo. In the bath tub the water looks light blue. Yesterday we went for a walk, like every day, till tea time. The sun was very warm, just like in Tobolsk, and in the evening, it penetrated the window of the second floor. We hope Kolya comes to play with you.

[Alexandra]: Papa reads to us a lot, Maria draws near the window and I rest lying down, as I always have a painful headache. Towards the evening, it is better and we stay in E.S.[283]'s room, playing bezique, Japanese

---

[283] Botkin

duraki[284], or kabbala. Today is two weeks since we left my dear ones. May God allow us to reunite soon. May Christ be with you. Papa and I kiss you affectionately and bless you. + Our best wishes to all.
Mama.

[Maria]: I am finishing the letter because there is nothing else to say. I hold you in my arms, my little souls. Warm wishes to everybody. May Christ be with you + Masha

Maria and Alexandra to Tobolsk

28 April/ 11 May, 1918. Good morning my dears. We just got up and kindled the fireplace, as it got very cold

[284] Card game "fools"

in the rooms. The wood is crackling cozily, reminds [me] of a freezing day in Tobolsk. Today we gave our dirty laundry to a washing woman. Nyuta also became a washer woman, washed Mama's kerchief, very well, and the dust rags. For a few days now, our guards are Latvians. It's probably not cozy for you, everything is packed. Did you pack my things, if you have not packed the book for births, then please ask N.T. to write. If it does not pan out, that is fine. Now you will probably be arriving soon. We don't know anything about you, really waiting for a letter. I continue drawing everything from Bem's book. Would you buy me some white paint. We have very little of it left. In the autumn, Zhilik got from somewhere a very nice one, flat and round. Who knows, maybe this letter will get to you just before your departure. May the Lord bless your journey and may He save you from all evil. Would like to know terribly who will be escorting you. Affectionate thoughts and prayers surround you – only to be together again sooner. I kiss you affectionately, my dear sweet ones and bless [you] +

[Alexandra]: Heartfelt regards to all and those who are staying [in Tobolsk]. I hope that Al. is feeling stronger and that the trip will not tire him out too much. Mama

[Maria:] We will take a walk this morning as it is warm. – They still do not allow Valya [to see us] - Tell Al. Regards to you and others. Was very sorry that did not have a chance to say goodbye. You will probably be terribly sad to leave that cozy house, etc., I remember all the cozy rooms and the garden. Do you still swing on the swing, or did the plank break? Papa and I kiss you all darlings. – May God keep you +. I send greetings to all in the house. Does Tolya come over to play? All the best and good journey if you are departing. Yours M.

From the 1918 diary of Nicholas Alexandrovich

1st May. Tuesday. We were overjoyed by the letters received from Tobolsk; I got one from Tatiana. We read each other's letters all morning. The weather was wonderful, warm. The guard was changed at noon, from the ranks of the same special frontier team—Russians and Latvians. The head—a presentable young man. Today they told us through Botkin that we are only allowed to walk one hour per day; and to the question why? The acting commandant replied "so that it is similar to a prisoner schedule." Food arrived on time. They bought us a *samovar*—at least we won't be dependent on the guards now. In the evening had four beziques during the game.

2 May. Wednesday. The application of "prisoner" schedule continued and expressed itself in that an old housepainter had painted over all our windows in all the rooms with lime. It started to seem like fog beyond the windows. Went to take a walk at 3 ½ and at 4.10 they chased us inside. There was not one extra soldier in the garden. The head guard did not speak to us once all this time one of the commissars was in the garden watching us, him and the guard! The weather was very nice, but the rooms got gloomy. Only the dining room benefitted because they took down the rug outside the window! Sednev has a cold with fever.

From the 1918 diary of Alexandra Feodorovna

Yekaterinburg. **2**/15 **May**. 10°. Wednesday... They were told not to go out this morning. An old man painted all the windows white fr. outside, so only at the top can see a bit of sky & looks as tho' there were a thick fogg [sic], not at all cosy...

Testimony of Ipatiev house guard Strekotin

The prisoners constantly tried to start conversations with the red guards. Once, during a walk, the Tsar quietly approached me and said: "Tell me, is this a large city- Ekaterinburg?"- "About as big as Moscow" – I responded, and having tossed the rifle up on the belt, I walked away.

Alexei to Kolya Derevenko

To Kolya. Tobolsk, **May** 1918. Dear Kolya. I send you my favourite cannon in exchange for yours. I think we will see each other before our departure. Regards to your Mama, Grandma and Feffffer. May God keep you and all of yours. + I kiss and cross you + Your Alexei

From the 1918 diary of Alexandra Feodorovna

Yekaterinburg. **3**/16 **May**. Thursday. They smeared over the therm[ometer]: so can't see temp; seems fine weather... Received coffee & chocolate from Ella. She has been sent out from Moscow & is at Perm (we read in the papers.)

From the 1918 diary of Nicholas Alexandrovich

3 May. Thursday. The day was grey but warm. One could feel the dampness in the rooms especially our two; the air entering the window flap was warmer than inside. I taught Maria to play trick-track. Sednev's fever is less, but he stayed in bed all day. Walked for exactly an hour. The guard order significantly increased, there were no more loiterers in the garden with us. During the day we got coffee, Easter eggs and chocolate from Ella in Perm. We lost electricity in the dining room, had supper with two candles in jars. In the hall, not everything had electricity either. Took a bath after Maria at 7 ½ o'cl.

From the 1918 diary of Alexandra Feodorovna

4/17 **May**. Great treat, cup of coffee... 3 weeks today we left Tobolsk. Maria wrote 22 times to the children -

& to Ella, & Zinochka Tolstaia (did not send it.)... Heard the children are already traveling...

Maria to Zinaida Tolstaya

Ekaterinburg, **4**/17 **May**, 1918. Christ Is Risen. My dear Z., Good wishes to you for this bright holiday. I apologize for [writing] so late, but we departed right before the holidays. It was very unexpected for us. Alexei happened to be sick, so the sisters had to stay with him. They are supposed to arrive here soon. Tell Rita that not that long ago we saw the little Sedusha. Today is three weeks since we left Tobolsk. It is so sad to be without the others, especially now during the holidays. We have settled in nicely here. The house is small but clean, shame that it's right in the city so the garden is rather small. When the others arrive, not sure how we will settle, there are not that many rooms. I live with Papa and Mama in one, where we spend almost the entire day. Just now we went out into the garden, the weather is grey and it is raining. On the way, the weather was wonderful. We used horses for 260 versts until Tyumen. The roads were awful, we were jolted terribly. The paper with which our things were wrapped rubbed out in places. Tobacco fell out of the cigarettes. But strangely no glass broke. We took the medicines with us and arrived safely. Rode for two days, stayed the nights in villages. Took horses across the Irtysh, and walked across the Tura on foot and a few *sazhens* to the banks—in a ferry. Mama withstood the journey surprisingly well, but now of course feels tired and has a headache almost daily. Doctor Botkin came with us, the poor man had kidney colic on the way, he was suffering a lot. We stopped in a village and they put him to bed there, he rested for two hours and continued with us. Luckily the pains did not happen again. And how are you all? The sisters wrote that we got news from you. If you want to write to me, my address is: Ekaterinburg, the Regional Executive Committee. To the Chairman, to be given to me. Have you had any news from Tili? Regards to all yours and Nik. Dm. I kiss you, Rita, and the children affectionately. I wish you all the best. May the Lord keep you. It was terribly sad that we were not able to go to the cathedral even once and venerate the relics of St. Ioann of Tobolsk.

From the 1918 diary of Nicholas Alexandrovich

4 May. Friday. It rained all day. Found out that the children left Tobolsk, but Avdeyev did not say when. He opened the door to the locked room, which we intended for Alexei. It turned out to be large and brighter than we thought, as it has two windows; our oven heats it well.

The steamer "Rus" on which Olga, Tatiana, Anastasia and Alexei traveled to Ekaterinburg to join their parents and sister

Took a walk for half hour due to rain. The food was plentiful, as it was this entire time, and came on time. The commandant, his assistant, head of the guard and electro-technicians ran around all the rooms, fixing cords, despite which we had supper in the dark.

5 May. Saturday. The weather was damp and rainy. The light in the rooms is dim and it is incredibly boring! During a game with Maria I got a real trick-track, - as rare as four beziques. Took a walk for half hour in the afternoon. Waited for supper from 8 o'cl. until 9 o'cl. The electric light in the dining room was fixed, but not in the hall.

Maria to Elizaveta Feodorovna[285]

5 May. Ekaterinburg. He Is Risen Indeed! We kiss you dearest, three times. Thank you very much for the eggs, chocolate, coffee. Mama drank her first cup of coffee with great pleasure, it was very good. It's very good for her headaches, and as it happens, we had not taken any with us. We learned from the newspapers that you have been sent away from your convent and were very sad for you. It is strange that we should all end up in the same province under arrest.[286] We hope that you will be able to spend the summer somewhere out of town, in Verkhoturie or in some monastery. We have so missed having a church. My address: Ekaterinburg, The Regional Executive Committee, To the Chairman for transmission to me. May God keep you + Your loving goddaughter

[285] Alexandra's sister, widow Nicholas's uncle Grand Duke Sergei, who was assassinated by terrorists in 1905

[286] Grand Duchess Elizaveta was sent to Perm, later to be transferred to Alapaevsk and ultimately murdered there along with other extended family members

From the 1918 diary of Alexandra Feodorovna

Yekaterinburg. **6**/19 **May**. Righteous Job the Long-Suffering. Sunday. Nicholas's 50th B.D... Cannot find out whether the children left or not – get no letters from anybody...

From the 1918 diary of Nicholas Alexandrovich

6 May. Sunday. I lived to 50 years, it seems strange even to me! The weather stayed wonderful, as if custom ordered. At 11 ½ the same Batushka with the deacon conducted moleben, which was very nice. Took a walk with Maria before dinner. In the afternoon sat in the garden for an hour and a quarter, basked in the warm sun. We do not get any news from the children and started to doubt, had they left Tobolsk?

8 May. Tuesday. In the morning we heard thunder; outside of the city [a thunderstorm] passed, but we had a few downpours. I read until dinner, the 4th part of "War and Peace", which I wasn't familiar with before. Took a walk with Maria. Avdeyev offered for us to look at two rooms near the dining room; the guard is now located in the cellar. Waited for our dinner and supper for over a half hour. Got a congratulatory telegram from Olga for 6th May.

From the 1918 diary of Alexandra Feodorovna

Yekaterinburg. **8**/21 **May.** Tuesday... Heard children probably come [sic] to-morrow or Thursday. Have given us a room for Baby, 1 for the gentlemen & 1 for the men (where the guard was at first) ...

From the 1918 diary of Nicholas Alexandrovich

9 May. Wednesday. A semi-clear day with some rain. Both Maria and I got into reading "War and Peace", and before tea enjoyed trick-track. Took an hour long walk. We still do not know where the children are and when will they all arrive? Tiresome unknown!

Last known photograph of Olga and Alexei, taken on steamer Rus

From Maria to Tobolsk

10 May. This morning we are going for a walk, as it is warm. Valya Dolgorukov is still not allowed to see us. Greetings to others. I am so sorry I was not able to say goodbye to them. You must be very sad to leave Tobolsk, such a pleasant house, etc.; I remember the cozy rooms and the garden. Do you play on the swing, or did the plank already break? Papa and I kiss you lovingly, my dears. May God keep you. I send greetings to everyone in the house. Best wishes and a safe journey if you are already leaving. Your Maria

From the memoirs of Pierre Gilliard

We reached Ekaterinburg in the night, the train being stopped at some distance from the station... The next morning... Nagorny, the sailor attached to Alexis Nicolaevitch [sic], passed my window, carrying the sick boy in his arms; behind him came the Grand Duchesses loaded with valises and small personal belongings. I tried to get out but was roughly pushed back into the carriage by a sentry... Tatiana Nicolaevna came last, carrying her little dog and struggling to drag a heavy brown valise. It was raining, and I saw her feet sink into the mud at every step.

Nagorny tried to come to her assistance; he was roughly pushed back by one of the commissaries. [sic]

From the 1918 diary of Nicholas Alexandrovich

10 May. Thursday. In the morning they announced during one hour that the children are a few hours from the city, then that they arrived at the station, and finally, that they arrived at the house, although their train stood here at 2 in the morning! Tremendous joy to see them again and embrace them after four weeks of separation and uncertainty. Mutual questions and answers were endless. Very few letters got to them and from them. They lived through a lot of emotional suffering, in Tobolsk as well as during the three days of travel. Snow fell overnight and stayed all day. Of all those who arrived with them, only the cook Kharitonov and Sednev's nephew were allowed to [join] us. In the afternoon we went out into the garden for about 20 minutes – it was cold and desperately muddy. Waited for delivery of the beds and necessary things from the station until late night, but in vain, so all the daughters had to sleep on the floor. Alexei spent the night in Maria's bed. In the evening, as if on purpose, he injured his knee and suffered greatly all night and prevented us from sleeping.

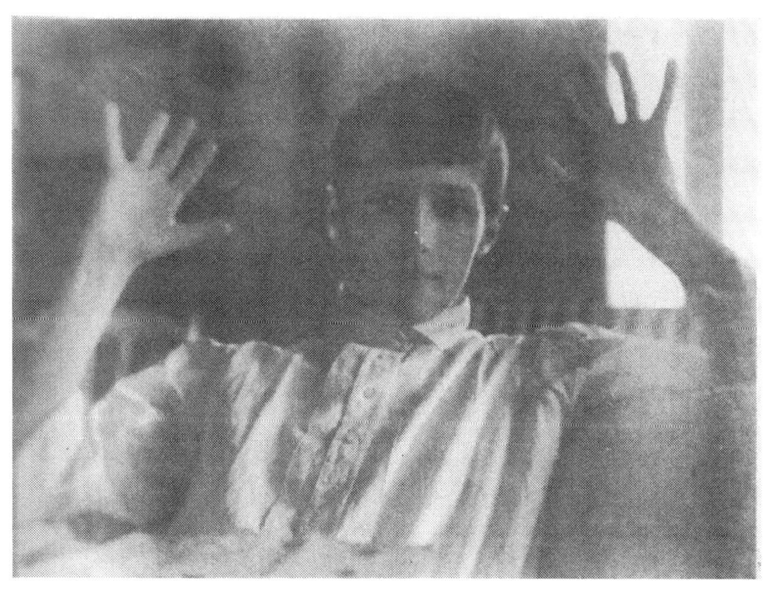

From the 1918 diary of Alexandra Feodorovna

Yekaterinburg. **10**/23 **May**. 1°. Thursday. All covered in snow. 4 weeks we left Tobolsk. – Towards 11 the girls suddenly turned up with Aleksei - thank God - such joy to have them again. Nobody else let in all day except for the cook Kharitonov & boy Sednyov, - only hand luggage brought – no news about the rest... Put Baby into Marie's bed, & arranged the 4 girls on cloaks & cushions on the floor in the adjoining room. Kharitonov on short sofa, Sednyov on two chairs, - after night Baby woke up every hour from pain in his knee, slipped & hurt it when getting into bed*. – Cannot walk yet, one carries him. Lost 14 pounds since his illness. – Saw fr. far in the night great fire burning. - * Tore sinews in the knee most probably. –

11/24 **May**. Ludwig's[287] B.D. May's[288] B.D. Friday. Baby & I had our meals in our bedrooms; his pains varied... Vladimir Nikolaevich[289] came to see Baby & change his compressings [sic] but in Avdeev's presence so he cld [sic] not say a word. – Chemodurov left as not feeling well – Was completely undressed & searched before leaving the house.- After supper Nagorny & Trup [sic] (& Joy) came – hours questioned & searched. All our other people are being sent back to Tobolsk, only won't know where Trina, Nastinka [sic], Tatischev, & Volkov[290] have been taken & Yevgeny Sergeevich wrote petition[291] for Avdeev to take to the Regional Committee to beg for Zhilik, as absolutely indispensable, he shld be with Baby, who suffers very much. - Baby slept in his room with Nagorny – the four girls next door, not all beds brought yet. Baby had bad night again.

---

[287] Louis of Battenberg, her brother in law

[288] Countess Maria Musina-Pushkina

[289] Dr Derevenko who also arrived in Ekaterinburg with his family

[290] Only Volkov survived the revolution, the other three were executed

[291] This petition was not granted

From the 1918 diary of Nicholas Alexandrovich

11 May. Friday. Since morning we waited for our people from Tobolsk to be let in and for the delivery of the rest of our luggage. Decided to let my old man Chemodurov go for a rest and temporarily take in Trupp. They only allowed him and Nagorny to enter in the evening and questioned and searched them in the commandant's room for an hour and a half. Although we all sat in the bedroom together, I was reading a lot; started "Unfinished novel" by Apukhtin.

12 May. Saturday. Everyone slept well, except Alexei, who was moved to his own room yesterday. He continues to have terrible pains, which alleviate periodically. The weather was completely appropriate for our mood, wet snow with 3° of warmth. We conducted talks though Evg.[eniy] S.[ergeievich] with the head of the Regional Soviet about allowing m-r [sic] Gilliard to join us. The children unpacked some of their things after an unbelievably long search of them in the commandant's room. Walked for about 20 minutes.

Testimony of Ipatiev house guard Yakimov

So, we were guarding Tsar Nicholas Alexandrovich with his family. All lived at the Ipatiev house, that is: the Tsar, his wife Alexandra Feodorovna, son Alexei and daughters – Olga, Tatiana, Maria and Anastasia. The non-family members who lived with them were: Doctor Botkin; "lady-in-waiting" as we called her, Demidova; the cook Kharitonov, and lackey Trupp. Botkin was older, grey, tall. He wore a blue set: jacket, vest and pants, starched undershirt and tie; short boots on his feet. Demidova was a tall, plump blonde, about 30-35 years old. She dressed well, not like a servant. She definitely wore a corset: by her figure one could tell that she was tightened... The cook was about 50 years old, short, stocky, strawberry blond [hair], dark moustache, not very long, he shaved his beard on his cheeks and chin, leaving it under and around the moustache; on one cheek he had a mole with long hair growing out of it. He wore a black jacket with a solid standing collar, black pants, short boots. The lackey was about 60 years old, tall, thin. He shaved the hair on his head and face. Wore some sort of a jacket, dark-grey pants and boots. Also, with the imperial family lived a boy, around 14 years old. I do not know his name. He was tall, thin, with a white face, long straight nose, wide mouth, thin lips, eyes not particularly large but deep set. He wore a dark-grey jacket with a standing collar, pants and short boots made from the same material, but I had also seen him in long boots.

Testimony of Ipatiev house guard Strekotin

The ex-emperor always wore the same military khaki uniform... he was taller than average, thick, fair-haired, with grey eyes, lively and impetuous, he twirled his ginger moustache often. The Tsarevich - Alexei, wore the same [uniform] as the Tsar in the same colonel rank, [he was] brunet, with black unhappy eyes, thin, ill-looking. His severe untreatable illness completely paralyzed both of his legs, apparently even before the revolution, which was why he was always carried outside by the Tsar himself. He carefully picked him up, pulled him close to his wide chest, and the other would grab his father's thick short neck with his arms, while his thin, whip-like weak legs hung limply. Two of the daughters were blonde with grey eyes, of medium height and looked very much alike. They were always together, and both seemed merry and talkative. The other two young ladies did not look like each other. One of them - Tatiana[292], a plump, healthy looking brunette. The other, i.e., the eldest Olga[293], was taller than average, thin, pale faced, ill looking, she did not take a lot of walks in the garden, did not socialize with any of her sisters, mostly stayed near her brother. The daughters always dressed well, changed dresses often, and accessorized with gold and diamonds.

From the 1918 diary of Nicholas Alexandrovich

13 May. Sunday. Slept wonderfully, except Alexei. His pains persist, but with long breaks. He stayed in bed in our room. There was no [religious] service. The weather was the same, snow on the roofs. As in all the recent days, V.N. Derevenko came to examine Alexei; today a dark gentleman was accompanying him, who we thought was a doctor[294]. After a short walk we entered the shed where our large baggage was dropped off with commandant Avdeyev. The search of some unopened chests continued. Started to read the works of Saltykov[-Schedrin] from the bookcase of the owner of the house. In the evening played bezique.

[292] Strekotin probably means Maria

[293] Strekotin probably means Tatiana

[294] This later turned out to be the new commandant, Yakov Yurovsky

Testimony of Ipatiev house guard Yakimov

About the Tsar, Avdeyev talked with malice. He cursed him in any way he could, called him “bloody” and “bloodthirsty”. The main thing he cursed him for was the war: that the Tsar wanted this war and for three years he spilled the blood of the workers, and that masses of these workers were shot in this war and also for the strikes. From his words we were to understand that he received the appointment as Commandant of the House of Special Purpose[295] as a reward from the revolution, because he prevented Yakovlev from taking away the Tsar. And it was obvious that Avdeyev was very satisfied with this appointment. He was so happy when he talked at a rally, and promised the workers: “I will take you all to the house and show you the Tsar”. Avdeyev was a drunkard. He loved drinking and drank all the time, ... here [Popov house[296]] and at the Ipatiev house. His associates drank with him. One time, Avdeyev got so drunk that he fell over in one of the lower rooms of the house. Right at this time, Beloborodov arrived and asked for him. Someone among Avdeyev’s associates lied that he stepped out.

[295] What Ipatiev house was referred to by the guard and their command

[296] House near Ipatiev’s where the guard and some of the suite who followed stayed

But the way he ended up on the lower floor was after visiting the imperial family in this drunk state, he went to see them that drunk. While drunk, they [Avdeyev and associates] made a lot of noise in the commandant's room, yelled, slept in a pile, wherever they fell, and made the place a dirty mess. Sang songs which could not have been pleasant to the Tsar. They sang "You fell victim in a fatal battle", "Let us reject the old world", "Walk together, comrades". At times when Avdeyev was absent, a member of the imperial family petitioned Moshkin with some request, and he always said that they need to wait until Avdeyev returns. When Avdeyev came back and Moshkin passed on the request, Avdeyev had the response: "To the devil with them!" Returning from the imperial family's rooms, Avdeyev would often tell us that he refused one of their requests. This refusal apparently gave him pleasure. He talked about it happily. For example, they asked him to permit them to open windows, and he was telling us how he refused it. I don't know how he referred to the Tsar directly, but behind his back he called him "Nikolashka".

From the 1918 diary of Nicholas Alexandrovich

14 May. Monday. The weather remained warm. I read a lot. Alexei feels better in general. Took a walk for an hour in the afternoon. After tea, Sednev and Nagorny were called in for questioning at the Regional Soviet. In the evening they continued inspecting the daughters' belongings with them present. The guard outside our window shot at our house, because he thought he saw that someone was moving by the window (after 10 o'cl in the evening) – in my opinion he was just fooling around with the rifle, as guards often do.

Testimony of Ipatiev house guard Yakimov

Avdeyev used to have conversations with his comrades about Rasputin. He used to say that there were a lot of rumours, and frequent newspaper articles, that the Empress slept with Rasputin.

From the 1918 diary of Alexandra Feodorovna

14/27 **May**. Coronation Day. Monday... Baby had again not a good night, Yevgeny Sergeevich sat up part of the night as to let Nagorny sleep... Baby spent the day in our room, Vladimir Nikolaevich did not come, don't know why. Children darning linen with Niuta - At 6:30 Sednyov & Nagorny were taken off to the District

Committee, don't know the reason. The others played cards with Baby. On the whole better, tho' at times very strong pains. Yevgeny Sergeevich spent the night with Baby.

15/28 **May**. Tuesday... Vladimir Nikolaevich came at last, can't speak to him as Avdeev always present. I asked when at last Nagorny will be let in again, as don't know how we shall get on without him- Avdeev answers does not know – fear that shant [sic] see him nor Sednyov again[297]. Baby suffered very much for a while, then after medic. & candle got better...

Digital recreation of the Grand Duchesses' room at Ipatiev house

[297] Both were murdered

Testimony of Ipatiev house guard Yakimov

Nothing was left of my ideas about the Tsar which I had before I became a guard. I started to think differently of them after I saw them with my own eyes. I started to feel pity for them as human beings. In my head an idea was born: let them escape; what can I do to allow them to escape. I never told anyone, but I had an idea to talk to the doctor, Derevenko, who used to visit them. But then I was wary of him, thought I don't know what kind of person he is. His face had no expression when he was leaving them, and he never said a word about them. So, I was too wary. Before I got hired as a guard, having not seen or known them, I was also somewhat guilty towards them. Avdeyev and the comrades would be singing revolutionary songs at times, and I would sing along with them a bit. But once I saw what's what, I quit all that, and almost all of us, if not all, used to criticize Avdeyev for that.

From the 1918 diary of Nicholas Alexandrovich

15 May. Tuesday. Today is a month since our arrival here. Alexei feels the same—only the restful breaks are longer. The weather was hot, stuffy, but cool inside. Had dinner at 2 o'clock. Walked and sat in the garden an hour and ¼. Alix cut my hair successfully.

16 May. Wednesday. The day was excellent. We took a walk in the morning and in the afternoon warmed ourselves in the sun for a long time. Alexei is feeling better. Vl. Nik. put a cast on him. Had supper at 8 o'cl. in daylight. Alix went to bed early due to a migraine. Nothing at all about Sednev and Nagorny!

18 May. Friday. It was raining during the night and during the day too. Started reading the second volume of Saltykov "The Lords Golovlyovs". In the rooms it was grey and tedious. Took a half hour walk. The fence was raised in front of Alexei's windows.

From the 1918 diary of Alexandra Feodorovna

18/31 **May**. Friday... Hammering hard, making wooden pailing [sic] before Baby's windows higher. Vladimir Nikolaevich not let in as Avdeev was not there. The others went out. Remained the whole day with shut eyes, head got worse towards the evening...

Testimony of Ipatiev house guard Strekotin

The prisoners were taken outside for a walk twice a day, at 10 in the morning and at 4 in the afternoon. 30 minutes each time. At this time, in the garden and in the yard, the guard was increased from among the volunteers in the team, there were always plenty of volunteers. The prisoners did not all always go outside for a walk. In particular, most rarely went out the four people who were imprisoned along with the imperial family. Another who rarely went out, and never for long, was the Tsaritsa. She was serious, haughty and silent. The Tsar was almost always wearing the same military uniform with a cockade in his military hat. The same with the Heir. The Heir was always carried by the Emperor himself during walks, he sat him into a wheelchair and wheeled him around the garden, stopping on paths to give him pebbles, he [the Heir] then tossed them into bushes, or he [the Emperor] picked flowers for him, or branches from bushes.

From the 1918 diary of Nicholas Alexandrovich

19 May. Saturday. The weather was grey and warm. I read all morning. Took a walk for an hour and some minutes before tea. Alexei has almost no pains. The greenery is getting there bit by bit. Supper was brought two hours [late] again – Kharitonov warmed it up for 8 o'cl. I played some trick-track with Maria.

Testimony of Ipatiev house guard Strekotin

The prisoners ate well and got plenty of rest. Their food came from the best cafeteria in town. Their clothes were washed well, starched and ironed. They were taken outside to the garden twice a day...

Testimony of Ipatiev house guard Yakimov

The imperial family's meals were brought from Soviet Cafeteria, the one on the corner of Voznesensky and Main Prospect... But later, still under Avdeyev, they were allowed to cook their own meals at home. Provisions for this were delivered from the Regional soviet by some special delivery man. The nuns from the monastery brought them milk, eggs and bread. There were prayer services in the house, but the entire time I stayed at the house, there were only three services. Twice they were given by the priest Storozhev and once by the priest Melendin. But there were services before us. I know this because I was the one who went to get the priests when there was to be a prayer service. During Avdeyev, there were two services at the house while I was there.

From the 1918 diary of Alexandra Feodorovna

20 May/2 June... Sunday... Dressed; took Baby into the big room with his bed & had *Obednitsa*. A new Priest...

Testimony of Father Ioann Storozhev

On Sunday, **20 May**/2 June, 1918, I performed the usual liturgy service at the Ekaterininsky Cathedral, and just having returned home at 10 o'clock in the morning, settled in to have tea, when someone knocked at the front door of my apartment. I personally opened the door and saw in front of me a soldier of nondescript appearance, with a red face and small shifty eyes.[298] He was wearing an old jacket of khaki color, on his head - a worn military cap. There were no epaulets, nor cockade, of course. No weapons could be seen on him.

---

[298] This was Yakimov

Father Ioann Storozhev

To my question of what he needs, the soldier responded: "You are requested to perform a service for Romanov." Not understanding whom he is referring to, I asked "Which Romanov?", "You know, the former tsar", he explained. From subsequent discussion it turned out that Nicholas Alexandrovich Romanov is asking to perform the next *obednitsa* - "He wrote over here asking for some kind of *obednitsa* service" the visitor announced. Structured *obednitsa* is usually performed for the military when for one reason or another it is not possible to perform a liturgy. Normally

this prayer service is combined with a subsequent liturgy, but is significantly shorter, as after *obednitsa* no Eucharist is offered. Having agreed to perform the service, I noted that it would be necessary to bring a deacon with us. The soldier insistently objected for a long time against inviting a deacon, stating that "the commandant" ordered to bring only one priest, but I insisted, and together with this soldier we went to the Cathedral, where I got everything needed for the service, invited deacon Buimirov, with whom, accompanied by the same soldier, we went to the Ipatiev house. Since the time the Romanov family was placed here, the house was surrounded by a double plank fence. The cabby stopped near the first outer wooden fence. In front walked the soldiers who accompanied us, behind them the deacon and I.
The external guard let us pass; having been delayed for a short time near the gate locked from within, on the side of the house that earlier belonged to Solomirsky, we entered behind the second fence right at the gate of the Ipatiev house.

Entrance to the Ipatiev house

Here stood numerous young men armed with rifles, dressed in general civilian clothes, on their belts hung hand grenades. These armed men apparently were the guards. They took us through the gates into the courtyard and from here through a side door into the ground floor of the Ipatiev house.

Having ascended the staircase, we entered the upstairs towards the main door, and then through the hallway - into the study which "the commandant" occupied. Everywhere, on the stairs as well as on the platform, and in the front room were guards - the same type of young men armed with same rifles and hand grenades in civilian clothes.

Inside the commandant's actual room we found two middle-aged men, who were wearing tunics. One of them was lying in bed and seemingly sleeping, the other was silently smoking cheap cigarettes. In the center of the room there was a table, on it a *samovar*, bread, butter. On the piano, which was also in this room, there were rifles, hand grenades and some other things. It was dirty, messy, disordered.

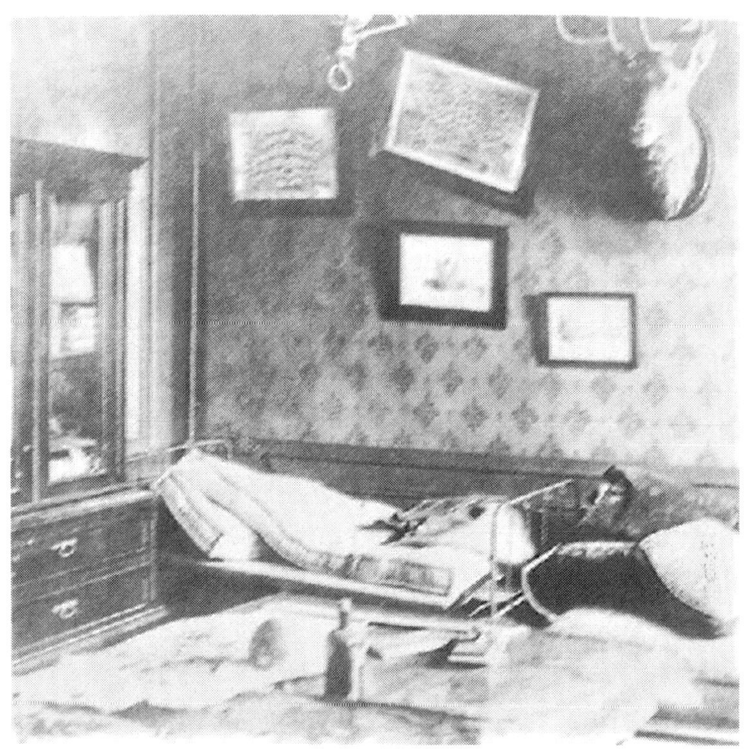

The best room on the lower floor, which was connected with the staircase, served as the commandant's office

At the moment of our arrival the commandant was not in this room. Soon some young man arrived, wearing a tunic, khaki pants with a wide leather belt with a holster in which was a large revolver; this man's appearance was that of a typical "workman". I did not notice anything unusual, nothing outstanding, attention grabbing or sharp either in this man's appearance, or his behaviour. I soon guessed, rather than understood, that this gentleman is "the commandant of the house of special purpose", as the

Ipatiev house was referred to by the Bolsheviks during the time the Romanovs were imprisoned there. The commandant stared at me silently, without greeting, I saw him for the first time and did not even know his surname, and now memorized it. To my question of which service we need to perform, he replied "they are asking for *obednitsa*". Neither I, nor the deacon engaged in any conversation with the commandant but I only asked if I would be allowed to offer *prosfora* to the Romanovs after the service, which I showed him. The commandant quickly looked over the *prosfora* and after a long thought returned it to the deacon, saying: "it can be given to them, but I must warn you there will be no other conversations". I could not help but respond that I do not plan to have any conversation at all. My response apparently bothered the commandant a bit and he said a few times "That's right, no other ones besides those about religious subjects". We got dressed with the deacon in commandant's room, meanwhile the bucket with burning coals was brought into the commandant's room by one of Romanovs' servants /not Chemodurov, - this one I never saw at the Ipatiev house, but met him later, after the Bolsheviks left Ekaterinburg/. This servant was tall, I remember, in a grey suit with metal buttons. .. Having dressed in holy robes, taking with us all that was necessary for the service, we walked out of commandant's room into the hallway. The commandant himself opened the door which led into the hall, letting me go in first, with me walked Father Deacon, and the commandant entered last. The hall into which we entered through an arch was connected with a smaller room - a sitting room, where close to the front corner I noticed a table set up for the service. But I was distracted from looking at the hall and the sitting room because as soon as we stepped into the hall we saw that three figures walked from the window: they were Nicholas Alexandrovich, Tatiana Nikolaevna and another older daughter, but which one exactly I did not have a chance to see.

The hall at Ipatiev house

In the next room, separated from the hall by an arch, was Alexandra Feodorovna, two younger daughters and Alexei Nikolaevich. The latter was lying down on a (folding) cot and I was amazed by his appearance: he was pale to a point of transparency, thin, and he surprised me by his great height. In general his appearance was extremely sickly and only his eyes were lively and bright and looked at me with obvious curiosity - a new person. He was dressed in a white undershirt and covered with a blanket down from his waist. His bed stood by the right wall from the entrance, just past the arch. Near the bed stood an armchair, in which Alexandra Feodorovna sat, wearing a loose dress, of dark lilac color.

Room “separated by arch from the hall”: recliner seen by the right wall probably used by Alexei or Alexandra

There were no jewels on her at all, and I did not notice any on the daughters either. Alexandra Feodorovna's great height was noticeable, as was her manner of holding herself, the manner that cannot be called anything but "majestic". She sat in an armchair but got up energetically and steadily when we entered and exited, as well as when during the service I preached "peace to all", read the Testament or when we sang the more important prayers.

Another view of the room past the hall

Next to Alexandra Feodorovna's chair, farther along the right wall stood both their younger daughters, and then Nicholas Alexandrovich himself; the elder daughters stood in the arch, and a bit away from them, behind the arch in the hall stood: a tall older gentleman and some lady /they later explained to me that this was Doctor Botkin and Alexandra Feodorovna's maid. Farther down stood two manservants: the one who brought us the bucket, and the other, whose appearance I did not notice and do not remember. The "commandant" stood in the corner of the hall by the farthest window the entire time, hence at a rather decent distance from the parishioners. No one else at all was either in the hall, or in the room past the arch. Nicholas Alexandrovich was dressed in a khaki tunic, the same color slacks and tall boots. On his chest was an officer's St George Cross. There were no epaulets. All four daughters wore dark skirts and simple white blouses. Their hair was cut rather short in the back; they looked cheerful, and I must say, almost merry. Nicholas Alexandrovich impressed me by his firm gait, his calmness and especially his manner of looking directly and openly into one's eyes. I noticed no sign of emotional oppression in him. It seemed to me that I saw some barely noticeable grey hairs in his beard, the beard was longer and wider when I was there this first time than on the fourteenth of July; when it looked to me like Nicholas Alexandrovich cut the beard all around. As for Alexandra Feodorovna, her appearance was somehow tired, even sickly. I forgot to mention one thing that constantly caught my attention - the special respect to my holy rank with which every member of the Romanov family bowed in response to my silent greeting to them at the exit of the hall after the service ended. The service - *obednitsa*, we performed in front of the table set up in the center of the room behind the arch. The table was covered with a silk cloth with ancient Russian style design. On the table, in proper order and the usual church symmetry stood numerous icons. There were small, medium and very small folding icons with vestments – all these of unique beauty in their ancient style and workmanship. There were simple icons without vestments, among them I noticed "Our Lady of the Sign [*Znamenie*]"/Novgorod, "It Is Truly Meet" icon, I cannot remember the rest.

Artist's (unknown) rendition of a prayer service at the Ipatiev house

I also noticed the icon of The Mother of God, which at the 20th May service took center place. This icon was apparently very ancient. I am afraid to insist, but I think this image was referred to as "Feodorovskaya". This icon was in golden vestments without jewels. This icon is not among those you showed me, - neither are folding ones, nor "*Znamenie*" nor "It Is Truly Meet", they are not here. The icon you are showing me without vestments, only with a metal frame, with a torn off crown - it is not called "Feodorovskaya" but "Kazanskaya" - this I insist on categorically. This icon was not at the first or at the second service, neither on the table nor on a wall. Having stood up at our spots in front of the table with the icons we started the service, and the deacon spoke the *ectenia*[299] petitions while I sang. Two female voices sang along with me /I think it was Tatiana Nikolaevna and one other among them/, occasionally Nicholas Alexandrovich sang along in a low bass/ he sang "Our Father" this way for instance and etc./ The service passed cheerfully and well, they prayed very zealously. At the end of the service I did the usual "release" with a holy cross and for a minute stopped in bewilderment: should I approach the parishioners with the crucifix so they could kiss it, or was this not allowed, and with this wrong step I could perhaps create difficulties for the Romanov family in being able to satisfy their spiritual needs by having future services. I snuck a look at the commandant, to see what he was doing and how he would feel about my intention to approach with the crucifix. It seemed to me that Nicholas Alexandrovich also threw a quick look towards the commandant.

---

[299] Litany

Father Ioann Storozhev's prayer book and crucifix used at the Ipatiev house service[300]

The latter stood in his spot, in the farthest corner and calmly stared at us. Then I took a step forward and simultaneously Nicholas Alexandrovich approached the cross first with firm and even steps, without moving his steady gaze away from me, and kissed the crucifix, behind him approached Alexandra Feodorovna and all four daughters, while I myself approached Alexei Nikolaevich lying in his bed.

He was looking at me with such lively eyes that I thought "doubtless he will now say something", but Alexei Nikolaevich silently kissed the crucifix. Father deacon gave him and Alexandra Feodorovna each a *prosfora*. Then Dr Botkin and the aforementioned

[300] Photos courtesy of Freeman's Auction House, Philadelphia, PA.

servants - the maid and two manservants, approached the crucifix.

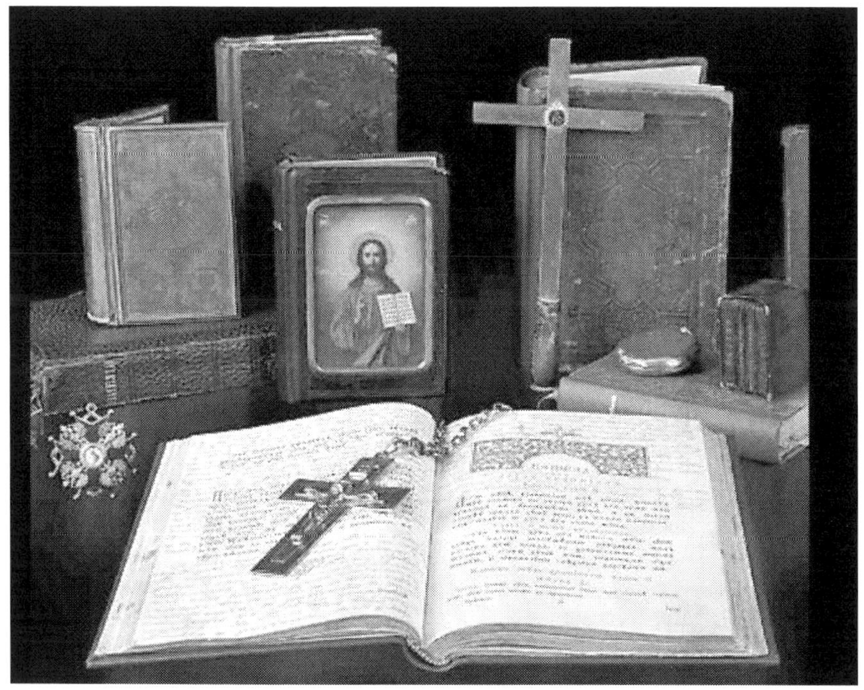

Actual prayer book and crucifix (and other items), used at the prayer service for the imperial family[301]

We undressed in the commandant's room, folded our things and went home, having been escorted through the gates and past the guards to the fence by some soldier.

301 Photo courtesy of Freeman's Auction House

From the 1918 diary of Nicholas Alexandrovich

20 May. Sunday. At 11 o'cl there was *obednitsa* for us; Alexei was there lying in his bed. The weather was marvelous, hot. Took a walk after the service and in the afternoon, before tea. It's intolerable to sit here locked up and be unable to go out into the garden when one wants to, and spend a nice evening in fresh air! Prison regime!

Testimony of Ipatiev house guard Yakimov

One thing I witnessed first-hand of the life of the imperial family: they used to sing sometimes. I had the chance to hear their spiritual singing. They sang the Cherubic hymn. They also sang some secular song. I did not hear the words, but the melody was sad... I heard only female voices, never any male ones... During the [prayer] service, from a distance I heard female and male voices: they must have sung themselves.

From the 1918 diary of Nicholas Alexandrovich

21 May. Monday. A wonderful warm day. Took a walk twice. Downstairs in the guardroom there was another shot; the commandant came to find out if the bullet went through the floor? Alexei had no pains at all; as usual, he is spending the day in bed in our room. I finished Saltykov's second volume. In the evening we played bezique.

Testimony of Ipatiev house guard Strekotin

The Tsar had a habit of coming over to the window and staring at the garden intensely, he ignored the guards' warnings. The red guard Safonov, V.Ya. decided to teach the Tsar a lesson. Once he warned him but the latter continued to stand at the window, so Safonov took aim at him, and when the Tsar turned around, apparently intending to walk away, he shot towards the ceiling right by the window... After this the Tsar never again approached the window.

From the 1918 diary of Nicholas Alexandrovich

22 May. Tuesday. Hot and stuffy in the rooms. Only took a walk in the afternoon. Around 5 o'clock a strong thunder shower passed and another in the evening. Alexei feels much better, and his knee got much smaller. My legs and back ached. And slept badly.

Testimony of Ipatiev house guard Strekotin

In the garden, hammocks were hanged for them, but they were used almost exclusively by the daughters.

The prisoners often attempted to start conversations with the guards, especially the daughters and the Tsar. They said for example: We are bored, it was merrier in Tobolsk. What is your name? Can you guess what this little dog's name is? (they always brought dogs outside with them, which lived with them, I think two or three dogs). Or: What is this? What is this for? They even showed photographs. For example: in one photograph, together with all the imperial daughters was Rasputin. Of course, any conversation with the prisoners was forbidden, but there was still some talk. Especially difficult was the indoor upstairs post where the prisoners lived. There, almost every minute, the prisoners walked by the guard post, and the daughters especially would smile at the guard every time and start a conversation, they would stop at the post and it was all very repulsive and annoying. I stood at that post only once, and declined after that.

From the 1918 diary of Nicholas Alexandrovich

23 May. Wednesday. We changed the clocks two hours forward. Today Alexei got dressed and was taken outside for fresh air through the main entrance. The weather was wonderful. Alix and Tatiana sat with him for an hour and a half. We took a walk in the garden at the usual time. My mood was sour. Went to bed while still daylight.

From the 1918 diary of Alexandra Feodorovna

23 May/5 June. Wednesday... Glorious morning. Baby did not sleep well, leg ached probably more because Vladimir Nikolaevich took it yesterday out of the splint wh. held the knee firm. Yevgeny Sergeevich carried him out before the house & put in my wheeling chair & Tatiana & I sat out with him in the sun before the entry [sic] with a pailing erected around- ... Are putting yet higher planks before all our windows, so that not even the tops of the trees can be seen- then one will have the double windows taken out & at last we can open the windows. – 4:15. The others went out...

24 May/6 June. My real B.D. ... Maria carried Baby out & put him on my basket long chair for half an hour. Olga & I sat with him, & after Nicholas & the other 3 went out into the garden. Very hot, awfully stuffy in rooms...

Alexei to Kolya Derevenko

[**Exact date unknown**] Dear Kolya, all the sisters send greetings to you, your Mama and Grandma. I feel well myself. My head was aching all day, but now the pain is gone completely. I embrace you warmly. Greetings to the Botkins from all of us. Always yours, Alexei THE END

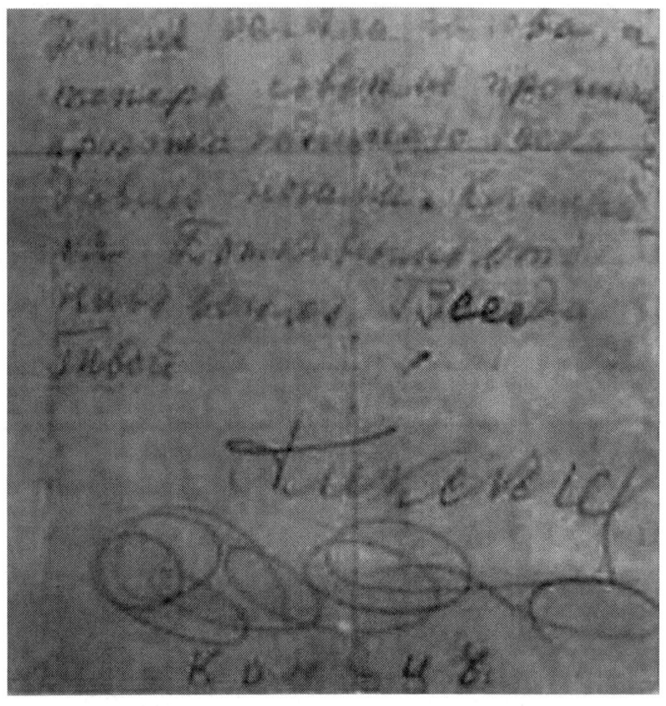

Letter from Alexei to his friend Kolya, believed to be his last letter. At the bottom Alexei signed it and wrote "THE END"

Recollection of Nikolai "Kolya" Derevenko

I was a little boy, just twelve years old. I knew nothing of the evil in people's souls. We were living at the Popov house near the Ipatiev house. In the middle of the summer of 1918, I was afraid and worried for

Alexei. I wanted to see him and at the same time I am sure he wanted to see me too.

Ipatiev house (right) and Popov house

From the 1918 diary of Nicholas Alexandrovich

24 May. Thursday. All day I was suffering with hem[moroidal] pains, therefore lay down on bed, as it was more convenient to make compresses. Alix and Alexei stayed outside in fresh air for about a half hour, and we did for an hour after them. The weather was wonderful.

25 May. Friday. Spent the birthday of dear Alix in bed with strong pains in the legs and other places. The next two days I felt better, was able to eat sitting up in a chair.

28 May. Monday. A very warm day. In the shed where our luggage chests are, they are constantly opening boxes and taking out various objects and provisions from Tobolsk. And all this without any explanation of reasons. All this makes one think that they can very easily take things they like home, and hence they will be lost to us! Disgusting! External relationships have also changed in the last few weeks: the jailers are trying not to speak with us, as if they are uncomfortable, and it seems as if they are anxious or cautious about something. Confusing!

Testimony of Ipatiev house guard Yakimov

When the [guards] moved into the Ipatiev house, they started to steal the Tsar's belongings. They would often go to the cupboards and take things from there into big bags, which they drove away in automobiles or horses. They brought these things to their houses.

From the 1918 diary of Nicholas Alexandrovich

29 May. Tuesday. Dear Tatiana turned 21 years old! since night time a strong wind has been blowing right into the window flap, thanks to which the air in our bedroom finally became clean and rather cool. We read a lot. Took walks again, in two shifts. Kharitonov served compote for breakfast, to everyone's joy. In the evening bezique, as usual.

Testimony of Ipatiev house guard Strekotin

The most eager to talk were the daughters (except Olga)... When they approached the red guard Sadchikov, N.S. with this type of talk, he rudely responded: "There is no need to distract me, you can just stomp along". They looked at each other fearfully, and continued walking along the path silently. Sometimes they lay down in the hammocks and, and one would ask: "Swing me", and if someone dared come over, she would unavoidably say: "I am bored".

Testimony of Ipatiev house guard Yakimov

I had the chance to see all the members of the family and everyone who lived with them. I saw them in the house, when they walked by to go to the lavatory or outside walking in the garden. They walked to lavatory past the commandant's room via the entrance hall and guard post № 1. They could have walked through the room where the kitchen was located, but for some reason they never went that way. If the Heir was already outside, they took the stairway which leads downstairs from the lavatory, then through the porch to the yard and from the yard into the garden. But when the Heir was going outside, then they all walked through the main entrance to the street, then through the main gate to the yard and into the garden. I never spoke to either the Tsar or any members of his family. I only saw them. These meetings were silent. Only once I heard and saw the Tsar talking with Shishkin. They were walking in the garden. The Tsar was walking around the garden. Moshkin sat in the garden on a small sofa. The Tsar approached him and started talking about the weather. The Tsar was no longer young. His beard had some grey in it. I saw him in a tunic, belted with an officer's belt with a buckle. The buckle was yellow, and the belt was yellow. Not light yellow, but dark yellow. The tunic was khaki. The same khaki color were his pants, and old worn looking boots. His eyes were nice, kind, as was his entire face. In general, he gave the impression of being a nice person, simple, sincere and talkative. He looked like he wanted to talk to us. The Tsaritsa did not seem anything like him. Her gaze was stern, her figure and manners were those of a proud and haughty woman.

At one time a group of us talked about what we thought of all of them, that Nicholas Alexandrovich was a simple man, while she was not simple: and that she looked like a Tsaritsa. She appeared older than him. On her temples grey hairs were noticeable, her face was not that of a young woman, but of an old one. He looked younger compared to her. It seemed that Tatiana was similar to the Tsaritsa. She also looked stern and proud like her mother. The rest of the Daughters: Olga, Maria and Anastasia did not have any haughtiness. One could tell by looking at them that they were simple and kind. The Heir was always ill, I cannot say anything about him. The Tsar would carry him out to the wheelchair, and in it he was covered by a blanket.

From the 1918 diary of Alexandra Feodorovna

31 May/ 14 June. Ascension of the Lord. Thursday ... Took Baby into the big room & placed the table with the images. They told us no Priest cld. come as such a big holiday!! ... Others told there would be no walk. – Avdeev came and said to pack up as might have to leave any moment. Spent rest of day & the whole evening packing. At midnight Avdeev again came & said we shld not leave before several days. Promised us Sednyov & Nagorny for Sunday, & Vladimir Nikolaevich for the journey. Said the rest of ours & Valia left 3 days ago for Tobolsk. –

From the 1918 diary of Nicholas Alexandrovich

31 May. Ascension. In the morning we waited for a priest for a long time for a service, in vain; everyone was too busy in different churches. In the afternoon we were not allowed out into the garden for some reason. Avdeyev came over and talked to Evg. Serg. for a long time. According to him, he and the Regional Soviet are afraid of anarchists' speeches, and therefore it is possible that a quick departure awaits us, most likely – to Moscow! He asked us to be ready for departure. Immediately we started to pack, but quietly, in order not to attract attention of the guard ranks, by special request from Avdeyev. Around 11 o'cl he returned and said that we will remain for another few days. Therefore, we stayed for 1 June as well, like bivouac, without unpacking. The weather was nice; the walk took place as usual, in two shifts. Finally, after supper Avdeyev, looking somewhat merrier, announced to Botkin that the anarchists were seized and that the danger had passed and our train was cancelled! After all these preparations it was even boring! In the evening we played some bezique.

3 June. Sunday. Again there was no service for us. This whole week I read and today finished history of "Emperor Paul I" by Shilder – very interesting. We keep waiting for Sednev and Nagorny[302], whom the promised to release today.

From the 1918 diary of Alexandra Feodorovna

4/17 **June**. Monday... 1:20. Luncheon, prepared by Kharitonov – he has to cook our food now. Worked, very hot, stuffy as no windows open & smells strong of kitchen everywhere- Baby in my wheeling chair going about the rooms. Man came with Avdeev to see about the windows... watched Kharitonov prepare for making bread. Baby was carried to his room... The girls needed [sic] the doe [sic] for the bread.

From the 1918 diary of Nicholas Alexandrovich

5 June. Tuesday. Dear Anastasia turned 17 years old. the heat outside and inside was excessive. I continue reading Saltykov III volumes – entertaining and intelligent. The whole family took a walk before tea.

[302] At this point, both were already executed, unbeknownst to the family.

Since yesterday Kharitonov is cooking our food, the provisions are brought every two days. The daughters are learning from him how to cook and in the evenings they mix the flour, and in the mornings they bake the bread! Not too bad!

From the 1918 diary of Alexandra Feodorovna

5/18 **June**. Anastasia's 17th B.D. Tuesday. Beautiful weather. The Children continued rolling & making bread & now its baking -... Lunched – excellent bread. Wheeled Baby into the garden & we all sat there for an hour – very hot, nice lilac bushes & small honeysuckle, quite pretty foliage, but as untidy as ever... Kind nuns[303] send now milk & eggs for Aleksei & us & cream.

From the 1918 diary of Nicholas Alexandrovich

9 June. Saturday. The last few days the weather remained wonderful, but very hot; very stuffy in our rooms. Especially at night. By a written request from Botkin, they allowed us hour and a half walks. Today during tea, 6 men entered, apparently from the Regional Soviet, to see which windows can they open? The resolution of this issue has taken around two weeks!

---

303 From nearby Novo-Tikhvensky monastery

Often various subjects would come over and silently looked over the windows in our presence. The scents from all the gardens in town are wonderful.

From the 1918 diary of Alexandra Feodorovna

10/23 **June**. Sunday. Glorious weather – Went with Tatiana to Yevgeny Sergeevich who had kidney pains & she made hm [sic] an injection of morphia suffers very much since 6 in the morning – lies in bed. Two of the soldiers came & took out one window in our room, such joy, delicious air at last & one window no longer whitewashed. Had the great blessing of a real *obednitsa* & vespers, first since 3 months – simply on the table with all our images & lots of birchtree [sic] branches. The first old Priest officiated- ...

From the 1918 diary of Nicholas Alexandrovich

10 June. Trinity Day. Was marked by various events: they opened one window for us in the morning, Evg. Serg. got ill with his kidneys and was suffering greatly, at 11 ½ we had a real *obednya* and *vechernya*[304] service, and at the end of the day Alix and Alexei had supper with us in the dining room. Besides this, we took a two- hour walk! The day was marvelous. Turned out

[304] Vespers

that yesterday's visitors were commissars from Petrograd. The air in the room became clean, and toward the evening it even got cooler.

12 June. Tuesday. Today and yesterday it was incredibly hot. In the rooms as well, despite the constantly open window! In the afternoon we took a walk for two hours. At dinner two strong thunderstorms passed, which refreshed the air. Evg. Serg. is much better, but he is still in bed.

From the 1918 diary of Nicholas Alexandrovich

14 June. Thursday. Our dear Maria turned 19 years old. the weather was still tropical, 26° in the shade, and 24° in the rooms, it is hard to tolerate! We spent an anxious night and stayed up and dressed... All this happened because the other day, we received two letters, one after the other, in which we were informed that we need to get ready to be kidnapped by some loyal people! But the days passed and nothing happened, and the waiting and uncertainty were very torturous.

Letter from "an Officer"[305]

When you...have heard the signal, close and barricade the doors against your captors, who will be blocked and frightened in the interior of the house. With the rope specially made for this, you will descend from the window, we will await you below.... In all these... the father, the mother, and... who descend, the girls after the .... of the suite. Reply... this is possible to us, and if you can make the appropriate rope... to be able to come the... you, is very difficult at this moment...

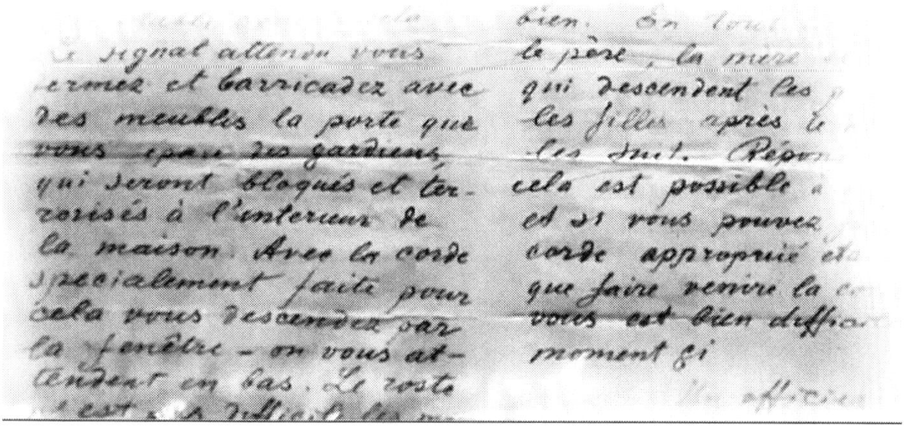
signal attendu vous
fermez et barricadez avec
des meubles la porte qui
vous sépare des gardiens
qui seront bloqués et ter-
rorisés à l'intérieur de
la maison. Avec la corde
spécialement faite pour
cela vous descendez par
la fenêtre – on vous at-
tendent en bas. Le reste

bien. En tout
le père, la mère
qui descendent les
les filles après le
Répon
cela est possible
et si vous pouvez
corde appropriée
que faire venir la
vous est bien diffi
moment ci

One of three letters[306] from "an Officer" written in French

[305] Translated from French by Nicholas B.A. Nicholson

[306] Nicholas's response to the third letter was: "We do not want to, nor can we escape..." These letters were a Cheka provocation

From the 1918 diary of Alexandra Feodorovna

14/27 **June**. Marie's 19th B.D. Thursday... Arranged things all day, tatted[307], Yevgeny Sergeevich sat with me often, as can sit up now; Baby wheeled about... Vladimir Nikolaevich did not come, but again the Military Commissar & Chairman of the Committee to look through the rooms, wont [sic] open another window, so Kharitonov and little Sednyov will sleep in Baby's room, being less hot than theirs near the kitchen. Heat intense. Supper 23° in the room, scarcely slept.

15/28 **June**. Friday... We hear the night sentry under our rooms being told quite particularly to watch every movement at our window – they have become again most suspicious since our window is opened & don't allow one to sit on the sill even now.

17/30 **June**. Sunday. Slept barely 4 hours, the sentry made so much noise. Alas cant [sic] have service. Arranged things, tatted, heart enlarged...

19 June/ 2 July... Now Avdeev has to come morning & evening to see if we are all there. In the daytime

---

[307] Making lace from thread

came to-day to ask if I don't go out because of my health, seems committee wont [sic] believe it. - ...

21 June/4 July. Thursday. Very hot, 21½° in the room at 9. During lunch the chairman of the Regional Committee came with some men, Avdeev is being changed & we get a new commandant (who came over to look at Baby's leg, & another time our rooms) with a young help who seems decent whereas the other vulgar & unpleasant. All our guard of inside left (probably one found out that they had been steeling [sic] our things out of the shed.) – Both men then made us show all our jewels we had on, & the young one wrote them all down in detail & then they were taken from us (where to, for how long, why?? don't know.) only left me my two bracelets of U. Leo's wh. I cant [sic] take off, & the children 1 bracelet each wh. we gave & can't be removed, neither Nicholas's engagement cld. he get off. – So the others only got out from 6-7. Olga remained with me. They took our kees [sic] wh. one had left us of the boxes in the hall but promised to return them. Very hot, went early to bed as awfully tired & heart ached more.

From the 1918 diary of Nicholas Alexandrovich

21 June. Thursday. There was a change of commandants today – during dinner Beloborodov[308] and others came in and announced that instead of Avdeyev, the one whom we mistook for a doctor has been appointed – Yurovsky.[309] During the day before tea, he and his assistants catalogued the gold jewelry – ours and the children's; the majority (rings, bracelets, etc.) they took with them. They explained that it was because there was an unpleasant incident in our house, mentioned our missing things. So, the suspicion about which I wrote on 28 May had been confirmed. I feel sorry for Avdeyev, it is not his fault that he was not able to hold back his people from stealing from the chests in the shed.

23 June. Saturday. Yesterday Yurovsky brought a box with all the seized jewels, asked us to check the contents and sealed it in front of us, leaving it with us for safekeeping. The weather became cooler, and it got easier to breathe in the bedroom. Yurovsky and his assistant are starting to realize what kind of people surrounded and guarded us, thieving from us. Not to

308 Alexander Beloborodov, chairman of the Ural Regional Soviet.

309 Yakov Yurovsky, the last commandant of the Ipatiev House and chief executioner of the Romanovs

mention our belongings, they even kept the major part of provisions delivered from the convent. Only now, after this change did we find out about this, because the entire amount of provisions started to end up in our kitchen.

Contemporary photo of Novo-Tikhvenky convent in Ekaterinburg, from where provisions were brought to the Ipatiev house in June and July of 1918

All these days I was reading a lot as usual; today I started VII volume of Saltykov. I really like his novels, short stories and articles. The day was rainy, we took an hour and a half walk and returned home dry.

Testimony of Ipatiev house guard Yakimov

Once Yurovsky took over the house, immediately he set up a machine gun post in the attic. Put a new guard post in the backyard. Ended the drunken antics. I never saw him drunk or drinking. But he did change something else, which worsened conditions for the imperial family. He decreased deliveries from the nunnery, or completely stopped them, I can't remember.

From the 1918 diary of Nicholas Alexandrovich

25 June. Monday. Our lives did not change at all under Yurovsky. He comes into the bedroom to check if the seals on the box are intact and looks out from the open window. Today, all morning, and until 4 o'cl they were checking and fixing electric lighting. Inside the house new Latvians are standing guard, while outside the same ones remained – part soldiers, part workers! Rumours have it that some of Avdeyev's men are already under arrest! The door to the shed with our luggage has been sealed. If only this was done a month ago! During the night there was a thunderstorm and got even cooler.

E.S. Botkin to his brother Alexander[310]

Ekaterinburg, **26 June** (9 July), 1918. My dear, good friend Sasha, I am making the last attempt to write a real letter, - at least from here, - although this caveat is completely redundant; I do not think that it is in the cards for me to ever write from anywhere else again, - my voluntary imprisonment here is limited to my existence on this earth. In actuality, I have died – dead to my children, my friends, my work... I have died, but have not been buried yet, or rather was buried alive, - whichever you prefer: the consequences are almost identical, i.e. both one and the other have their negative and positive sides. If I were literally dead, that is to say, anatomically dead, then according to my faith I would know what my children are doing, would be closer to them and undoubtedly more useful than now. I rest with the dead only civilly, my children may still have hope that we will see each other sometime in this life, while I, other than thinking that I can still be useful to them somehow, do not personally indulge myself with this hope, do not humour myself with illusions, but look directly into the face of unadorned

[310] Dr Botkin started this letter on date indicated but continued writing it on subsequent days. It is thought that he was writing the letter at midnight of 16-17 July, when he heard the knock on his door, which was why letter ended abruptly. It was never finished or mailed

reality. Although for now, I am as healthy and fat as always, to a point where I feel disgusted every time I look in the mirror. I only console myself with the thought that if it would be easier for me to be anatomically dead, then this means that my children are better off, because when I am separated from them, it always seems to me that the worse off I am, the better off they are. And why do I feel that I would be better off dead, - I will explain this to you with small episodes, which illustrate my emotional being. The other day, i.e. three days ago, when I was peacefully reading Saltykov-Schedrin, which I often read with pleasure, I suddenly saw the face of my son Yura in diminutive size, as if from far away, but [it was] dead, in a horizontal position, with closed eyes... The last letter from him was on 22 March o[ld] s[tyle], and since that time postal connection from the Caucasus, which even earlier faced great difficulties, probably stopped completely, as neither here nor in Tobolsk had we received anything else from Yura. Do not think that I am hallucinating, I have had these types of visions before, but you can easily imagine, how it was for me to experience this particular thing in the current situation, which in general is quite comfortable, but to have no chance not only to go to Yura, but not even to be able to find out anything about him. Then, only yesterday, during the same reading, I suddenly heard some word, which to me sounded like "Papulya"[311], which was uttered in Tanyusha's[312] voice, and I almost broke down in sobs. Again, this was not a hallucination, because this word was uttered, the voice was similar, and not even for a second did I think that this was my daughter speaking, who was supposed to be in Tobolsk: her last postcard was from 23 May – 5 June, and of course these tears would have been purely egotistical, for myself, that I cannot hear and, most likely will never again hear that dear little voice and feel that affection that is so important to me, with which my little children spoiled me so. Again, the horror and sorrow which gripped me during the vision I described were purely egotistical too, since if my son had truly died, then he is happy, but if he is alive, then it is unknown what kind of trials he is going through or is fated to live through. So you see, my dear, that my spirit is cheerful, despite the torment I live through, which I bear, just described to you, and cheerful to a point where I am prepared to do this for many more years... I am encouraged by the conviction

[311] Diminutive affectionate term for "Papa"
[312] Botkin's daughter, Tatiana

that "one who bears all until the end is saved", and the awareness that I remain loyal to the principles of the 1889 graduates. Before we graduated, while still students, but already close friends who preached and developed the same principals with which we started life, for the most part we did not view them from a religious point of view, I do not even know if too many of us were religious. But each codex of principals is a religion already, and for some it is most likely a conscious thing, while for others subconscious, - as it basically was for me, as this was the time of, not exactly uniform atheism, but of complete indifferentism, in the full sense of the word, - it came so close to Christianity that our full attitude toward it, or at least of many of us, was a completely natural transition. In general, if "faith is dead without work", then "work" cannot exist without faith, and if faith joins any of our work, then this is just due to special favour from God. I turned out to be such a lucky one, through the path of heavy trials – the loss of my firstborn, the year-and-a-half-old little son Seryozha. Since that time, my codex has been widened and solidified significantly, and I took care that each task was not only about the "Academic", but about the "Divine". This justifies my last decision as well, when without any hesitation I left my children completely orphaned, in order to do my physician's duty to the end, like Abraham did not hesitate to sacrifice his only son to God on His demand. I strongly believe that the same way God saved Isaac, He will save my children too and be a father to them. But since I do not know how He will save them, and can only find out about it in the next world, my egotistic torment which I described to you, due to my human weakness, does not lose its torturous severity. But Job did bear more, and my late Misha always reminded me about him, when he was afraid that I, bereft of my dear little children, would not be able to bear it. No, apparently I can bear it all, whatever God wills to burden me with. In your letter, for which I ardently thank you once more (the first time I tried to convey this in a few lines on a detachable coupon, hopefully you got it in time for the holiday, and also my physiognomy – for the other?), you were interested in my activities in Tobolsk, with a trust precious to me. And so? Putting hand on heart, I can confess to you that there, I tried in every way to take care of "the Divine, as the Lord wills" and, consequently, "not to shame the graduates of year 1889". And God blessed my efforts, and I will have until the end of my days this bright memory of my swan song. I worked with my last strength, which suddenly grew over there thanks to the great happiness in the life [we had] together with Tanyusha and Glebushka[313], thanks to the nice and cheerful climate and relative mildness of winter and thanks to the touching attitude towards me from the townspeople and villagers. As a matter of fact, in its center, albeit a large one, Tobolsk presents as a city that is very picturesquely located, rich with ancient churches, religious and academic institutions, [but] at the periphery it gradually and unnoticeably transitions into a real village. This circumstance, along with noble simplicity and the feeling of self-respect of Siberians, in my opinion gives the relationships among the residents and not visitors, the specific character of directness, naiveté and benevolence, which we always valued and which creates the atmosphere necessary to our souls. In addition, various news spreads around the city very fast, the first lucky incidents for which God helped me be of use brought out such trust towards me, that the number of those wanting to get my advice grew with each day, up to my sudden and unexpected departure. Turning to me were mostly those with chronic illnesses, those who were already

[313] Botkin's son Gleb

treated again and again, [and] sometimes, of course, those who were completely hopeless. This gave me the opportunity to make appointments for them, and my time was filled for a week or two ahead in each hour, as I was not able to visit more than six - seven, in extreme cases eight patients per day: since all these cases needed thorough review and much and much pondering. Who was I called to besides those ill within my specialty?! To the insane, to those asking to be treated for drunkenness; [they] brought me to a prison to see a kleptomaniac, and with sincere joy I remember that the poor wretch of a lad, who was bailed out by his parents on my advice (they are peasants), behaved decently the rest of my stay... I never denied anyone, as long as the supplicants accepted that certain illnesses were completely beyond the limits of my knowledge. I only refused to go to those recently fallen ill if, of course, they needed emergency help, since, on the one hand I did not want to get in the way of regular physicians of Tobolsk, which is very lucky to have them in the capacity and most importantly, quality of relations. They are all very knowledgeable and experienced people, excellent comrades and so responsive that the Tobolsk public is used to sending a horse or cabby to the doctor and receive him immediately. More valuable is their patience towards me, who did not have the ability to fulfill these types of requests, but on the contrary, was forced to make them wait a long time. It's true that soon it became commonly known that I never refuse anyone and keep my word sacredly, a patient could wait for me with peace of mind. But if their illness did not allow them to wait, then the patients went to local physicians, which always made me happy, or to Doctor Derevenko, who also possessed their vast trust, or they headed to the hospital, and this way it would happen that when I arrived at a time of prescheduled appointment, I did not find the patient there, but that was always convenient, since most of the time my schedule was so extensive that I wasn't able to accomplish everything, at times debts formed, which I paid off when I did not find someone there. To see [patients] at the house where I was staying was inconvenient, and anyway there was no room, nevertheless from 3 until 4 ½ - 5, I was always home for our soldiers, whom I saw in my room, the walk-through room, but since only our own [people] passed though there, it did not discomfort them. During the same hours, my town patients came to see me too, either for a refill of a prescription or to make an appointment. I was forced to make exceptions for peasants who came to see me from villages tens or even hundreds of versts away (in Siberia they don't pay attention to distance), and who were in a hurry to get back. I had to see them in a small room before the bathroom, which was a bit out of the way, where a large chest served as an examining table. Their trust was especially touching to me, and their confidence, which never betrayed them, that I will treat them with the same attention and affection as any other patient, not only as an equal but as a patient who has every right to my care and services, gave me joy. Those who were able to spend the night, I would visit at the inn early the next morning. They always tried to pay, but since I followed our old codex, of course I never accepted anything from them, so, while I was busy in an *izba*[314] with a patient, they hurried to pay my cabby. This surprising courtesy, to which we are not used to at all in large cities, was occasionally highly pertinent, as at times I was not in a position to visit patients due to lack of funds and fast-growing cab costs. Therefore, for our mutual benefit, I widely took advantage of another local tradition and asked those who had a horse, to send it for me. This way, the streets of Tobolsk saw me riding in wide bishop's

[314] Peasant house generally made of logs

sleighs, as well as behind beautiful merchant trotters, but most often drowning in hay in most ordinary burlap. My friends were equally varied, which perhaps was not to everyone's liking, but it was no concern of mine. To Tobolsk's credit I must add that there was no direct evidence of this at all, and only one indirect, which in addition was not unquestionable. One evening the husband of one of my female patients came to see me with a request to visit her right away, because she had strong pains (in the stomach). Luckily, I was able to fulfill his wish, albeit at a cost to another patient, for whom I did not schedule a visit, but rode with him to his house in a cab in which he came to get me. On the way he starts to grumble at the cabby, that he is not going the right way, to which the latter reasonably respon... [letter ends abruptly]

Dr Evgeny Botkin with his children Tatiana and Gleb

From the 1918 diary of Nicholas Alexandrovich

28 June. Thursday. In the morning, around 10 ½ o'cl three workers approached the open window, picked up the heavy screen and attached it outside the frame – without any warning from Yurovsky. We are liking his type less and less! Started reading VIII volume of Saltykov.

30 June[315]. Saturday. Alexei took his first bath since Tobolsk; his knee is getting better, but he still cannot straighten it completely. The weather is warm and pleasant. There is no news at all from outside.

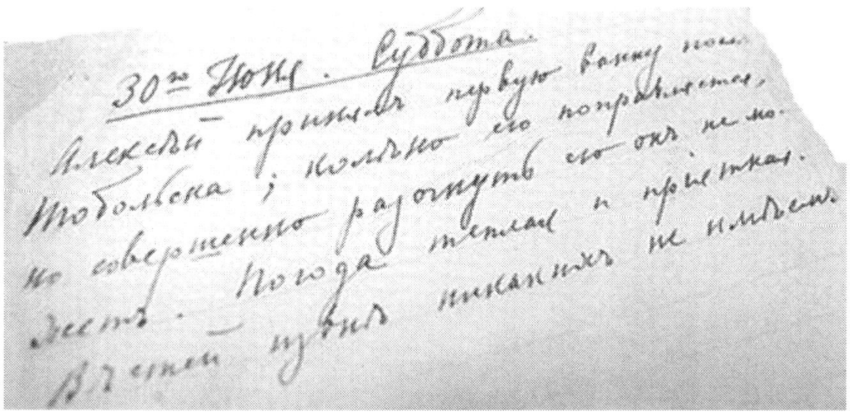
30-го Июня. Суббота.
Алексей принял первую ванну после Тобольска; колено его поправляется, но совершенно разогнуть его он не может. Погода теплая и приятная. Вестей извне никаких не имеем.

The last diary entry ever written by Nicholas Alexandrovich, dated **30th June**, 1918 (Old Style)

[315] This was the very last diary entry written by Nicholas

From the 1918 diary of Alexandra Feodorovna

30 June/ 13 July. Saturday. Beautiful morning. I spent the day as yesterday lying on the bed, as back aches when move about. Others went out twice. Anastasia remained with me in the afternoon. One says Nagorny & Sednyov have been sent out of this government, instead of giving them back to us. – at 6:30 Baby had his first bath since Tobolsk. He managed to get in & out alone, climbs also alone in & out of bed, but can only stand on one foot as yet. 9:45 I went to bed again. – Rained in the night. Heard three revolver shots in the night.

Testimony of Ipatiev house guard Yakimov

Something confusing happened with the priest. The prayer service under Yurovsky happened just once. This was on Saturday, 13 July[316] [**30 June**], Yurovsky called me to him and instructed me to find a priest. First, he asked me which priests are serving. I named f. Meledin and f. Storozhev. Then he asked me to get one of them. Back then Meledin lived the closest (Vodochnaya 168), so on that same Saturday evening I asked him. In the morning... Yurovsky [found out] and

[316] From here on, the dates used are in the New Style

sent me to tell Meledin not to come, [to tell him] that *obednitsa* was cancelled. And if he asks who cancelled it, "tell him that it was them, not I. Instead of Meledin, go ask Storozhev", [he said]... So, I went to Storozhev and asked him. What this meant, I do not know.

Testimony of Father Ioann Storozhev

On 30 June/**13 July** I found out that the next day, 1/14 July, on Sunday, f. Meledin had to perform a liturgy at the Ipatiev house, that he already had a warning about this from the commandant, and the commandant at the time was infamously cruel, a certain Yurovsky - former military medic.

The last commandant of the Ipatiev house – Yakov Yurovsky

I assumed that I would replace f. Meledin at the cathedral and perform a liturgy for him on 1-14 July. Around 8 o'clock in the morning on **14 July**, a soldier came to see me, and requested for me to serve *obednitsa* at the Ipatiev house. At 10 o'clock, I was already at the Ipatiev house with deacon Buimirov. Inside, behind the fence, at the bottom of stairs and inside the house, there were lots of armed young men, standing on guard. When we entered the commandant's room, we saw disorder, dust and mess. Yurovsky was sitting at the table, drinking tea and eating bread with butter. Another man was sleeping on the bed, fully dressed. Having entered the room, I said to Yurovsky: "The clergy was invited here, so here we are. What do we need to do?" Yurovsky directly stared at me without a greeting, and said "Wait here, then you will serve *obednitsa*" I asked "*Obednya* or *obednitsa*?" "He wrote *obednitsa*", said Yurovsky. When we dressed and a bucket with coals was brought in, Yurovsky invited us into the hall for service. I was the first to enter the hall, then the deacon and Yurovsky. Simultaneously, Nicholas Alexandrovich with two daughters came in through a door that led into inner rooms. Yurovsky asked Nicholas Alexandrovich: "Are all of you gathered?", Nicholas

Alexandrovich answered firmly "Yes – all". Ahead, behind the arch, already standing were Alexandra Feodorovna with two daughters and Alexei Nikolaevich, who was sitting in a wheelchair, wearing a sailor jacket. He looked pale. Alexandra Feodorovna, wearing a dress, looked livelier than in the past. Olga Nikolaevna, Tatiana Nikolaevna, Maria Nikolaevna and Anastasia Nikolaevna were wearing black skirts and white blouses. Their hair reached their shoulders in the back.

To me, Nicholas Alexandrovich, as well as his daughters, looked exhausted this time. During the service the family members arranged themselves [this way]: Alexandra Feodorovna's chair stood next to the wheelchair of Alexei Nikolaevich, which was farther away from the arch, hers was a bit behind his. Behind Alexei Nikolaevich stood Tatiana Nikolaevna. Olga Nikolaevna, Maria Nikolaevna, Anastasia Nikolaevna stood near Nicholas Alexandrovich, who took his usual place on the right side of wall arch. Behind the arch, in the hall stood Doctor Botkin, the maid and three servants. At the far corner window stood Yurovsky. We performed the service at the table set up in the center of the room behind the arch. This table was covered with a silk cloth with ancient Russian style design. On the table, in proper order and the usual church symmetry stood numerous icons. There were small, medium and very small folding icons with vestments – all these of unique beauty in their ancient style and workmanship: "Our Lady of the Sign [*Znamenie*]", "It Is Truly Meet", the Icon of the Holy St Ioann of Tobolsk...

Our Lady of *Znamenie* icon

In front was a large plant and to me it looked like among its branches was an icon called "Saviour Not Made By Hands", in the usual style, without vestments. The deacon and I started the *obednitsa* service. The ritual of *obednitsa* is usually performed for the military, when for one reason or another it is impossible to do a liturgy. In its substance this prayer service is similar to the ritual of liturgy, but is significantly shorter, as at *obednitsa* the Holy Eucharist is not offered. According to the ritual of *obednitsa*, it is customary to read "at rest with the saints" at a certain point. For some reason instead of reading, the deacon sang this prayer. But as soon as we started singing, I heard that the Romanov family members, who were standing behind us, fell to their knees, and here I suddenly felt a deep spiritual comfort afforded by shared prayer.

Artist's rendition of the Romanov family at their last prayer service

On an even deeper level one felt this when at the end of the service I read a prayer to the Mother of God, where in highly poetic touching words the supplication of a tormented person is expressed to support him in his sorrows, to give him strength to bear with dignity the cross sent by God.

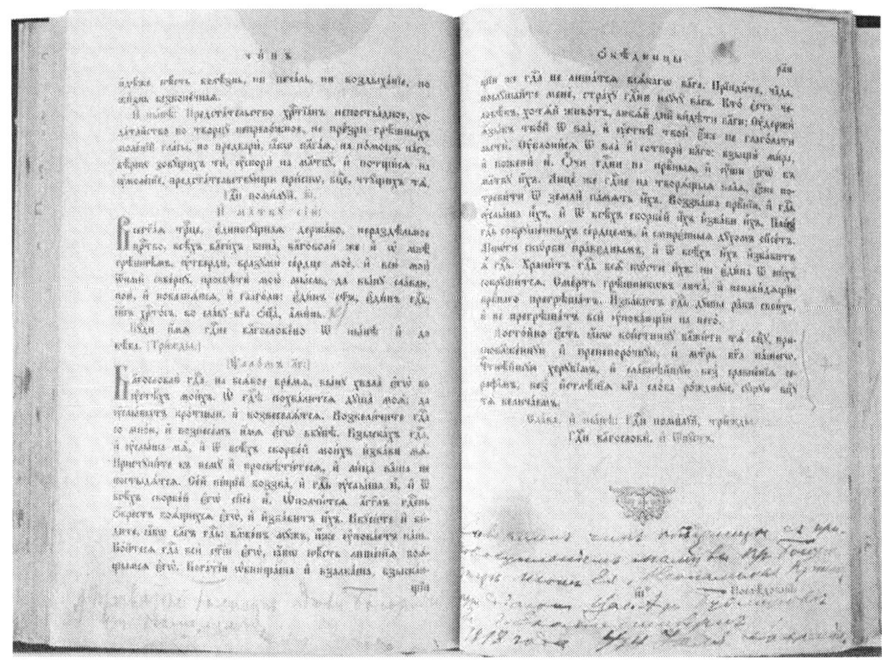

Pages from the actual prayer book used for the last *obednitsa* service performed for the imperial family on **14 July**, 1918 (with Father Storozhev's writing mentioning the event)

After the service all kissed the Holy Cross. When I was leaving and walked very close by the former Grand Duchesses, I heard barely audible words "Thank you". Silently the deacon and I reached the art school building, and here he said to me, "You know Father Protoirei[317], – something happened with them in there". In these words there was confirmation of my own impression, I stopped and asked him why he thinks so. "Not sure. It is as if they are different

[317] Archpriest

somehow. And no one sang." And I must say that for the first time no one in the Romanov family sang with us at the prayer service on 14 July. What an amazingly subtle perception of the situation. Only now do we know what happened to the family from the testimonies of the eyewitnesses. But those who performed the service understood with a joint perception of the praying people. As far as deviation from the canon law in following the ritual of *obednitsa*: singing "at rest with the saints" represented a funeral service for those praying while they were still alive! How this happened, for what reason – is only known to the Supreme Being, but it happened just prior to the murder of the prisoners of the House of Special Purpose. They had their funeral service. That evening was blessed: it passed in warm sincere conversations.

From the 1918 diary of Alexandra Feodorovna

1/**14 July**. Sunday. Beautiful summers [sic] morning. Scarcely slept because of back & legs. 10:30. Had the joy of an *obednitsa* – the young Priest for the 2nd time. 11:30-12:00. The others walked – Olga [stayed] with me. Spent the day on the bed again. Tatiana stayed with me in the afternoon. Spir. Readings, Book of the Prophet Hosea, ch. 4-14, Pr. Joel 1-end. 4:30. Tea –

tatted all day and laid patiences. Played a little bezique in the evening, they put my long straw couch in the big room so it was less tiring for me. 10:00. Took a bath - & went to bed.

2/**15 July**. Monday. Marie's B.D. Greyish morning. Later sunshine. Lunched on the couch in the big room, as women came to clean the floors, then lay on my bed again & read with Maria J. Sirach 26-31. They went out twice as usual. In the morning Tatiana read to me Spir. Readings. Still no Vladimir Nikolaevich – at 6:30 Baby had his second bath – Bezique. Went to bed 10:15. - 11 1/4° of warmth at 10:30 evening. Heard the report of an artillery shot in the night & several revolver shots.

Testimony of Ipatiev house guard Yakimov

On **15 July**, Monday, in our barracks at the Popov house the boy who lived with the imperial family appeared, he used to take the Heir around in his wheelchair. It caught my attention then, the other guards also noticed it. Nevertheless, no one knew what it meant, why the boy was brought here. But it was undoubtedly done on Yurovksy's orders.

From the report of Yakov Yurovsky

[On] **16 [July]** ... A telegram was received from Perm about extermination of the Romanovs, and at 6 o'cl in the evening Filipp Goloschekin signed for it to be enforced. At midnight, a truck for moving the corpses was supposed to arrive. At 6 o'clock, the little cook Sednev was taken away, which really worried the Romanovs and their children. Dr Botkin came over to ask, what brought this on? He was told that the boy's uncle, who was arrested, had escaped, now he has returned and wants to see his nephew. The next day the boy was sent to his hometown /I think in the Tulsk province/.

From the 1918 diary of Alexandra Feodorovna

3/**16 July**. Irina's[318] 23rd B.D. Tuesday. Grey morning, later lovely sunshine. Baby has a slight cold. All went out ½ hour in the morning. Olga & I arranged our medicines. Tatiana read Spir. Readings. 3:00. They went out, Tatiana stayed with me & we read: Bk. of the Pr. Amos and Pr. Obadiah. Tatted. Every morning the Command. comes to our rooms, at last after a week

318 Irina Alexandrovna, daughter of Nicholas's sister Ksenia, wife of Felix Yusupov

brought eggs for Baby. 8:00. Supper. Suddenly Lyonka Sednyov was fetched to go & see his Uncle & flew off – wonder whether its [sic] true & we shall see the boy back again! Played bezique with Nicholas. 10:30 to bed. 15 degrees.

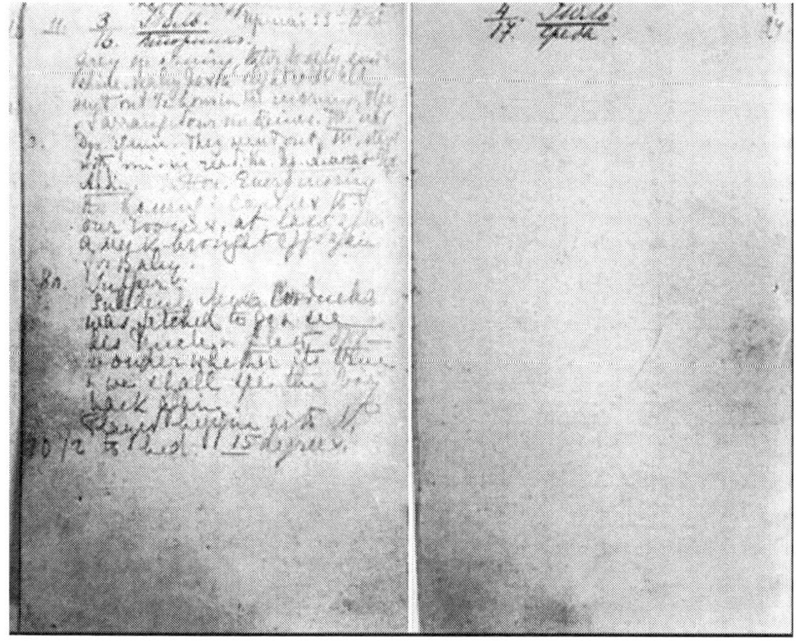

Last page of Alexandra's diary

Testimony of Ipatiev house guard Yakimov

The last time I saw the Tsar and his daughters was **16 July**. They were taking a walk in the garden at four o'clock in the afternoon. I cannot remember if I saw the Heir at this time. I did not see the Tsaritsa, she did not go out then.

From the testimony of Yakov Yurovsky

[**16 July**] ...Meanwhile, all the preparations were made: 12 men were selected /including the Latvians with revolvers, who were supposed to execute the sentence/. 2 of the Latvians refused to shoot the girls. When the truck arrived, everyone was sleeping. We awoke Botkin, and he [awoke] all the rest. The explanation was given as follows: "in light of the disturbances in the city, it was necessary to move the Romanov family from the upper floor to the lower one.

Testimony of Ipatiev house guard Yakimov

[**17 July**]... Just after midnight, old style time, or after 2 new style time, which the Bolsheviks changed to two hours forward, - some people came down into the lower rooms and started walking towards the room marked "I" on the map of the lower floor [the cellar]. In front walked Yurovsky and Nikulin. Behind them walked the Sovereign, the Empress and the daughters: Olga, Tatiana, Maria and Anastasia, and also Botkin, Demidova, Trupp and the cook Kharitonov. The Sovereign himself was carrying the Heir. Behind them walked Medvedev and the “Latvians”, i.e. the ten men who lived in the lower rooms who were recruited by Yurovsky through the Extraordinary [committee]. Among them were two Russians with rifles.

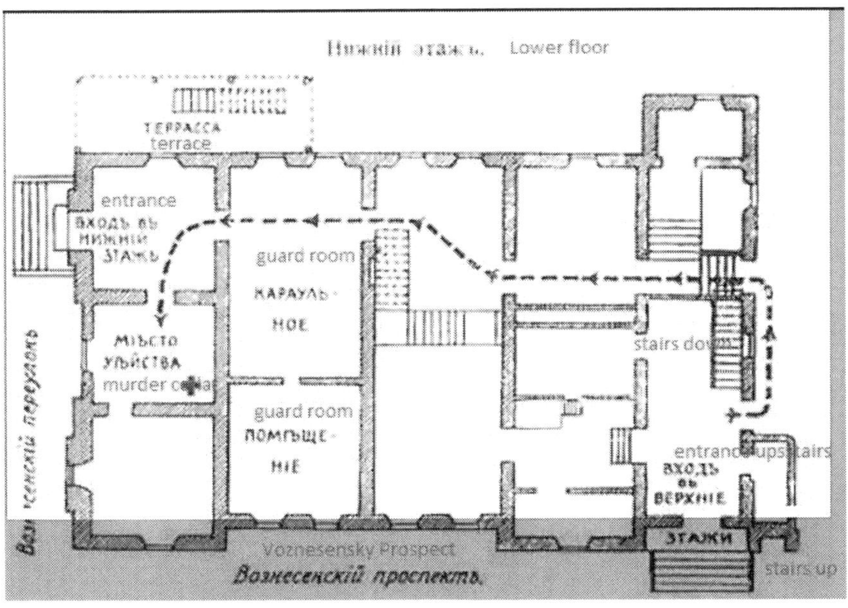

Plan of the lower floor of the Ipatiev house, showing the path the prisoners were led on towards the cellar

From the report of Yakov Yurovsky

[**17 July**] They dressed for about a half hour. Downstairs a room with wooden paneling was chosen to avoid ricochet/all furniture was taken out from it. The team was ready in the room next door. The

Romanovs did not suspect anything. The commandant went to get them personally, alone, and brought them down the stairs to the lower room. Nicholas carried Alexei in his arms. The rest carried with them little cushions and various small things. Having entered the empty room, A.F. asked: "so, there is no chair? May we not sit?" The commandant ordered two chairs to be brought in. Nicholas sat Alexei on one, A.F. sat on the other. The rest were ordered by the commandant to line up.

Steps leading down to the ground floor

Courtyard through which one had to pass in order to get from the main house to the cellar. Entrance to the cellar is on the right of the photo.

Steps leading to the cellar; artist's rendition of the Romanov family descending these steps on the night of 16-17 July, 1918

Doors to the cellar room (shut and open)

From the report of Yakov Yurovsky

[**17 July**]. When they lined up, the team was called in. After the team entered, the commandant said to the Romanovs, that in light of their relatives' continuous offense on Soviet Russia, Ural-ispolkom[319] made the decision to execute them by shooting. Nicholas turned his back to the team, facing his family, then, as if he realized what was happening, turned to the commandant, with the question "what? what?". The commandant quickly repeated and ordered the team to get set. Earlier the team was assigned who will shoot whom and were ordered to aim directly in the heart, to

[319] Urals executive committee (abbreviation)

avoid too much blood volume and to finish faster. Nicholas did not utter anything else, again turning to the family, the others uttered a few incoherent exclamations, all this lasted a few seconds. Then the shooting started, which lasted two-three minutes. Nicholas was killed by the commissar himself, immediately after A.F. and Romanovs' people died/ 12 people were shot in total: Nicholas, Alexei, A.F., the four daughters Tatiana, Olga, Maria and Anastasia, Dr Botkin, lackey Trup [sic], cook Tikhomirov[320], another cook (Kharitonov) and a lady-in-waiting[321], whose surname the commandant forgot/. Alexei, their [sic] his three sisters and Botkin were still alive, and they had to be finished off.

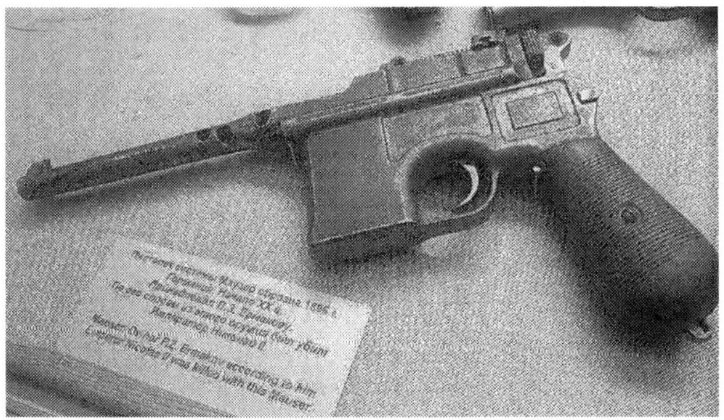

Revolver used to shoot Nicholas Alexandrovich

[320] It is unclear whom he meant here, there was only one cook: Kharitonov
[321] The maid Anna Demidova

This surprised the commandant because they aimed directly into their hearts, it was also surprising that the revolver bullets bounced off someone and ricocheted like hail around the room. When they tried to finish the girls off with bayonets, the bayonet could not go through the corsage[322] [sic]...

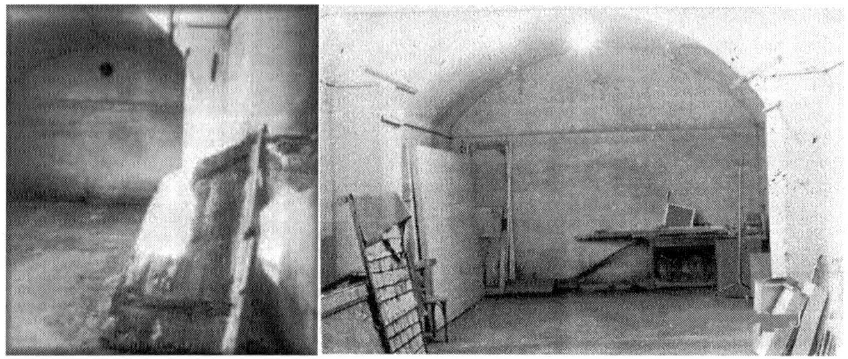

Photos of the cellar room taken a few weeks after the murders

Then [we] started carrying out the corpses and loading them into the truck, covering with cloth, in order to prevent blood seepage. That's when theft started; was forced to get 3 reliable comrades to guard the corpses during the transfer/the corpses were carried one by

[322] He meant corset

one...

Truck that was used to carry the bodies

"The team" of murderers of the Ipatiev house prisoners near their burial spot

Pyotr Ermakov posing near the burial spot

Recollection of Nikolai "Kolya" Derevenko

Until that sad day of **17 July**, 1918, my father, Gilliard, Gibbes, and others knew everything, but I knew nothing. Something terrible was going to happen, but I didn't know what it was... In the last week of July 1918, myself, my father, Gilliard, Gibbes, and others entered the Ipatiev house. There was a terrible scene... The house was in complete chaos; diaries, letters, albums, and other things were strewn all around in the house... "But where is Ieskela*?" I asked my father, but he stayed silent. Ieskela's diary was found by a White guard, I think his name was Nemetkin, I am not sure. But Leonid Sednev... I saw him. He cried. His cries were so loud... so loud! I was confused. “Papa, where is my Ieskela?” – I asked. “They killed him”, he said, and I started to cry. “But how?” – I replied. “They killed the Tsar, the Tsaritsa, and the Grand Duchesses too. They are all dead.” – said my father. “But I don’t understand. Where... where are their bodies?” “We don’t know, maybe we will never find them”.

Kolya Derevenko, with Alexei, and in his old age

I then realized how brutal life could be... I found Ieskela’s last letter written to me. One sentence in particular in that letter – “I hug you tightly” – made me cry so much. I thought “and I hug you tightly too, my dear friend, my Tsar...” I was in shock. In the following years, I thought about him. “Why did they kill you? In the USSR, there was no place for my Ieskela. We will be friends forever, my dear Tsesarevich... If I could see you just one more time, then I can die in peace...

Photo of inside of Ipatiev house taken after the murders

Воскресенье, 28-го (15) Іюля 1918 года.

Панихида по мученически убіенномъ

Всероссійскомъ Императорѣ

НИКОЛАѢ II.

Имѣетъ быть совершена въ Каѳедральномъ соборѣ архіерейскимъ служеніемъ въ воскресенье 15—28 іюля, послѣ поздней литургіи (около 12 ч. дня).

Newspaper notice about the "*panikhida* for the martyred Emperor of All the Russia Nicholas II", taking place on Sunday, **28**(15) **July**, 1918. At this time, it was still believed that the rest of the family was alive

Nikolai Sokolov[323] and his team at the site where attempt to burn the bodies took place

[323] Investigator of the murders of the Romanovs and their people, appointed by the Whites

ADDENDUM

TSARSKOE SELO

Alexander Palace

Formal reception room (Alexander Palace)

Portrait hall (Alexander Palace)

Maple Room (Alexander Palace)

Maple Room (Alexander Palace)

Nicholas's study (Alexander Palace)

Alexander Palace during world war ii German occupation

Damage to the palace during the Second World War

Alexei boating on a canal in Alexander Park

Catherine Palace

Contemporary drawing of Feodorovsky Cathedral

Imperial entrance of Feodorovsky Cathedral

Parade entrance of Feodorovsky Cathedral

Entrance to the Lower Chapel at Feodorovsy Cathedral (private chapel of the imperial family)

Feodorovsky Cathedral fell into disrepair after the revolution and during Second World War

It was fully restored in 2005

Contemporary postcard of Feodorovsky Gorodok

Chapel at the Brethren Military Cemetery of Tsarskoe Selo

Above: Brethren cemetery chapel consecration, which took place on 5 October, 1915

ST PETERSBURG

Alexei in the courtyard of the Winter Palace

Study of Nicholas II (Winter Palace)

Sitting room of Alexandra Feodorovna (Winter Palace)

Nicholas II's pool ((Winter Palace)

Tea at Grigori Rasputin's apartment on Angliysky Prospect 3

Entrance to Angliysky Prospect 3, where Grigori Rasputin resided in St Petersburg

Windows of Grigori Rasputin's last residence on Gorokhovaya St, as seen from the courtyard. Photo circa 1914

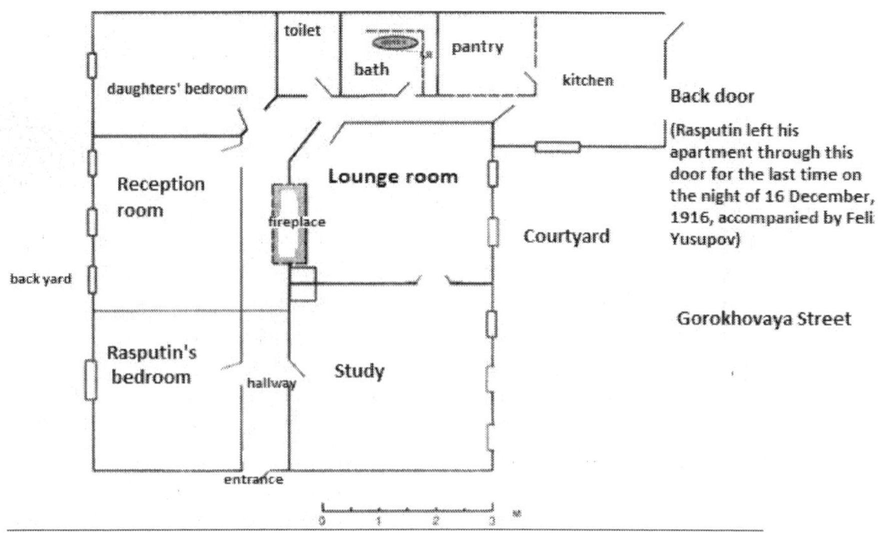

Floor plan of Rasputin's last apartment on Gorokhovaya Street 64

Yusupov Palace on Moika Canal, circa 1916

Cellar room of Yusupov Palace used for Rasputin's murder

Above: Yelagin Palace, residence of Dowager Empress Maria Feodorovna, prior to the revolution

Below: Yelagin Palace post World War II

Matilda Kschessinska's mansion on Angliyskaya Embankment

GATCHINA

Above and below: Tsar Alexander III and family at Gatchina

From the 1917 diary of Grand Duke Michael

7 April. Friday. Gatchina. In the morning read "The New Times". In the afternoon Natasha, Georgiy, J and I went to Kurakinsky gates, and from there walked around the lake and to the greenhouse, where we bought flowers and strawberries...

8 April. Saturday. Gatchina. Spent the morning on the terrace, Georgiy read a newspaper. At 12 o'cl Sonia D and Vera Orbeliani came over. In the afternoon we all went to the Kurakinsky gates, and from there walked

around the lake and got into an automobile by the greenhouses...

30 April. Sunday. Gatchina. At 11 o'cl Natasha and Praskovia Iv. went to church at the Realnoye school, and Georgiy, J, Koka and I drove in the "Rolls-Royce " to the palace park, where we sat near the lake and basked in the sun...

18 January. Wednesday. Gatchina. At 10 ¾ drove to Ditz's in an auto, and from there [went] hunting with him in a troika. The troika slid off the road (caught) on the way to Salezi. Ditz held the right out-runner, I did the left one, but this didn't help, and we ran full steam ahead, luckily did not hit or encounter anyone. Having

ridden this way for about a half of verst, Epifan turned the root into a ditch, where we stopped successfully. On the way to Korpikovo 4 pheasant corrals were set up, Ditz killed 9, and I 15. By 1 ¼ I was already home. Krestyanov had breakfast with us and stayed until 2 ½. In the afternoon I jogged around the park.

1 October. Sunday. Gatchina... At 3 o'cl we all drove in the "Packard" to the edge of the Tsarskoselsky forest, from there took a walk back to the village, then drove to Remiz and walked to the Tea house. Meet up five people with rifles and a dog. These anyone who wishes can hunt, having paid 17 rubles for a ticket.

Almost all game has been exterminated. We returned home at 5 1/4 and had tea on the terrace...

From the 1918 diary of Grand Duke Michael

16 January. Tuesday. Gatchina. ... From 3 1/2 to 4 1/2 o'cl Natasha and I took a walk on Nikolaevskaya, on Baggovutskaya ran into Elena K, who took a walk with us, walked on Lyutsevskaya for a bit, then on Alexandrovskaya and returned home at 4 1/2, and at this time Maria Ferdinandovna with Nadezhda D came over to see us, and also Andrei I. The guests stayed until 6 1/4. After the English dictation I did gymnastics. After dinner J[ohnson] and I played two games of billiards, then miss Nim massaged my head, as usual...

Villa on Nikolaevskaya Street 24, where Grand Duke Michael Alexandrovich resided with his family in 1917, prior to his arrest

11/24 February. Sunday. Gatchina. In the morning I practiced with Domenichi for ¾ hour, then walked on skis with Vasily for an hour and a half, walked through the field, around the cemetery, across M. Zagvozdka to Priorat, there we came down the hill between pine trees, walked past J's and went home. At 2 o'cl. arrived: Alyosha, Dvorzhitsky and Naryshkin. Around 3 ½ Natasha, Margarita V, Dvorzhitsky, Naryshkin, Boris Yak. and I took a walk to Olginskaya, a bit via Priorat and home via Nikolaevskaya...

17 [February]/2 March. Saturday. Gatchina. In the morning walked on skis with Vasily for an hour, - from Gernetovskaya we entered the Zoo, walked along Berezoviy, then to the left towards the river, along to cascade and back home...

Contemporary postcard with view of "The Zoo" at Gatchina

31 December. Saturday. Gatchina. At 10 ¾ Vyazemsky and I went to get J and with him through the Matrossky gates to the palace park, where we took a walk and went around the lake. By the palace near the Turkish gazebo we met up with Natasha and prince V's children and a few times slid down the hill, which was built there for Krestianov's children. In the afternoon Vyazemsky and I took a ride in a sled: The Zoo, Black gates, Priorat. After tea I rested a little, and at 6 ½ we lighted the tree in the dining room, which the children cut down at the Zoo.

Michael Alexandrovich with Sergei Rachmaninoff. Gatchina, 1910

PETERHOF

Olga and Tatiana at Peterhof, circa 1913

From the 1913 diary of Olga Romanov

Tuesday. 3 June. Peterhof. Got up late due to Bekker. Had breakfast with Papa, Mama and Bagration. At 2 o'cl. 10 min. went to *Znamenie*, and then to the [train] station. At 3 ½ arrived in Peterhof. Chilly, rather windy. Had tea with Papa and Mama, had dinner with them and Aunt Olga. Went to bed late. Papa read to us. Mama is well, thank God. We are lodging in 2 rooms upstairs.

Saturday. 27 July. Fireworks. We 2 walked around Peterhof with Aunt and Lori Yertsen. They took pictures of the most beautiful sites. Sunny. At 9 1/2 Papa left for maneuvers and returned at 2 o'cl. Had tea with Papa, Mama and the Aunt. Had dinner with Mama and the Aunt. Papa had dinner with the French. [We] played tennis with Anya. It started to rain but then it ended. Went to church. Mama's face aches, but her head[ache] is better. Played cards and smoked.

Tatiana and Olga with Lori Yertsen in Peterhof

Farm palace

Bathtub fountain by the Farm Palace

TYUMEN

Below: various views of the Tyumen Port where the imperial family boarded a steamer in 1917

№ 9. Гор. Тюмень. Пристань на рѣкѣ Турѣ.

Тюмень. № 3.

POKROVSKOE VILLAGE

Григорій Распутинъ у себя на родинѣ, въ селѣ Покровскомъ, Тюменскаго уѣзда, Тобольской губерніи.

Contemporary newspaper clipping with a feature on Pokrovskoe and Rasputin, with his writing

Rasputin and his three children: Matryona, Varvara and Dmitri

Matryona and Varvara Rasputinas, the reverse of the second photo is signed (possibly in their father's hand): "To dear unforgettable friend, to remember from Matryosha and Varya"

Varvara and Matryona Rasputin

Pokrovskoe Village. Above: Rasputin with neighbors. Below: streets of the village

Home of Rasputin's parents, in front of which the escort with Tsar, Empress and Grand Duchess Maria stopped to change horses on the way to Ekaterinburg in April of 1918. From this spot Maria made a sketch of Rasputin's own house which stood directly across the street. Today this house is the Rasputin Museum

Inside Rasputin's house: the original chair in this photo can be seen at the Rasputin Museum

Fishing in Pokrovskoe

All Pokrovskoe photos were taken by Anna Vyubova during her visit in 1914

Rasputin with fellow Pokrovskoe residents. The two women are Praskovia, Rasputin's wife (left) and Maria "Munya" Golovina, Rasputin's admirer and close friend of Felix Yusupov, Rasputin's future murderer. Photo was taken by Vyrubova

Pokrov Cathedral of the Holy Mother of God in Pokrovskoe (contemporary photo by Prokudin-Gorsky). Cathedral was destroyed after the revolution

Medallion with the image Our Lady of Kazan: a gift from the Tsar and Empress to Rasputin in 1912

Grigori Rasputin to Nicholas II[324]

Dear friend/ one more time [I] say a terrible cloud is above Russia/ affliction/ much misfortune/ darkness with no light in sight/ a sea of tears/ there is no recourse but blood? What will I say? There are no words/ indescribable horror/ I know everyone wants wars from you most likely not seeing that it will mean death. Heavy will be God's punishment when he takes away reason/ it is the beginning of the end. You the Tsar father of the people/ do not allow insanity to triumph and ruin yourself and the people. they will win over Germany but Russia? Just think/ truly there was not bitterer suffering for ages/ they will all drown in blood/ great ruin/ endless grief / Grigori

[324] Written sometime in the first half of 1914

+

милой друг еще разъ
скажу грозна туча натъ
расеей беда горя много
темно и просвету нету. слез
то море и меры нет а крови?
что скажу? словъ нету неописуемы
ый ужасъ. знаю все отъ тебя
войны хотятъ и верныя не
зная что ради гибели. тяжко
Божье наказанье когда уж
отыметъ умъ тутъ начало конца.
Ты Царь отецъ народа не
попусти безумнымъ торжествовать
и погубить себя и народъ
вотъ Германию победятъ а
Расея? подуматъ такъ воистину
не было отъ веку горшей
страдальницы вся тонетъ
въ крови велика погибель
бесъ конца печаль

Григорий

Rasputin's letter translated above

ALAPAEVSK

FRONT

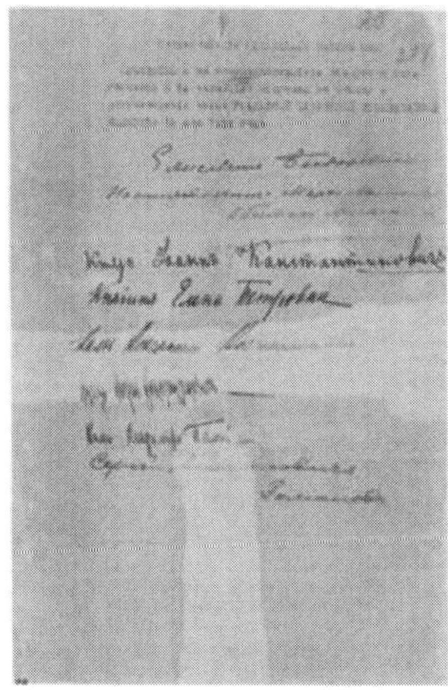

Decision of the REGIONAL SOVIET: WE ARE NOTIFIED AND WE, the undersigned, commit to be ready by 9 ½ o'clock for the departure to the train station accompanied by the member of the URAL REGIONAL EXTRAORDINARY COMMITTEE on 19 May, 1918.

[Signed]:

Elisaveta Feodorovna, Mother Superior of Marfo-Mariinsky Convent

Prince Ioann Konstantinovich

Princess Elena Petrovna

Prince Konstantin Konstantinovich (the younger)

Prince Igor... Konstantinovich

Prince Vladimir Palei

Sergei Mikhailovich Romanov

The prisoners arrived in Alapaevsk on 20th May 1918, and were housed in 'Napolnaya school' on the edge of the town. The stone building had four large and two small rooms with a series of hallways. One of the corner rooms to the left of the entrance was occupied by the guard. Further down the same side of the hallway were three additional rooms.

Napolnaya School: building where the Alapaevsk prisoners were held before their murder

Sergei Mikhailovich and Vladimir Pavlovich Palei with their servants shared the first room. In the next room lived Konstantin and Igor Konstantinoviches. The second corner room was occupied by Elizaveta Feodorovna and two novice nuns of the Marfo-Mariinsky Order: Varvara Yakovleva and Ekaterina Yanysheva. Ioann Konstantinovich lived in the first corner room on the right of the entrance, in the next room on the right was the footman Kalin, and the next room was the kitchen.

Memorial Museum of Grand Duchess Elizaveta Feodorovna

Elizaveta Feodorovna and Ioann Konstantinovich

Konstantin and Igor Konstantinoviches

Vladimir Pavlovich Palei and Sergei Mikhailovich

Sister Varvara Yakovleva

Executioners posing at the abandoned mine where the Alapaevsk prisoners were thrown in

In October, 1918, the bodies of the following were removed from the mine shaft: Feodor Remez, Varvara Yakovleva, Vladimir Palei, Konstantin Konstantinovich, Igor Konstantinovich, Sergei Mikhailovich, Elizaveta Feodorovna and loann Konstantinovich. The bodies were clothed. In their pockets were various articles and documents they always carried with them during imprisonment. Elizaveta Feodorovna wore around her neck an icon with precious stones. Reportedly Tsar Nicholas II prayed to this icon before his abdication, and later gave it to his sister in law. On the reverse is the inscription 'Palm [Sunday] 13th April, 1891'.

Results of the autopsies[325]

The body of Elizaveta Feodorovna: In the cranial cavity, on dissection of the skin, bruises were exposed; in the forehead area [a bruise] the size of a child's palm, and in the region of the left parietal bone [a bruise] the size of an adult's palm. There are bruises in the cellular tissue, the muscles and on the surface of the cranium. The skull bones are intact. A bruise is visible in the aura mater of the parietal area.'

[325] From The Alexander Palace Time Machine website

The body of Sergei Mikhailovich: 'On dissection of the cranial skin in the left parietal area [there is] a bruise in the muscle and cellular tissue; in the right parietal bone there is a round hole the size of the *groshina* (1/2cm in diameter); the channel of this wound runs downwards and backwards. On removal of the cranium, on the inner surface of the right parietal bone there is a hole 1cm in diameter corresponding with the first; around the hole are splinters of bone. In the aura mater there is a disruption of the fabric in the form of a [not quite] round hole corresponding with the holes in the skull bone.'

The body of Ioann Konstantinovich: 'In the region of the right temple, on dissection of the skin, a bruise is visible in the muscle and cellular tissue, which occupies the whole region of the temple. On removal of the cranium a bruise was exposed in the aura mater in the same right temple region. There is a bruise within the thickness of the muscle over the whole of the frontal chest wall. In the cavities of the pleura is an extensive haemorrhage. In the abdominal region, on dissection of the skin, a bruise is visible in the thickness of the muscle and fatty tissue, which has spread over the whole frontal wall of the stomach.

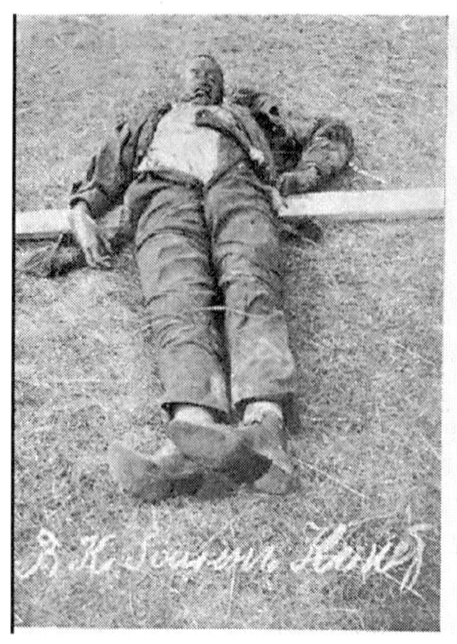
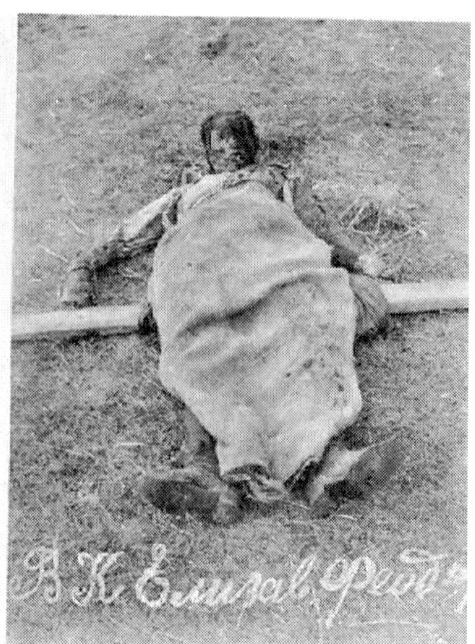

Bodies of Ioann Konstantinovich and Elizaveta Feodorovna

The body of Konstantin Konstantinovich: 'On the parietal is a large torn wound in the skin running from right to left, with a length of 9cm and a width of 3cm. 2cm behind this is a second torn wound 2cm long. On the right temple and parietal (bones) and on the parietal itself is an extensive bruise the size of a palm. On removal of the cranium a bruise was discovered on the aura mater, the parietal and the occiput. In the thoracic cavity, on dissection of the skin, a large bruise was found which has penetrated the muscle and cellular tissue of the front wall of the thorax.

The body of Igor Konstantinovich: 'In the cranial cavity, on dissection of the skin, a bruise [was found] occupying the entire right hand, half of the forehead; [There is] a crack in the bones of the skull starting in the centre of the upper edge of the right orbit and running along the centre line of the frontal bone. The crack runs rearwards into the (posterior fontanelle) and on to the occiput. On dissection of the cranium, the brain [was found to be] a grey mass. On removal of the brain, [a] crack was seen running over the upper wall of the right orbit to cross the (internal occipital protuberance). In the thoracic cavity, on dissection of the skin, a large bruise was found, which has penetrated the muscle in the lower part of the front wall of the thorax. On dissection of the abdominal cavity, a large bruise [was found] in the thickness of the abdominal wall.'

The body of Vladimir Pavlovich Palei: 'In the cranial cavity, on dissection of the skin, [was found] a large bruise occupying both parietals and the occipital regions. On dissection of the skin about 4-5 cubic cm of blood ran out . . . On dissection of the cranial cavity a haemorrhage [was found] under the aura mater in the occipital region. The rearward parts of the brain are a gruel-like red mass. In the thoracic cavity [is] a large bruise in the thickness of the muscle and cellular tissue.

The body of Fyodor Semyonovich Remez: 'In the region of the chest muscles [is] a severe bruise, which has spread over the whole thoracic cavity . . . [There is] a haemorrhage in the region of the right pleura. . . In the region of the right temple, on dissection of the skin, a large haemorrhage [was found]. A bruise has spread over the entire occipital region . . . Under the dura mater in the region of the left temple [there is] a haemorrhage.

The body of Varvara Yakovleva: 'On dissection of the skin of the head a bruise was found in the region of the right temple, and a second bruise in the occipital and parietal regions. The bones of the skull are intact. There is blood in the sutures. On removal of the cranium a bruise was found under the aura mater in the occipital region. On dissection of the skin a bruise [was found] in the region of the sternum.

Experts determined that the death of **Sergei Mikhailovich** was caused by 'haemorrhage into the aura mater and disruption of the brain tissue as a result of a gunshot wound'.

All the others were thrown alive into the shaft and their deaths were caused by 'haemorrhages as a result of their injuries'.

EKATERINBURG

Ipatiev house in the 1970s. Popov house can be seen in background

For a time, Ipatiev house became the "Museum of the Revolution"

Inside the Museum of the Revolution

Some original artifacts from the house survived, such as this fireplace

Ipatiev house was demolished in September 1977, on orders of the Soviet government. It was too controversial to keep intact, even as a museum

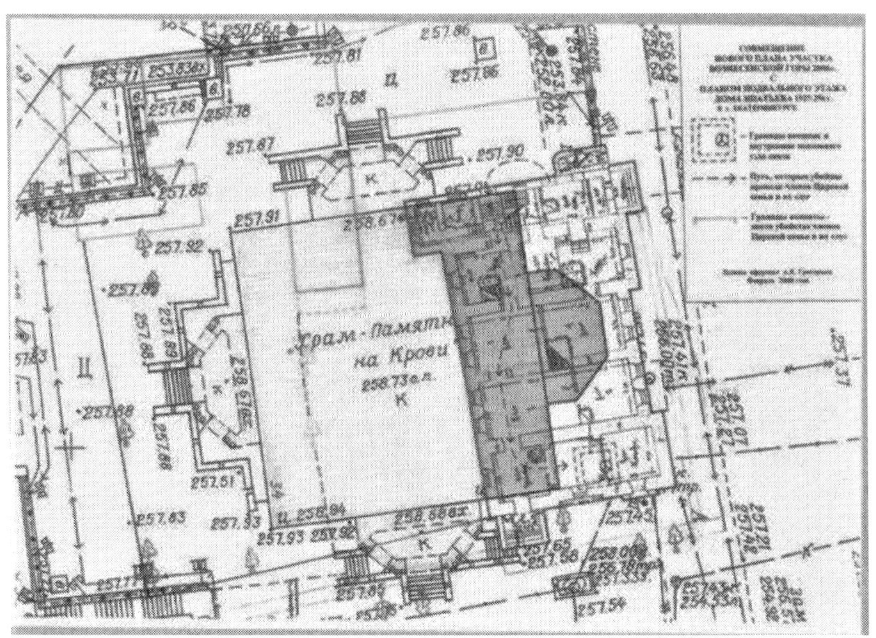

Plan showing where Cathedral on the Blood stands today (K) and where the cellar room was actually located (outlined darker on the right)

Cathedral on the Blood

BIBLIOGRAPHY

Alexander Palace Time Machine website (http://www.alexanderpalace.org/palace/)

Romanov collection. Beinecke Library at Yale University.

Buligin, P.P. *Ubiystvo Romanovykh.* M., 2001

Hoehnebart, Victor. Private letter collection

Ispoved tsareubiytz. *Podlinnaye istoria velikoi tragedii. Ubiystvo Tsarskoi Sem'yi v materiyalakh predvaritenogo sledstviya i v vospominaniyakh litz, prichastnykh k sovershеniyu etogo prestupleniya.* M.: OOO Izdatelskiy Dom Veche", 2008

Nepein, I.G. *Pered Rasstrelom: Poslednie Pisma Tsarskoi Sem'yi.* Omskoe Knizhnoe Izdatelstvo, 1992

Romanov Papers. Hoover Institution at Stanford University.

Rossiyskiy Arkhiv: *Istoria Otechestva v Svidetelstvakh i Dokumentakh* XVIII-XX vv. L.A. Lykov

Khrustalev, V.M. *The Last Diary of Tsaritsa Alexandra.* Yale University Press. New Have. 1997.

Sokolov, N.A.: *Predvaritelnoe Sledstvie 1919-1922.* M., 1998

State Archive of Russian Federation (GARF)

Tsarskiy Venetz. *Pisma Tsarskoy Semi iz Zatocheniya.* Veche, 2013

Yakovlev, V.V. "*Transfer of Nicholas Romanov from Tobolsk to Ekaterinburg*". GARF F. 601, Op. 2

In the steps of the Romanovs

www.getours.com.au/tours

Our tour focuses on the final two years (1916-1918) in the life of Russia's last imperial family Romanov. Their photographs, diaries and letters are used to help us relive their experiences, from the revolution-torn Petrograd to the "Red" Ekaterinburg.

We start in Tsarskoe Selo with their wartime efforts at the infirmaries, their daily attendances of prayer services at local churches, their visits to orphanages, and burials of their beloved patients. We visit places where they went regularly such as Anna Vyrubova's house, Peterhof and Yelagin Palace. We go inside the apartment where their 'friend' Grigori Rasputin lived just prior to his death, tour the Yusupov Palace and descend into its cellar room, where he was murdered in late 1916.

We relive the Tsar's abdication and retrace his sad last ride from the imperial train station to the Alexander Palace. We experience the family's life under house arrest by walking around the Alexander Park - where they planted a vegetable garden, broke ice on canals, cut trees for firewood and took walks followed by guards.

During our time in St Petersburg we visit additional locations, including the cathedral where the remains of the imperial family are currently entombed.

We follow the Romanovs east to Siberia and enter the Governor's mansion in Tobolsk where the family lived in captivity for almost a year. We then head back west, towards Urals through Tyumen, making a stop in Pokrovskoe village, Rasputin's hometown. We stand in the same spot the Romanovs stood - in front of Rasputin's house, when in April of 1918 they changed horses during their transfer to Ekaterinburg.

We make a detour to Alapaevsk, where Grand Duchess Elisaveta, the Tsarina's sister, and other members of the extended Romanov family were imprisoned and ultimately murdered.

Our journey concludes in Ekaterinburg, where 'The House of Special Purpose' - the last prison of the Russian imperial family - once stood. We pay respects in the exact spot they were murdered a century ago, and remember and honour them at their original burial site in the woods outside the city limits.

For more information on the Romanov family, please visit **TheRomanovFamily.com**.

Made in the USA
Lexington, KY
15 June 2018